A California State of Mind

A California
State of Mind

*The Conflicted Voter
in a Changing World*

Mark Baldassare

UNIVERSITY OF CALIFORNIA PRESS
Berkeley · *Los Angeles* · *London*

A Joint Publication with the
Public Policy Institute of California

University of California Press
Berkeley and Los Angeles, California

University of California Press, Ltd.
London, England

Library of Congress Cataloging-in-Publication Data

Baldassare, Mark.
    A California state of mind : the conflicted voter in
a changing world / Mark Baldassare.
    p. cm.
Includes bibliographical references and index.
ISBN 0-520-23648-3 (alk. paper)
1. California—Politics and government—1951–
2. Political participation—California. 3.
California—Economic conditions. I. Title.

    JK8741 .B35 2002
    324.9794'053—dc21   2002019474
Manufactured in the United States of America

10 09 08 07 06 05 04 03 02
10 9 8 7 6 5 4 3 2 1

"We're not prepared to handle growth."

"The whole government system's a bureaucratic mess."

"Growth is not the problem—lack of planning and poor authority is."

"No higher taxes for better schools. We throw money at them."

"I'd like it if we could vote on everything, so they don't make decisions for us."

"This whole episode with the energy crisis has totally shaken my belief in the government having a grip on what's going on."

Focus groups conducted with adult residents living in Los Angeles, Sacramento, San Jose, and San Diego in May 1999 and April 2001.

Contents

List of Tables

Foreword

When the PPIC Statewide Survey was launched in 1998, we knew that public opinion would play a key role in understanding the resolution of future public policy debates. Voters had already targeted tax policy, term limits, affirmative action, and many other social policies to be changed through the initiative process. We did not fully appreciate, however, that the ballot initiative was just the tip of the iceberg when it came to understanding the public's frustration with government. Whether it springs from California's role in the early frontier days and a respect for nineteenth-century individualism or from roots set deep in the 1960s during the Vietnam and civil rights era, Californians don't trust government. The distrust is manifest in their recent history of fiscal conservatism, a pattern of restricting the autonomy of state legislators and local representatives, and a tendency to believe that government wastes such huge amounts of money that additional taxes are not needed to launch new spending programs.

In 2000 Mark Baldassare focused the PPIC Statewide Survey on Californians and their government. Over an eighteen-month period, he interviewed some 22,000 residents of the state, probed their knowledge about public policy, and invited their perspectives on the best way to solve the numerous problems facing the state. Two of his many findings are worthy of special note. First, state residents frequently change their ranking of key public policies, readily shifting from budget surpluses or the importance of K–12 education to the energy shortfall or recession. This fickle behavior is due in part to the crisis mentality of the media and in part to the public's sense that government has been established to deal with each specific policy plight as it emerges. These shifting priorities leave only small windows of opportunity for decisionmakers to improve programs. Whether these decisionmakers act quickly to revise policy strategies or work gradually to improve outcomes over a longer term, the voter is a harsh judge.

Second, the harsh judgment of elected officials is largely based on promises that politicians make—and so often fail to keep when political reality sets in. Whether it was the failure of energy deregulation or the apparent inability to decide how best to use huge budget surpluses in the late 1990s, the voter saw a representative government that apparently could not handle the job. Taking a measure of the public's concern about such policy shortfalls and its shifting demands on government to deliver, Baldassare finds a populace in California that is deeply distrustful of government. It is not surprising, then, that voters consistently rate the initiative process as a preferred option for resolving contentious policy debates in the state.

A California State of Mind: The Conflicted Voter in a Changing World raises serious questions about the future role of representative government in California—and, by extension, in the other forty-nine states. Baldassare is not sanguine that the increasing racial, ethnic, and regional diversity of the voting population will result in a closer match between the people and their politicians. In spite of the national crisis raised by the events of September 11, 2001, Californians are still a very conservative lot of voters when it comes to spending and taxes. As of this writing, approval ratings of the governor and president may be riding high on a wave of patriotism. But the opinion that government is not to be trusted dies hard, whether the belief stems from the nineteenth century or the 1960s.

If there is a single message from this latest book by Mark Baldassare, it is that distrust of government is the wild card in California politics. Even in the flush economic times at the end of the twentieth century, that distrust kept California voters from granting government more resources—even for such cherished goals as improving K–12 education. A reading of this book suggests that as long as distrust persists, California voters will be conflicted about their government and its ability to serve their best interests.

David W. Lyon
President and CEO
Public Policy Institute of California

Acknowledgments

My intention in writing this book was to understand the relationship between Californians and their government during times of social and economic change. I was interested in the policy preferences and political attitudes surfacing in the 2000 elections and in the ballot choices voters made. A presidential election is an ideal setting to see the link between the people and the governments that serve them, and the 2000 race had two candidates with very different views about government's role. Moreover, Californians are asked to do more work at the ballot box because our state and local initiative process enables them to participate directly in policymaking. There were decisions to be made about state funding, taxes, and new public programs. Voters were in the midst of enviable circumstances in California: large budget surpluses and a strong economy. Yet a lingering distrust of government was evident, and the public was anxious about the state's abilities to deal with a future full of growth and change.

My plan for writing this book worked fine until Election Day. After that, there were some unforeseen events. First, the presidential election was not decided until December. Then, California encountered an electricity crisis in early 2001. The 2000 U.S. Census provided new information on the amount of growth and demographic change in California, and the population shifts were more dramatic than expected. The terrorist attacks on the World Trade Center and Pentagon in September 2001 led me to reconsider the issue of government trust in light of public reactions to this tragic event. Finally, the state's surplus dwindled and was replaced by a huge budget deficit in early 2002. These circumstances gave me greater understanding of themes surrounding Californians' distrust in government.

I could not have completed such an ambitious project without the help and support of others. I am deeply indebted to the Public Policy Institute of California, which funded my two-year project Californians and Their Government. PPIC provided me with the support to conduct waves of large-scale public opinion surveys leading up to the 2000 elections and with the time to write this book after the elections were over. To this, I owe special gratitude to David Lyon, the president of PPIC, for setting the standards for high quality and objective research. I thank the PPIC board of directors, and especially Arjay and Frances Miller, for the gift of an endowed chair. We at PPIC are all indebted to William Hewlett, who provided PPIC with the endowment that makes our work possible.

I benefited from the expertise and writings of my colleagues at PPIC. I would like to acknowledge Julian Betts, Michael Dardia, Claudine Gay, Elisabeth Gerber, Zoltan Hajnal, Hans Johnson, David Lesher, Paul Lewis, Max Neiman, Deborah Reed, Belinda Reyes, Kim Rueben, Fred Silva, and Jon Sonstelie. I consulted with Joyce Peterson, Abby Cook, Gary Bjork, and Michael Teitz on each survey. Jon Cohen, Lisa Cole, Christopher Hoene, Eric McGhee, and Mina Yaroslavsky provided research assistance.

Joyce Peterson and Michael Teitz read an early draft and provided many useful suggestions. The revised draft benefited from editing by Joyce Peterson and Gary Bjork. I wish to thank the reviewers of the University of California Press for their suggestions. Special thanks to Naomi Schneider, Executive Editor at the University of California Press, for her enthusiasm and encouragement at the right moments during the process.

This book is largely based on information provided through focus groups and public opinion surveys conducted from the spring of 1999 through early 2001. Discovery Research Group of Utah conducted the telephone interviews for the eleven survey waves, which included over 22,000 adult Californians. I wish to thank Steven Jenson and Mary Spain for all of their thorough and careful work and for their timely and consistent efforts.

Relationships with other organizations extended the scope and resources of the original plans for this project. The C2K Project, which was funded by the James Irvine Foundation and the William and Flora Hewlett Foundation, organized the May 1999 focus groups. I was involved in the planning and design of the focus groups with David Booher, Deborah Drake, Gail Kaufman, Dan Schnur, Donna Lucas, Lee Ann Buchanan, and the NCG Porter Novelli staff. I collaborated with the Great Valley Center for the Central Valley Survey in November 1999, the David and Lucile Packard Foundation for the Environment Survey in June 2000, and the San Diego Dialogue for the San Diego County Survey in July 2000. The Hewlett, Irvine, and Packard foundations provided funds for focus groups in April 2001, and the sessions were moderated by Kay Lavish.

My survey advisory committee provided me with many useful ideas and important feedback about survey topics, questions, and findings. At various times, the committee members included Ruben Barrales, Mary Bitterman, Angela Blackwell, Nick Bollman, Paul Brest, Molly Ann Brodie, Bruce Cain, Matt Fong, Dennis Collins, William Hauck, Sherry Bebitch Jeffe, Monica Lozano, Jerry Lubenow, Donna Lucas, Max Neiman, Jerry Roberts, Dan Rosenheim, Richard Schlosberg, Carol Stogsdill, Cathy Taylor, Steven Toben, Raymond Watson, and Carol Whiteside. I am very grateful to Sherry Bebitch Jeffe and Max Neiman for reviewing the survey reports.

There are many scholars and authors whose works influenced my thinking about the themes of Californians' distrust of government. These individuals include Bruce Cain, Jack Citrin, Michael Dear, Steven Erie, Bill Fulton, Elisabeth Gerber, Sherry Bebitch Jeffe, Joel Kotkin, Max Neiman, Harry Pachon, Jack Peltason, Susan Rasky, Gregory Rodriguez, David Sears, Ray Sonenshein, Peter Schrag, and Dan Walters.

I also wish to thank Bruce Cain, Jerry Lubenow, and the entire staff at the Institute of Governmental Studies Library at the University of California, Berkeley. They provided me with a steady stream of relevant books, journal articles, and government reports, which have found their way into many of the pages of this book.

I benefited from using questions and seeking advice from several national pollsters. I became reacquainted with Daniel Yankelovich early in 2000, and he was an important role model and source of advice. I also benefited from the work of Molly Ann Brodie at the Kaiser Family Foundation, Richard Morin and Claudia Deane at the *Washington Post,* Andrew Kohut at the Pew Research Center, and Kathy Frankovich of CBS News. I appreciated the opportunity to converse with Mark DiCamillo of the Field Poll and Susan Pincus of the *Los Angeles Times* Poll about their surveys. Paul Maslin and Stephen Kinney offered insights and information on partisan surveys about candidates.

I am certain that my knowledge has been expanded by the conversations I have had with national and state political columnists, commentators, editors, and reporters. I learned quite a lot in discussions with Mark Barabak, Jim Barnes, Mitchel Benson, Dan Borenstein, David Broder, Ron Brownstein, Amy Chance, Zachary Coile, David Lesher, Scott Lindlaw, John Marelius, Carla Marinucci, Warren Olney, Mark Paul, Todd Purdum, Bill Rosendahl, Robert Salladay, Bill Schneider, Scott Shafer, Mark Shields, George Skelton, Peter Schrag, Steve Scott, James Sterngold, Cathy Taylor, and Dan Weintraub. I thank them for asking such thoughtful questions and for sharing their insights on politics and elections. I am also grateful to Mark Paul from the *Sacramento Bee* and Cathy Taylor from the *Orange County Register* for providing me with an opportunity to write about California issues for their editorial-opinion pages.

I also benefited from conversations with several people in state government about the issues surrounding Californians and their government. These included California State Treasurer Phil Angelides, California Secretary of State Bill Jones, State Senator John Vasconcellos, Phil Trounstine in the Governor's Office, Phil Garcia in the Lieutenant Governor's Office, and Alfie Charles in the California Secretary of State's Office.

During and after the 2000 election, I gained insights from conversations with individuals who have a strong working knowledge of political campaigns in California, including Gary Hunt, Leslie Goodman, Gale Kaufman, Julie Buckner Levy, Donna Lucas, Dan Schnur, Gary South, Larry Thomas, and Ron Unz. Kim Alexander and the California Voter Foundation offered valuable information on initiatives and campaign funding.

I would like to thank Cheryl Katz for her help at every stage. We thought through the topics and questions for the focus groups and surveys, and her expert advice on data collection and statistical analysis was crucial. As usual, she was a good listener and provided honest feedback while I was working on the book. As for our two children, Benjamin at thirteen and Daniel at eight, I can't express enough gratitude for their inquiring about which page of the book I was working on and their need for explanations on the workings of the electoral college, on why California was having an electricity problem, and on where the 50 million people in California will live in 2040. I hope the book is useful to their generation, as we look toward making decisions today for the state's future.

Mark Baldassare
San Francisco, California
May 2002

CHAPTER I

Introduction

The last years of the twentieth century seemed like the best of times in California. Yet its citizens expressed the worst of fears about the future of the Golden State. What could explain this strangely dissonant outlook in the nation's most economically important and politically influential state—and how has it played out in the political and policy arena? These questions are the focus of this book, especially as they relate to voters' choices in the 2000 election.

At the turn of the twenty-first century, two major, competing forces had emerged as the yin and yang of California political life—we might call it the New Economy meets the New Demography. A booming economy and new wealth generated a euphoric mood, and talk about the present was thus enthusiastic. Yet the state's residents also saw signs of troubling long-term trends, many of which—like congestion, pollution, and increasing income inequality—are related to the state's growth and changing demography. People's concerns about these trends and future quality of life were compounded mightily by another trend that emerged, paradoxically, during times of plenty—a widespread distrust of government. Californians, by and large, did not believe that government had the ability to handle problems or that it even had their best interests at heart.

The confluence of these trends could have many political implications for California. It could affect what issues matter to people and could make them think differently about what government should be doing to solve problems. In a state where policymaking for the past twenty years has been guided by the political principle "smaller is better," it could conceivably alter views about resources the government needs and how involved government should be in serving the public good. Ultimately, it could alter people's thinking about the kinds of leaders they need to elect, change the fortunes of political parties, and give new purpose to exerting policy influence through the initiative process.

How these trends affected and may affect California politics is evident in voters' issues and priorities leading up to the 2000 election and is recognizable in the election outcomes. The 2000 election provided choices for Californians who wanted to express their feelings about new directions for public policy. Voters could have broken with the twenty-year "tax revolt" and supported candidates and ballot measures that stood for more taxes and government spending. The outcome could have signaled the start of a new era for the Golden State: one in which the public, comfortable with the present, would look to government to solve tomorrow's problems. In fact, this election was not all that different, and the reasons why distrust undermined confidence in the future during this time of plenty offer important insights into California's future.

CALIFORNIANS AND THEIR GOVERNMENT STUDY

This book documents a large-scale study, Californians and Their Government, conducted by the Public Policy Institute of California (PPIC) over the course of the 2000 elections and followed up in spring 2001. We began this journey with focus group interviews around the state to gauge the public's mood and concerns. We then conducted a comprehensive series of public opinion surveys before, during, and after all the votes were tallied. We asked Californians about a wide range of issues, including the elections, tax-and-spending policy, public policy issues that were being debated at the time, and, most important, how they felt about their federal, state, and local governments. In spring 2001, we conducted another set of focus groups.

One of the common complaints about a public opinion poll is that it offers only a snapshot of voters' opinions before an election. In other words, polls are accurate only insofar as they can tell us how people say they will vote on a specific issue at a certain time. The goals we had in mind for this investigation were quite different from the goals of those engaging in preelection polling. We were not interested in predicting a winner, either in the presidential race or for other items further down on the ballot, nor were we concerned about who was ahead and by how much at a given point in time.

Our purpose was to find out how the unusual mix of current prosperity, future worries about growth and change, and voters' distrust in government was affecting policy preferences and ballot choices in 2000. We needed to take multiple measures of each of these dimensions at different times. We also needed to make sure that we interviewed a sufficient number of people to be able to break out the results for important demographic and political subgroups and regions. In the end, we provided an in-depth portrait over time of California voters' opinions during the 2000 elections.

As noted previously, we conducted a series of focus groups in several of the major regions of the state. Focus groups are not intended to be scientific and representative surveys of public opinion. They use qualitative methods and seek to engage groups of people in a structured conversation about issues and experiences. I used the conversations generated in these focus groups for two distinct purposes. First, they helped me to develop survey topics and specific questions on population growth, ongoing change in the state, and the role of state and local government. Second, they provide quotations to bring to life some of the issues and concerns revealed by the surveys. Generally speaking, what we heard in focus groups was largely similar to what we learned from the surveys.

The first set of focus groups was conducted in collaboration with a nonpartisan group called California 2000, which was funded by major state foundations. We joined forces since their interests coincided with the larger goals of my Californians and Their Government project. The focus groups were carried out by the Nelson Communications Group.[1] Eight focus group interviews were conducted in May 1999 in Sacramento, Santa Clara, San Diego, and Los Angeles. In April 2001, with the California elections a fading memory and the state in the midst of an electricity crisis, I returned to Santa Clara, Los Angeles, and Sacramento to conduct a second set of six focus groups.[2] In all, we talked with about 170 individuals in the course of these interviews, focusing on such issues

1. The results of the focus groups referred to in this book were summarized in a client report, "California 2000," prepared by the Nelson Communications Group (1999). I also had the audio and videotapes available for further analysis and use in this book.

2. Kay Lavish moderated and provided analysis for these focus groups.

as California's growth trends and the state's future, distrust of government, the role of state government, and elections.

The major data collection effort, however, consisted of a series of large, comprehensive public opinion surveys. One purpose of the surveys was to provide an in-depth profile of political, social, and economic attitudes; public policy preferences; and ballot choices. Another purpose was to build on my previous work on government distrust and to develop a deeper and more thorough understanding of Californians' perceptions of how their government works and what it does, the role it plays in their lives, how well it currently performs, and the place they would prefer for government to have in their lives. This was, of course, in the context of a federal and state government that had surplus funds at its disposal.

I conducted eleven surveys, which included the responses of over 22,000 Californians, over the course of a year and a half. Four statewide surveys were conducted in September and December 1999 and in January and February 2000, in advance of the March 7 primary. There was also a special survey on the Central Valley region, conducted in November 1999, and a special survey on San Diego County in July 2000. Four more statewide surveys were conducted in June, August, September, and October 2000, prior to the November 7 general election. These included a special survey on attitudes toward the environment in June 2000. The tenth survey was conducted in early January 2001, two months after the election and a month after the presidential election was finally decided.[3]

The surveys involved random-digit-dial telephone interviews, each with a minimum of 2,000 adult residents. Every survey included the responses of at least 400 Latinos, with the interviews conducted in English or Spanish as needed, so that we could represent this increasingly large and politically influential group. Individual surveys were also large enough to break out the results for the major regions throughout the state (i.e., Los Angeles, the rest of Southern California, the San Francisco Bay Area, the Central Valley), voter groups (i.e., Democrats, Republicans, independents), and demographic subgroups.

We interviewed both voters and nonvoters, so that all Californians were represented, but we also separately analyzed the results of "likely"

3. See *www.ppic.org* for the methods and questions for each PPIC Statewide Survey.

voters for the questions pertaining to the March primary and November general election. Every survey was about twenty minutes in length and included a range of attitudinal and factual questions. Some of the questions were repeated from national surveys, thus offering a comparison with California. Other questions were repeated in the course of the series and thus provided an opportunity to look at responses over time. Since the surveys were conducted over a relatively short time frame and many of the responses remained in a narrow range, we were also able to merge the responses of survey questions that were repeated over time—such as optimism about the state, political ideology, policy preferences, and demographic characteristics—thus providing a large data base that included the responses of over 22,000 Californians during the 2000 election cycle.

This book, then, offers evidence from two original sources—focus groups and statewide surveys—supplemented with published data from a variety of other organizations. For instance, there are the exit polls of state voters from the major news organizations, such as the Voters News Service and the *Los Angeles Times* poll. We also analyze the actual vote tallies in the March primary and November general election, as prepared by the California secretary of state. There are demographic and economic data from the U.S. Census, the California Department of Finance, and other sources. Finally, there are public opinion surveys from state and national polling organizations that provide further context on the state and national mood during the 2000 elections.

THE PROBLEM OF DISTRUST IN GOVERNMENT

The scholarly literature on trust in government has a long and important history in the social sciences. Its status has been elevated by a keen interest in evidence of deep public distrust in government and elected officials that first surfaced in the United States during the tumultuous era of the Vietnam War and the Watergate presidential scandal in the 1970s. Other Western nations had, or have since, experienced distrust in government. Measuring the public's trust in government is no simple task. There are scholars who take a critical aim at the mixed meaning and ambiguous wording of survey questions on trust, the lack of analysis of specific *trust* concepts, and the misinterpretation of results of studies that seek to measure the causes and consequences of government mistrust through a variety of multiple-measure indices in national surveys (see Barber, 1983).[4]

Over the course of several decades, distrust in government has commonly been defined in two different ways: one is through the level of confidence that people have in the public institutions that serve them, such as the executive and legislative branches of state, federal, and local government; the other is through the general perceptions that the public has toward the ways that the government and its elected officials perform their duties, such as their effectiveness, responsiveness, efficiency, fairness, and honesty. In tandem with these efforts to measure trust in government are the common questions on job approval ratings of current office holders and global satisfaction with the nation's direction; in many ways, these answers also reflect the public's confidence and trust.

Whichever of the two ways one defines and measures trust in government, the results have been consistent over time. There was a high level of trust and confidence in government in the mid-1960s, that is, in the years after the assassination of President John Kennedy, the beginning of the Great Society by President Lyndon Johnson, and the era of strong economic growth and a Cold War threat. Over the next ten years, the national government faced a series of important crises—the Vietnam War, urban race riots, high crime rates, an oil embargo, inflation, and the Watergate scandal—and by the mid-1970s, all measures of trust and confidence in government were showing significant declines. Since then, the public's reports about their trust in government have been fairly negative throughout economic recessions and recoveries, approval and disapproval of specific office holders, and changes of party control and presidential leadership. Many observers say that trust in government reached its lowest point in 1994, the so-called year of the angry voter, during which the Republicans took control of the legislative branch of the federal government, and also a time of deep economic recession. Then trust is thought to have steadied when the economy recovered and even rebounded somewhat for the remainder of the 1990s through 2000. Still, distrust in government was running fairly high by the longer historical standards throughout the entire 2000 presidential election. The measures

4. This section relies on a wealth of political science literature on this topic, including Citrin (1974); Citrin and Luks (1998); Citrin and Muste (1999); Erber and Lau (1990); Hardin (1996); Howell and Fagan (1988); Levi and Stoker (2000); Lipset and Schneider (1983, 1987); Miller (1974a, 1974b); Nye, Zelikow, and King (1997); Sears et al. (1978); Warren (1992, 1996, 1999); and Wendy Rahn's conference paper cited in Nye, Zelikow, and King (1997:291).

of trust in federal government showed significant improvements immediately after the terrorist attacks in New York and Washington on September 11, 2001.

There has been a considerable amount of attention devoted to the *causes* of the public's distrust in government. Some studies have sought to link personal characteristics such as age, education, gender, income, and occupation with attitudes toward government, but others argue that trust in government cannot really be explained by these factors (see Baldassare, 1986; Barber, 1983; Lipset and Schneider, 1983). A few have examined the effects of living in urban and suburban communities on trust in government and have found at most modest effects (Baldassare, 1986; Fischer, 1975, 1984). Some have looked at media biases and a lack of knowledge as the causes of mistrust. Other scholars have focused on the role that historic events, policy decisions, and their outcomes have on the mood of the people toward their government (Citrin, 1974; Miller, 1974a) in light of office holders' responses to crises, emergencies, wars, scandals, economic booms, and fiscal failures; focusing on these causal factors has by far seemed the most promising in terms of explaining time trends in distrust.

In essence, we take the position shared by others that trust in government is an attitude reflecting the sum total of experiences and knowledge the public has toward its government institutions and its elected officials at any given time. It is a composite feeling of how the public feels about the responsiveness, effectiveness, competence, caring, efficiency, honesty, fairness, and other attributes of its government and leaders. Of course, this judgment will be based on a mixture of direct and indirect experiences: few people meet their president, but many learn about the president and Congress from reading newspapers and watching television and from interpreting the news with friends and family; likewise, people from time to time do have experiences with government agencies, such as the U.S. Postal Service, military, Social Security Administration, or Internal Revenue Service, and these personal events can also shape trust in government. In other words, we would argue that distrust in government, as measured in public opinion surveys, is largely a rational response to people's experiences with government and their interpretation of all of the information they are receiving from the media and other sources about how their government and elected officials are functioning at a given time. This influence of external events can explain why levels of trust in government can shift suddenly in some places, while holding steady in certain Western societies over a lengthy period of time.

Why is trust in government an important issue for us to consider? It is because distrust can have profound *consequences* for the ability of public officials to govern. Many scholars have argued that a government and its leaders cannot function without some minimum level of trust from the public; exactly how much trust is required is a subject of controversy. The need for trust in government is, of course, especially true in a democratic society. If voters are to elect their representatives to make public policy choices in their interest, then they have to trust the representatives to do so. If people do not trust their elected officials, then they might not respect the laws the officials make, and this may lead some members of the public to question the need to comply with the rules and regulations governing their society, such as paying taxes. If the public does not trust the government, then it might elect people who want to restrict the role of government, its size and spending, or its abilities to plan and act on behalf of the public. A lack of government action could hinder, or even endanger, the well-being of the public. Or, if voters have the ability through state and local initiatives, they may take lawmaking into their own hands and make policy decisions on their own.

The study reported in this book builds upon the large body of literature on trust in government and contributes to knowledge in several important ways. In our surveys, we repeat many of the questions about the federal government that have been asked in national surveys over time, specifically, those concerned with attitudes toward the effectiveness, efficiency, and responsiveness of government. We also refocused the typical survey questions so that we could measure the California public's trust in state and local government, which are important public institutions in people's lives that have received much less attention in the scholarly literature. In analyzing distrust in government, we agree with those scholars who argue for looking at individual questions rather than composite indices. Having established the high levels of distrust in federal, state, and local governments, we then go on to explore how these underlying doubts about government have expressed themselves in public policy preferences, candidate selections, and certain ballot choices during the 2000 elections.

There is no doubt that the issue of distrust in government has a rich history in the California political context. The state is the home of the tax revolt in the late 1970s, the birthplace of the Reagan Revolution in the 1980s, and the headquarters of many political causes of the left and right in the 1990s that have challenged the political status quo and questioned the decisions of governmental authorities. Most important, the state's residents have time and again demonstrated a profound distrust of government through their active and creative use of the state's initiative process. Indeed, the voters enacted the citizens' initiative in the early twentieth century in response to state government corruption and incompetence. Californians have voted in favor of initiatives that have changed their state constitution and thus exerted their authority over the executive, legislative, and judicial branches of state government. They have voted for initiatives that limited the terms of state office holders, restricted the amount of money they pay in local property taxes, mandated the amount of funding the state legislature must earmark for programs they like, eliminated government programs they did not care for, decriminalized the use of drugs that the government deems illegal, determined the length of prison sentences so that judges and legislators cannot use their discretion, and changed the voting rules for primaries so that parties cannot determine who votes for candidates. Sometimes, the public's distaste for government dictates has led to legal battles that have been resolved by courts' overturning their initiatives, resulting in more distrust of government. In all, the extent, roots, and consequences of the state residents' seemingly profound distrust in government offer us an excellent and special case to study.

The unique circumstances of California at the turn of the century offer another reason to study the public's distrust of government in this state's setting. California has enormous private resources within its state's borders, yet its public institutions have not kept pace with the enormous demands created by a fast-growing population (Schrag, 1998). In almost every category of state spending—schools, highways, prisons, infrastructure—California lagged well behind other states in the nation. A lack of planning and preparedness is at least partly a result of limits the public placed on government itself through restrictive initiatives, though those limits placed on government could also be viewed as a reaction by voters who were disappointed in the past performance, efficiency, and responsiveness of their state government.

As we shall see later, the public's expectations for what needed to be done to accommodate growth and change by their government were high at this time. There was widespread recognition of the immensity of the tasks at hand and the shortcomings of current efforts. During times of prosperity and obvious needs, would the public overcome its fears of government failure and give its elected officials more resources to tackle problems or would it continue to be reluctant to see its government act in a bigger, bolder way? The public's well-being could depend on the resources the voters will allow their government to have in its efforts to be prepared for the state's challenging future. How Californians resolved this problem of distrust is the focus of our inquiry.

WHY THE 2000 ELECTION PROVIDED IMPORTANT INSIGHTS

The 2000 election was an especially important and revealing event. The state and nation were in an unprecedented, long period of economic prosperity and job growth. The nation was at peace, and the federal government had a large budget surplus. Yet the national political scene was anything but stable. President Bill Clinton had lied under oath about an affair with a White House intern while under investigation for other alleged, but never proven, wrongdoings. After the 1998 midterm election, Clinton was impeached by a U.S. House of Representatives that voted along party lines. The Clinton presidency survived a trial in the U.S. Senate that was also largely decided along partisan lines. This left many voters in an ambivalent mood, still liking the job Clinton was doing in office but tiring of his personal antics. Other voters were equally disturbed by the Republican leaders in Congress, whom they saw as pursuing an effort to "get" Bill Clinton, which most of the public did not want. These were not normal times, and this would turn out to be a highly unusual election.

California's presidential primary has historically been a political nonevent, but the script was changed in 2000. The primary is typically held on the first Tuesday in June. By that late date, other state primaries have been decisive in choosing the standard-bearers for the Republican and Democratic parties. In 2000, California moved its primary up to early March so that it could be a player in the presidential selection process. Both parties had competitive presidential primaries in the early going— Vice President Al Gore and former U.S. Senator Bill Bradley on the Democratic side and Governor George W. Bush and U.S. Senator John McCain on the Republican side. The state's voters thus received an earlier and steadier dose of political campaigning than they had in the past. They were exposed to a range of issues and policy discussions beginning in the fall of 1999.

California would be holding its first open, or "blanket," primary for president. The voters had passed an "open primary" initiative in 1996, and the state held its first primary under the new rules in the statewide election of June 1998. This meant that all voters received the same ballot, which included the names of all candidates for each race. This would allow independent voters to participate in the selection process of partisan candidates as well as allowing crossover votes, in which candidates could receive support from voters who belonged to a different party. In the presidential race, this added an element of uncertainty. It was a chance to see the candidates' strengths in maintaining party loyalty and in attracting independent voters. March 2000 would be the first and last time that voters could cross party lines and vote for any candidate in a race. The U.S. Supreme Court, acting on a court challenge by the parties, outlawed this practice a few months later.[5]

After the primary season was over, the political parties and the presidential nominees did not abandon the Golden State. They spent considerable time and resources courting the California voter, along with the state's big prize of fifty-four electoral college votes. The Democrats concluded that they could not win without taking California. The Republicans were never willing to give up on the Golden State, since there had never been a time in the twentieth century that the GOP took the White House without winning in California. So the Bush campaign spent millions of dollars on television advertising, while the Gore campaign countered by sending Clinton in during the closing days.

There were many other factors that also propelled national politics to center stage for the state's electorate. The presidential campaigns made regular pilgrimages to the Silicon Valley, both because it was a source of campaign funds and because it had become the symbol of the New Economy. The Democratic national convention took place in Los Angeles in mid-August. Also, the candidates used the backdrop of the state's ethnic and racial diversity—especially the increasingly large Latino community—to display their skills at the politics of inclusion. Voters heard their plans for tax cuts, spending the budget surplus, improving the schools, and protecting the environment. This intense activity provided us with an up-close view of the electorate's moods, politics, and priorities.

In twenty-two of the twenty-five presidential elections in the twentieth century, the candidate who won in California became the occupant of the White House for at least four years. Not this time. In California, Gore won the state over Bush by a huge margin of 1.3 million

5. See Cain and Gerber (2002) for discussion of California's blanket primary.

votes. Gore ended up winning the national popular vote by about a half-million votes, but he fell a few "chads" short of taking the state of Florida. What followed was a suspenseful and strange few weeks of recounting the Florida ballots, interrupted by legal maneuverings. Eventually, the U.S. Supreme Court overruled the Florida Supreme Court and the counting stopped. Again, political turmoil seemed to be the undercurrent in these prosperous times. The electoral college vote gave the presidency to George W. Bush.

The presidential election was the main event, but there were several other noteworthy ingredients to the 2000 election that required our close attention. There was a U.S. Senate election for the seat held by Dianne Feinstein. The Republican primary offered up moderate and conservative choices, while the Democratic incumbent was unchallenged. The declining political fortunes of Republicans in statewide elections had been partly blamed on the fact that their conservative primary voters were choosing candidates who were too far to the right for the state's overall electorate. The open primary was supposed to change all of this, since more moderate voters from the independent ranks and other parties could participate in the GOP primary. The winner on the GOP side was a moderate, pro-choice politician from the Silicon Valley—U.S. Congressman Tom Campbell. The plan seemed to be working for the GOP, until their moderate candidate lost by a landslide of over 2 million votes in the general election, providing further evidence of the troubles that Republicans now have winning against Democrats in the Golden State.

The legislative races around the state provided us with an opportunity to better understand the political mood and shifting landscape on the ground in California. The state's fifty-two U.S. House members represent the largest delegation that any state sends to the U.S. Congress. Those federal seats were up for grabs, as were all eighty of the seats in the state assembly and twenty of the forty seats in the state senate. With the balance of power narrowly in favor of the Republicans in the U.S. Congress, there was national attention and considerable statewide interest in a half-dozen hotly contested seats. Once again, these legislative races provided an opportunity to test the importance of issues and ideas for voters. As it turned out, voters were more comfortable with the approach of the Democrats than with the Republican leaders in Congress. The Democrats won most of the closely watched contests and extended their already sizable leads in the U.S. House, state senate, and state assembly. Of equal importance, the changing demography—in the form of a growing Latino and Asian vote—seemed to be playing an important role in tipping the vote in legislative districts away from Republicans and into the Democrats' column.

California voters were also served a full course of state ballot propositions during the 2000 primary and general election. There were twenty state propositions on the March 2000 primary ballot. They included eight citizens' initiatives, two referenda that sought to overturn existing state laws, and ten measures offered by the state legislature. Twelve passed, and eight failed. In November 2000, there were eight state propositions, including three from the state legislature and five that were citizens' initiatives. Five passed, and three failed. Millions of dollars were spent on initiative campaigns, and a major element of media election coverage was devoted to ballot items.

The statewide initiatives in the 2000 elections offered us a feast of information on Californians' views on specific issues, policy priorities, and spending preferences. We picked a few controversial initiatives and closely followed them with our surveys through the March primary and November election: three ballot measures concerned with educational reform, since voters had been telling us in surveys that schools were their top issue, and a citizens' initiative regarding a socially conservative cause, that is, the ban on gay marriages. While they were not a specific focus of our surveys, the votes on multibillion-dollar state bond measures on water and parks were also informative, since they told us how distrustful voters viewed the prospects of substantially increasing the state's debts to deal with their environmental concerns during prosperous times.

There were also a substantial number of growth control initiatives on local ballots in 2000 that are very revealing of voters' main concerns and policy interests. Indeed, there were more local growth measures on the ballot in California than anywhere else in the nation and more initiatives in this election than had been evident for many years in the state. Not only were there more ballot measures, but many were bolder and broader than in the past, such as seeking to ensure that voters always have their say in growth. Many attributed the increase in local growth initiatives to an improved economy, which generated traffic problems and suppressed fears about growth controls.

In California, the trend was for voters to take decisions about growth away from their local elected officials. They wanted to take land use matters into their own hands, once again indicating that voter distrust is a powerful force in shaping policy choices. We know from the overall results of the local elections that local growth initiatives went over well with the voters in 2000. We also know that local growth initiatives achieved their greatest successes in the areas of the state that were the most upset with traffic and growth and the most content with the economy. Clearly, these local ballot measures reflected expressions of voter distrust with local officials charged with the duty of maintaining the quality of life in times of growth and change.

RELEVANCE OF THE CALIFORNIA EXPERIENCE

What happens in California politics and elections is important to the nation and world. The state has political and economic significance beyond its borders. It has the largest electoral college vote in presidential elections. It sends the biggest delegation to the U.S. Congress. The state's economy is larger than all but four nations on the planet. It has become the destination and home to people throughout Asia, Latin America, and Europe. California has the added status of being a premiere social and cultural trendsetter, making what is happening in the state worth watching for the entire nation. Thus, the events surrounding the 2000 election in California have broader significance than on California only.

Nonetheless, it has become popular in the national press to declare that California is irrelevant to the rest of the nation. It is no longer a trendsetter, they say. Rather, it is a demographic, geographic, and political oddity. "California Doesn't Matter" was the conclusion of a leading political pundit (Barnes, 2000). The status of being a unique state is not new, dating back at least to the classic book *California: The Great Exception* (McWilliams, 1949). During the 2000 elections, East Coast political pundits seemed fixated on a new idea—California's lack of significance for national politics.

Here is the basic logic for the state's political irrelevance: California is too big and diverse to matter in elections anymore. In other words, its population is too large and ethnically and racially mixed to reflect the nation or predict what will happen in any other state. Most recently, its politics have been viewed as too Democratic-leaning to have much relevance for a nation that is evenly divided along political party lines. Consider the fact that the national presidential election ended in a statistical dead heat, the U.S. Senate in a 50–50 tie, and the House of Representatives narrowly controlled by the GOP. Is it time to look for another national trendsetter, say Florida or Oregon? In California, statewide elections and political power are solidly in Democratic hands. What can we possibly learn from an analysis of the 2000 election in the Golden State?

I would argue that California remains centrally important because of its size. One in seven Americans calls the state home. No state comes close to California in the size of its population, and none had more of a population gain in the last few decades. Its media markets in a dozen geographic regions contain every possible version of urban, suburban, and rural locales that is available on the national landscape. As for the economy, it is often said that if California sneezes, the nation catches a cold. When the lights went out during California's electricity crisis, businesses elsewhere worried about the impact, and the national press, reflecting the state's relevance, covered the story on a daily basis. In the realm of politics, no state has as many members in the U.S. Congress; after the 2000 Census, California was awarded fifty-three Congressional seats. Nor does any state have close to as many members in the electoral college: in 2004, California will have fifty-five electoral college votes. Certainly, in Bush's defeat of Gore in 2000, we learned that it is possible to win in the presidential electoral college without California, but we saw how difficult it is to do so.

Although California is ahead of the curve in becoming a "majority-minority" state in its racial and ethnic makeup, the 2000 U.S. Census surprised us in showing that Asian and Latino immigration is a fact in many states that have traditionally been predominantly white with minority black populations.[6] Overall, the Latino population in the United States now outnumbers the black population, and the Asian population is the fastest-growing group. It seems certain that many other states can learn from California as they too face a major change in their racial and ethnic mix. Among other things, California's experience tells others how the political landscape can be altered by increasing diversity.

California is also worth watching for its ability to create, innovate, and experiment. Even now, the rest of the nation waits to see the latest trends coming out of the Silicon Valley. The state has been an economic hotbed for software, multimedia, and Internet start-up companies. Its residents lead the nation in computer, email, and Internet use and in discovering new ways to incorporate the Internet into their everyday lives. The political arena is no different. The initiative process allows policies and lawmaking to move much more quickly, and in an unconventional

6. For the sake of brevity, the designation *whites* will be used in place of *non-Hispanic whites* throughout the book; the designation *blacks* will refer to people who call themselves black or African American and the designation *Latino* to people who describe themselves as Latino or Hispanic.

fashion, bypassing the executive and legislative arena. The state gets to try out new ideas that the voters accept, including tax limits, term limits, casino-style gambling on Indian reservations, use of marijuana for medical purposes, or elimination of bilingual education in public schools. The residents of other states can and sometimes will imitate California's political trends. So it is worth taking note of how Californians' distrust of government surfaced in prosperous times.

SUMMARY OF CHAPTERS

This book is divided into nine chapters. In this first chapter, I offer an introduction to the theme of this book, which is the persistence of public distrust in government during the immediate circumstances of budget surplus and economic prosperity, and the long term trends of dramatic social and economic change. I then review the way we approached this issue, which was to conduct multiple, large-scale surveys during the 2000 elections. I review the basic knowledge on distrust in government and discuss the context of the 2000 election. In addition, I consider the continued relevance of California's experiences with political, social, and economic trends for the rest of the nation.

In Chapter 2, "Sunny Today, Cloudy Tomorrow," I provide an overview of the public's mood during the 2000 elections in California: I consider the unique nature of the state's "politics of prosperity" in light of previous thought about how the public reacts to government in more affluent conditions. In sum, the voters were feeling economically secure and yet highly pessimistic about their future quality of life in the state. I hypothesize that this combination is a result of Californians' distrust of elected officials and government and that it leads to hesitation about expanding the government's role.

In Chapter 3, "The Tax Revolt and the Golden State," I address the central questions of what happens when voters' distrust from the twenty-year tax revolt and confronts the reality of federal and state budget surpluses. I reexamine what is known about public attitudes toward tax and spending. I look at the public's reactions to campaign and policy proposals to spend the surplus, including providing more funds for government programs in general and specific programs that are seen as popular and useful to the general public and to reducing taxes and paying down the national debt.

In Chapter 4, "Schools, Schools, and Schools," I examine the strong emphasis Californians placed on improving the quality of the public school system. Voters told us that schools were their top priority for government action, yet when I look at how Californians responded to education initiatives on the 2000 ballot, I find they are concerned about the prospect of their taxes increasing for schools.

In Chapter 5, "Growth and Environmentalism," I consider the political focus on growth and environmental issues in good economic times. I follow the reemergence of the growth control initiatives on the local scene, after a hiatus during the recession of the 1990s, as evidence that residents distrust local elected officials and want to make the land use and growth decisions on their own. Moreover, environmental problems were much on people's minds in 2000, challenging the public to think about the government's role in addressing regional, state, and global environmental issues.

In Chapter 6, "The Latino Century Begins," I look at the population group expected to be the largest racial and ethnic group in the state by the 2020s. Latinos continued their pattern of increased voting in the 2000 elections. Thus, they played an important role in the outcome of statewide elections, and many Latinos won in federal and state legislative races. Latinos differ from other groups, expressing more trust in government and a desire for government to play a more active role in their lives. If trends persist, growth in the Latino population could result in a shift in Californians' distrust of government.

In Chapter 7, "The Un-Party State," I explore the common misconception that California has become a one-party state ruled by the Democrats. Actually, there has been no shift in the voter registration toward either of the major parties. Instead, the partisan leanings of the increasing numbers of voters outside of the major parties explain the current election trends. Moreover, distrustful Californians prefer to make new laws by voting on citizens' initiatives, rather than having partisan elected officials making policy decisions. I look at how the voters reacted to the 2000 elections, including the presidential vote and ballot controversy in Florida, and the state's initiative process.

In Chapter 8, "Lights Out for California?" I offer some thoughts about how Californians reacted to an obvious and serious government failure. Californians were thrown into uncertainty by an electricity crisis that threatened higher utility bills, rolling blackouts, and a slowing economy. The problem had its roots in a flawed deregulation law passed by the governor and legislature. This episode reinforced Californians' distrust in government, their perception that the state is unprepared for its future, and their desire to take lawmaking into their own hands.

In Chapter 9, "Insights after a Golden Moment," I provide an array of observations about what we have learned about distrust of government from viewing this phenomenon during a time of budget surplus and economic prosperity, and then during an electricity crisis that nudged the public's mood toward further pessimism, followed by the terrorist attacks of September 11, 2001, that shook American lives from coast to coast. I also offer some recommendations for making California's unique democratic system work—a critical first step in restoring public confidence in government and elected officials.

CHAPTER 2

Sunny Today,
Cloudy Tomorrow

After a particularly bad recession in the early 1990s, California found itself in unusually good economic times as it approached the twenty-first century. Unemployment was at an all-time low, new millionaires were minted daily in the dot.com Land of Oz, the stock market seemed unable to go anywhere but up, and the real estate market was building large equity nest eggs for home owners. It seemed truly like a brave new economic world. There were even those who claimed that the New Economy was not liable to the old rules. Generally, Californians were happy about the present and optimistic about the near future. Nevertheless, there was a growing concern about challenges in the more distant future and about government's ability to cope with those challenges.

VOICES OF CONCERN

Why Californians perceived a dark lining to their golden cloud came out in the focus groups and the surveys we conducted beginning in 1999. The 1999 focus groups previewed public response in the 2000 elections. It was surprisingly easy to get the people who live in the Golden State to verbalize what was wrong with an otherwise perfect picture of prosperity. We heard the same story from people again during the focus groups in April 2001. In a state known for divergence of opinions across its many large regions, there was a remarkable convergence of opinions about the future. The consensus was pessimistic, and the culprit was a belief that government was not up to the challenge.

Almost everyone we talked with had noticed growth in their own region and expected growth to continue, no matter if the state's economy went boom or bust. One respondent commented, "We're not prepared to handle growth"; another one asserted, "We're growing too fast"; and someone else added, "I'm worried about the quality of life in California." When asked to envision the future, these Californians presented an image more like a nightmare than utopia. The scenes in the science-fiction movie *Bladerunner* come to mind. "We're going to be packed in like sardines," commented one Californian; and another added, "We'll be one big parking lot." In one of the groups, a participant wondered out loud, "Where are future Californians going to live?"

These negative feelings about the effects of growth and related trends extended far into the future. While most people were worried about themselves in the tomorrowland of California, many also fretted over the legacy that would be left for future generations. One parent of a young child told us: "I worry about what kind of life my child will have." An older Californian wondered, "Will future generations have to leave?" A commonly held view about California was that the state's problems were unmanageable and that California would become unlivable in the future.

A cynical view of government and a distrustful eye on politicians were major contributors to the gloom-and-doom scenarios of the future. One resident concluded, "I don't believe the state or local governments are ready for the growth we're going to see." Another individual firmly believed that "we don't have leadership to deal with these growth issues." When asked to describe the future and our ability to control the state's destiny, one resident said, "I'm getting nervous. Politicians never think beyond their own terms." Largely, it seems, thinking about government and elected officials made people feel worse about the future. This is typified by the resident who stated, "If we don't have good planning, we'll be a mess."

At this juncture, the public viewed its government and elected representatives more as part of the problem than as part of the solution. The public perceived that the ship of state was heading into a storm without a competent captain at the helm. Clearly, these attitudes suggest that political distrust is likely to continue shaping policy preferences, if it could so powerfully affect them even during good economic times. As Geoffrey Chaucer said in a different time and place, "If gold rusts, what will iron do?"[1]

THE NEW POLITICAL CULTURE:
RETHINKING THE POLITICS OF PROSPERITY

In the midst of a happy reversal of fortune, one could hardly be faulted for expecting an appreciative electorate that would smile on government. The idea that economic conditions affect voters' moods, preferences, and ballot choices is common knowledge in both the political world and scholarly literature.

It is generally the rule that incumbents are rewarded with reelection when voters go to the polls in a happy and confident mood. Angry voters facing job insecurities and an economy that is failing them tend to punish their elected officials by turning them out of office. The most vivid example in recent times was the experience of George H. Bush in 1992. Bush saw his sky-high approval ratings following the Gulf War take a nosedive soon after, when the economy faltered. What once seemed like a certain reelection ended in defeat. Moreover, voters are known to gravitate toward pocketbook issues, such as government programs that will offer them needed funds and services when the economy is tanking or tax cuts that might put more money in their hands.

In good economic times, voters have been known to be more willing to give their government the green light on spending more money. In California, for instance, the legislature has a tendency to place state bond measures on the ballot when times are good, since people are feeling relatively more generous about their government's borrowing more money. In bad economic times, voters feel stingier about the big price tags of public projects, so the state's leaders are reluctant to ask for permission to borrow. The decline in opposition to state bonds is not the same as the public's gaining more trust in government. Rather, the public is less risk averse about debt in good times.

This received wisdom seems at odds with both Californians' expressed distrust of government and the outcomes of the 2000 election that we discuss later on. However, both may be explained to some degree by what political scientist Robert Inglehart (1998) has identified as "post-

1. From "The Prologue to Canterbury Tales," line 500, by Geoffrey Chaucer (2001). I thank Joyce Peterson for pointing out this reference.

materialist values" and their effect on voters' political decisions in Western nations, or what sociologist Terry Clark calls the "New Political Culture." Both refer to the emergence of a new type of voter in more well-heeled local communities. Essentially, the idea is that affluent voters have the luxury of not having to worry about how government will provide for their basic material needs, such as jobs, food, housing, and clothing. They can focus their attention on "quality of life" issues, such as traffic and the environment. They can attend to "lifestyle" concerns, such as how to achieve greater personal freedom and self-fulfillment through the political process.

Clark and other social scientists also point out that distrust in government is an important ingredient of these postmaterialist values. People become more wary of the actions of traditional political institutions—such as central governments, interest groups, and political parties—as they have less personal need for government intervention. Their voting is focused on candidates and ballot initiatives that mirror their specific concerns, and their quality of life concerns lead them to seek more local authority and solutions.

California has long been a hotbed for postmaterialist values, according to other recent studies. The state's voters—largely upscale and suburban compared with the overall population—have the basic characteristics that fit the socioeconomic profile, while the dominant politics of liberalism on social and environmental issues and conservatism on fiscal and "law and order" issues is the hallmark of the New Political Culture.[2]

How would Californians weigh their political options and policy choices in the context of prosperous times? While the voters may be somewhat less stingy when they feel economically secure, their negative feelings about the fiscal performance of their government are persistent. While they may be more receptive to the idea of long-term public investments for the good of the state, their leanings are often toward solving matters in their locality and, preferably, through the citizens' initiative process. We can expect a hot-and-cold reaction to government intervention: confidence and a desire to tackle obvious future worries but deep ambivalence about the ability of government to follow through on promises. It is also likely that distrust in government will contribute to worries about the state's future.

2. See also Clark (1994); Clark and Ferguson (1983); Clark and Hoffman-Martinot (1998); and Clark and Rempel (1997).

THE PUBLIC'S MOOD: CURRENT OPTIMISM,
FUTURE PESSIMISM

In most ways, the series of public opinion surveys conducted in the course of the year leading up to the 2000 elections confirmed what we heard from residents in focus groups, only with more precision and in greater detail. Residents were in a consistently positive mood about the state for over a year leading up to the November 2000 presidential election, yet many expressed deep concerns about the future of California.

One simple question, oft-repeated in preelection surveys, was whether voters thought their state was headed in the right or the wrong direction (see Table 2-1). Generally, a "right direction" response is an indication of a content electorate, whereas a "wrong direction" response signals a frustrated electorate that probably wants change. In the course of six surveys, about six in ten Californians said that things in their state were going in the right direction, while about three in ten said that things were going in the wrong direction. These numbers reflected a very stable and optimistic view of the state in the moment and in the near term.

This optimistic view of the current state conditions was not only pervasive over time but also across demographic groups and geographic regions. There were some variations in survey responses, predictably, depending upon personal circumstances. Latinos expressed more happiness with the state than whites did. San Francisco Bay Area residents were more upbeat than were people living in the Central Valley. Income, age, and education all mattered to some degree. Nevertheless, in no groups were there more people expressing a negative opinion than a positive opinion.

It is important to point out that Californians are not always in such a steady, happy mood. Since these kinds of survey questions are commonly asked in election cycles, there is a long history of responses. In my own work, I had monitored the mood of the electorate in a very different time, during the deepest and darkest days of the recession in the early 1990s. During the 1994 election, twice as many Californians were negative as were positive toward the way things were going in their state. In essence, the state's mood was the polar opposite in the months before the 2000 election.[3]

3. The results on the "right direction/wrong direction" question were similarly upbeat and consistent during the 1998 election. This points to the fact that this positive mood trend stretches back even further in time (Baldassare, 2000).

TABLE 2.1   OVERALL
CURRENT MOOD

*"Do you think things in California are generally going
in the right direction or the wrong direction?"*

	Right Direction	Wrong Direction	Don't Know
September 1999	61%	34%	5%
December 1999	62	31	7
January 2000	66	26	8
February 2000	65	27	8
August 2000	62	30	8
October 2000	59	32	9

SOURCE: PPIC Statewide Survey (1999b, 1999d, 2000a, 2000b, 2000e, 2000g).

The source of this positive mindset was the state's strong economy. (See Table 2-2.) At least in the short term, California was seen as headed for smooth sailing. Throughout the year leading up to the election, roughly three in four residents believed that the state's economy would be in good shape for the next twelve months, while less than one in four was expecting bad times. Again, one could find more optimism in one group or region than another during a given survey. Still, the vast majority of Californians in all age, income, and racial and ethnic groups were optimistic about the economy.[4]

These more general feelings about the state's conditions and economy were reflected in people's assessments of their own financial situations. Consumer confidence was strong and climbing as we took a series of measurements in the course of a year. Nine in ten people described their financial situation as the same as or better than the year before, while only one in ten residents felt that his or her economic circumstances had worsened. Nine in ten people felt that their finances were stable or improving going into the next year, while only about 5 percent expected their circumstances to get worse.

4. Multiple regressions were analyzed for the "right direction" question, with age, education, income, gender, home ownership, region, and race and ethnicity in the equation. The following B values and significance levels (in parentheses) are for the significant variables from the final equations with all variables, with positive correlations indicating a correlation with "right direction": Education = .13 (.001), Income = .04 (.01), San Francisco Bay Area = .23 (.001), Latinos = .35 (.001), Whites = −.21 (.01), Blacks = −.28 (.01) and Central Valley = −.17 (.001).

TABLE 2.2   CURRENT ECONOMIC
CONDITIONS

*"Turning to economic conditions in California,
do you think that during the next 12 months we will
have good times financially or bad times?"*

	Good Times	Bad Times	Don't Know
September 1999	72%	23%	5%
December 1999	76	19	5
January 2000	78	15	7
August 2000	72	21	7

SOURCE: PPIC Statewide Survey (1999b, 1999d, 2000a, 2000e).

Sometimes, a good economy has the side effect of diminishing the way that people rate their quality of life. When people feel more secure in their financial circumstances, they are inclined to be more critical about their residential and neighborhood environments. With their basic needs taken care of, they can focus their complaints on lifestyle issues. Moreover, growth spurts can have real consequences for quality of life. A rapidly growing job market can increase the rush hour traffic and add to the stress of daily commutes. In the 1980s, perhaps for both of these reasons, we saw evidence that Californians thought their economy was great but that their quality of life was lacking (Baldassare, 1986).

This trend was not evident at any time before the 2000 election. Californians rated quality of life in glowing terms. Indeed, they were more positive about their quality of life in January 2000 than they were two years earlier. In the January survey, about eight in ten said that things in California were going very well or somewhat well, compared with seven in ten who held such positive perceptions in May 1998. The quality of life ratings were highly favorable across all regions of the state, identical for Latinos and whites, and very strong across all of the major demographic groups.

Adding to the euphoria was the perception that the crime rate was declining. In fact, crime rates dropped sharply in the 1990s, as mentioned earlier, but people were finally perceiving that their state was safer. By the beginning of 2000, Californians were becoming less worried about crime. While half said that crime was a big problem in the state, this was a sharp decline from the 66 percent who held this view just two years earlier. More people than in May 1998 rated crime as only "somewhat of a problem" (42% versus 28%), while there was little change in the numbers of people who thought that crime was no problem at all (7% to 4%). The percentage saying that crime was a problem fell in every region, but residents in the San Francisco Bay Area were the least concerned about this threat. Latinos were much more likely than whites to perceive crime as a big problem. Fear levels among whites dropped sharply over time.

Similarly, Californians were much less likely than they were two years earlier to say that crime is increasing in the state. Still, fewer than four in ten believed that crime rates were really on the decline in the past few years, while one-third felt there had been no change. Across the regions of the state, it was the San Francisco Bay Area residents who were the least likely to think that the crime rate had been increasing. Even though Latinos were more likely than whites to think that crime rates were increasing, most in this group also thought that crime rates had either dropped or stayed the same.

Despite the euphoria about the present and the near-term direction of the state, Californians were negative about long-term trends and future conditions. In a survey conducted in December 1999, we found that most Californians lacked the facts about the current population and future growth of their state, but this did not prevent them from holding negative perceptions of the consequences.

California's then-current population of 34 million was apparently a well-kept secret. Only one in seven Californians placed the state's population within the 30 million to 35 million range. Almost half of the residents thought the state's population was actually below 30 million, one in five believed it was more than 35 million, and one in four were unwilling to even venture a guess. Most people thus have a perception of the state's population that is very dated. The state's population reached 10.6 million in 1950, 20 million in 1970, 23.7 million in 1980, 29.8 million in 1990, and 33.9 million in 2000. Yet 22 percent of residents thought the state had 10 million or fewer inhabitants, and 24 percent said that between 11 million and 29 million people lived in California. In this survey, we did not correct their misperceptions before we asked them to ponder their state's future.

When asked for their best guess about California's population in 2020, residents gave some widely varying and some highly unlikely estimates. The California Department of Finance (1998) estimates that there will be 45 million residents in 2020. Only 10 percent of Californians expect the state's population to be between 40 million and 49 million. Twenty-seven percent expected the population to be under 30 million, less than the actual California population in 2000. Twenty-two percent expected the state's population to reach 60 million or more by the year 2020, while current California Department of Finance forecasts do not put the state's population at that level for more than another twenty years—after 2040. To put these results further in perspective, consider how many Californians have a grasp of both the current population figures and future growth projections. Only 4 percent say that the state population is between 30 million and 35 million today and will be between 40 million and 49 million in 2020. The other 96 percent underestimate or overestimate the current and future populations or are unwilling to make a guess.

Although people may have been lacking knowledge of basic facts about the state, there was a general consensus about what to expect in the regions where they lived. Most people felt that the population would be growing rapidly in the years ahead. When asked to look ahead to what life would be like in their regions in the year 2020, Californians saw cause for both hope and concern (see Table 2-3). Solid majorities believed that the public education system, race and ethnic relations, and job opportunities and economic conditions would improve. However, large majorities also believed that the gap between the rich and the poor would grow, that the quality of the natural environment would decline, and that the crime rate would increase.

We considered the possibility that pessimism about the quality of schools, race relations, the economy, the environment, crime, and the gap between the rich and the poor may go together. They appear to be fairly distinct attitudes. In analyzing the intercorrelations, the five future perceptions are correlated with each other but not very strongly. In particular, negative perceptions of the growing gap between the rich and the poor and toward crime and the environment were only weakly related. In contrast, optimism on race relations, education, and the economy were more closely related. Nor could we find any consistent trends that suggested more negative attitudes about these domains among relative newcomers compared with the state's longer-term residents or among the more affluent residents compared with those with lesser incomes.

More important, many Californians were pessimistic in their general long-term outlook for the state. Nearly half expected California to be a

TABLE 2.3   SPECIFIC HOPES
AND FEARS ABOUT THE FUTURE

"Looking ahead to the year 2020, which is more likely to happen in your region?"

	Will Improve	Will Get Worse	Other/ Don't Know
Public education system	63%	34%	3%
Race and ethnic relations	61	34	5
Jobs and the economy	60	35	5
Crime rate	41	55	4
Quality of the natural environment	37	60	3
Gap between rich and poor	23	72	5

SOURCE: PPIC Statewide Survey (1999d).

worse place to live in the year 2020, while only one in four expected it to be a better place (see Table 2-4). This amounts to an 18-point gap between pessimists and optimists. Thirty percent expected no change.

In every major region, those expecting California would be a worse place to live outnumbered those who thought things would be better. Latinos were more optimistic about the state's future than whites were. Latinos were equally likely to say that California would be a better place, a worse place, or that there would be no change. In contrast, whites were more likely to think it would be a worse place than a better place. Otherwise, this grim view was consistent across age categories and other demographic groups.[5]

Pessimism was greatest among those with the most accurate sense of the state's future population. Of those who thought the state's population will reach the expected 40 million to 49 million by 2020, half believed the state would be a worse place to live, while only one in six were looking for California to be a better place to live in the future. Those who said the state's population in 2020 would reach the predicted 40 million to 49 million were also more likely than others to believe that

5. Multiple regressions were analyzed for the "overall outlook in 2020" question, with age, education, income, gender, home ownership, region, and race and ethnicity variable in the equation. None of these factors were significant at the .01 level or lower. However, specific perceptions of conditions in 2020 were highly correlated with the overall outlook question, after controlling for these same demographic variables.

TABLE 2.4   OVERALL
OUTLOOK FOR 2020

"Do you think that in 2020 California will be a better place to live than it is now, or a worse place to live than it is now, or will there be no change?"

	All Adults	Latinos	Whites
Better	25%	34%	21%
Worse	43	31	48
No change	30	33	29
Don't know	2	2	2

SOURCE: PPIC Statewide Survey (1999d).

the income gap would grow, and they were less likely to think that race and ethnic relations would improve.

Californians' pessimism about the future was compounded by their lack of faith that either the federal or the state government could solve their important problems. Only one in ten said they had "a lot" of confidence that when the government in Washington sets out to solve a problem, the problem will actually be solved; half of the state's residents said they had "some" confidence in the federal government's abilities to solve problems, and four in ten reported their confidence in the federal government amounted to "just a little" or "none at all." The responses varied somewhat by political party, demographic groups, and race and ethnicity. Democrats were more likely than Republicans and independent voters to have at least some faith in the federal government's abilities. Those residents who were less likely to routinely participate in the political process—younger adults, Latinos, people with lower incomes, and people with no college education—were a little more optimistic than others. Still, few residents in any of the political or demographic groups expressed a lot of confidence that the federal government can set out to solve a problem and actually solve it.[6]

As for their faith in state government, fewer than one in ten expressed "a lot" of confidence that the government could solve a problem when it decides to do so. About half said they had some confidence, while one in three said they had little or no confidence. Democrats were a little

6. The question was asked in October 2000 (PPIC Statewide Survey, 2000g).

more likely than Republicans and independent voters to have at least some confidence, but no demographic or political group expressed a great deal of confidence in state government. Moreover, we found no evidence that the public's trust in the state's problem-solving abilities had increased over time: indeed, a similar question asked in the fall of 1998 found a little more confidence in the state government's solving problems than did the survey after the 2000 election (69% to 63%).[7]

Distrust of government correlated highly with negative views of the future. Those who said they could trust the government to do what is right "always or most of the time" were optimistic about the future, while those who thought they could trust the government "only sometimes or never" were pessimistic. Two in three residents held the latter, negative view in this measure of government distrust, so the gloomy outlook on the future prevailed. Similarly, most residents who thought the governor and state legislature were doing an excellent job had a positive outlook on the state's future, while others were more negative. However, most residents rated both their state officials and the state's future in less-than-glowing terms. While these responses fall short of proving a direct causal link, there is certainly a strong association between government distrust and pessimism about the future.

GETTING HERE FROM THERE

What explains these fears for the future and this profound distrust of government in the midst of such prosperous times? As the focus group comments suggest, in some ways Californians were seeing the state as a victim of its prosperity and the future as hostage to its growth. As for distrust, much of that may spring from government's perceived and actual performance—in both bad and good times.

Happy Days Were Here Again

As the 2000 election approached, California was experiencing an unusually long period of economic well-being. Not too long before, doomsayers had given California up for dead after the end of the Cold War devastated the state's aerospace and defense industry, leading to massive civilian job losses and economic shocks from military base closings.

7. See PPIC Statewide Survey (2001a), reporting findings from January 2001.

Moreover, the collapse of the savings and loan industry helped to push the real estate market and construction industries into a deep recession. All of this took place in the midst of a terrible series of natural and man-made disasters in the state, including fires, floods, earthquakes, riots, and a county government bankruptcy. Like the phoenix, the state of California rose from its ashes in the mid-1990s, more powerful than ever. As a result of its preeminence in computers and the Internet, the state was once again a global economic superpower. There was a steady stream of good economic news leading up to 2000, leaving many to believe the state's economic boom would go on.

The state's employment figures are indicative of California's powerful economic rebound during the 1990s (see Table 2-5). The state began the decade with a nonfarm payroll employment of about 12.5 million. Then the recession hit. For the next few years, the state's workforce shrank by almost a half million and reached a low of 12 million by 1993. The unemployment rate climbed from 5.8 percent to 9.4 percent. The economy hit bottom in 1993, and then there were annual employment gains every year through 2000. At first, the gains were small, but they accelerated to large employment increases and a steady drop in the state's unemployment rate. Between 1995 and 2000, the state's nonfarm payroll employment grew by over 2 million—from 12.5 million to 14.5 million. In the year before the 2000 election alone, the state gained over 500,000 jobs. In the meantime, the unemployment rate fell to a near-historic low of 4.9 percent.[8]

The availability of jobs was not the only thing going right for California in the late 1990s. Personal incomes also showed an impressive increase by the year 2000, meaning that Californians had more money in their pockets to spend on goods and services (see Table 2-6). Per capita personal income had reached about $22,000 in 1991 and stayed within the $20,000 to $23,000 range during the recession of the early 1990s. However, per capita incomes started showing substantial, positive annual changes of at least 4 percent beginning in 1995 and carrying through every year for the rest of the decade. Per capita personal income had reached close to $30,000 by 1999 and was growing at a rate of almost 6 percent a year—at a time when inflation was well below that figure. Thus, income growth resulted in real increases in Californians' ability to spend money.

8. I was helped by discussions with Michael Dardia and Fred Cannon, who provided some of the economic statistics. See also Dardia (1995) and Dardia and Luk (1999).

TABLE 2.5   EMPLOYMENT AND
UNEMPLOYMENT IN CALIFORNIA,
1990–2000

	Nonfarm Payroll Employment (in thousands)	Unemployment (in thousands)	Unemployment Rate
1990	12,499	874	5.8%
1991	12,359	1,172	7.7
1992	12,153	1,431	9.3
1993	12,045	1,441	9.4
1994	12,159	1,328	8.6
1995	12,422	1,209	7.8
1996	12,743	1,120	7.2
1997	13,129	1,005	6.3
1998	13,596	968	5.9
1999	13,991	864	5.2
2000	14,518	833	4.9

SOURCE: California Department of Finance (2001a).

People started flocking back to the Golden State by the late 1990s. The state's population stood at about 29.9 million after the 1990 census; and for a few years, even in the early part of the recession, the state was still gaining large numbers of migrants. Most of these new residents were from abroad. However, for several years, beginning in 1993, the state had a net out-migration. This is a rare event in California's modern history and indicative of how deep and painful the economic recession was for the state's residents. While immigration from other countries was continuing, a sizable number of California residents decided to move to other states. However, the out-migration ended in 1997, when the state experienced the highest annual net in-migration of the decade, followed by equally impressive gains in 1998. A good economy was once again attracting immigrants and keeping current residents in-state. According to both the 2000 U.S. Census and the state's figures, California had a net gain of about 4 million people, reaching a population of about 34 million residents.[9]

9. I was helped by discussions with Hans Johnson about state migration trends. See California Department of Finance (2000a, 2000c) and Johnson (1996, 1999, 2000).

TABLE 2.6   PER CAPITA
PERSONAL INCOME IN
CALIFORNIA, 1991–1999

	Amount	Annual Change
1991	$22,024	0.6%
1992	22,722	3.2
1993	22,927	0.9
1994	23,473	2.4
1995	24,496	4.4
1996	25,563	4.4
1997	26,759	4.7
1998	28,280	5.7
1999	29,910	5.8

SOURCE: California Department of Finance (2000b).

Those who owned homes in California were rewarded by the strong showing the economy made in the late 1990s (see Table 2-7). The rising prices for homes, in turn, added to the net worth of many of the approximately six in ten households owning their homes. In 1991, the median price for a single-family home in California reached $200,000. For several years, a weak economy and consumer pessimism led to median home prices slipping more than 10 percent to about $177,000 by 1996. After that, home prices showed steady gains each year through 2000, clearly coupled with ongoing trends in employment, income growth, and the net in-migration that we have already reviewed. Home prices grew by almost $10,000 between 1996 and 1997, $15,000 between 1997 and 1998, $16,000 between 1998 and 1999, and an astounding $26,000 between 1999 and 2000. At the time of the 2000 election, the median price of a single-family home in California was about $243,000. This latest figure reflects more than a 10 percent annual increase from 1999 to 2000 and over a 20 percent increase for the decade for those fortunate long-term home owners.

Clearly, the return on investments for home owners was substantial in the 1990s. The news was also positive for most of the state's residents who owned stocks or stock mutual funds. Based on the results of our statewide surveys, we estimate that about half of Californians are invested in the stock market. All of the stock indices—including the Dow

TABLE 2.7   EXISTING
SINGLE-FAMILY
MEDIAN HOME
PRICE, 1990–2000

1990	$193,770
1991	200,060
1992	197,030
1993	188,240
1994	185,010
1995	178,160
1996	177,270
1997	186,490
1998	201,440
1999	217,510
2000	243,390

SOURCE: California Association of Realtors (2001).

Jones, Standard and Poor's, and high-tech-oriented Nasdaq showed solid gains in the 1990s. Californians who were stock owners were reaping the rewards of a bull market that, in many ways, was a reflection of the state's publicly owned computer and Internet companies that had led to the state's economic rebound. Californians with stock holdings felt very good about their investments, which appeared to be doing well on paper, if not in real cash terms.[10]

At rare moments, everything seems to be going in the right direction. California in the late 1990s was having this kind of moment. Over the past few decades, Californians have considered crime to be one of their most worrisome problems, yet the crime rate in California was dropping sharply. Some claim credit is due to politicians who passed a tough Three Strikes law in the early 1990s, requiring mandatory lockup of repeat offenders. Others claim the strong economy reduced the motivation for crime; yet others point to demographic trends such as aging. Whatever the reason, the violent crime rate declined by more than 40 percent between 1993 and 1999, and the property crime rate fell by 50 percent—from 2,309 cases per 100,000 people to 1,166 per 100,000. At least from a statistical standpoint, California had become much safer for the public, at the same time that people were also enjoying the per-

10. This was reported in an August 2000 survey (PPIC Statewide Survey, 2000e).

sonal benefits of a strong economy and prosperity (California Secretary of State, 2000a).

The Downside of Prosperity and Growth

Whatever explains the public's mood, in the prosperous late 1990s, a number of trends were making Californians wish they could trust government to act in the public interest or at least to respond competently to problems. The fear that we heard in focus groups that the state's population was growing larger at a furious pace was confirmed through the 2000 Census figures. (See Table 2-8.) California has gained more than 4 million residents since 1990, adding more people to its landscape in the last decade than are present in either the second or third largest cities in the United States—Chicago or Los Angeles.

There is almost unanimous consensus that California's ongoing population surge will not stop any time soon. Of course, it is anyone's best guess what the population will be in the future. According to well-regarded estimates by the California Department of Finance, the state is expected to add 10 million people by 2020, reaching 45 million. Looking further out, the department predicts 50 million residents some time in the 2030s. The exact number of new Californians has proven to be difficult to predict. More important, the overwhelming belief among demographers today is that the state will continue to add millions of residents per decade for the foreseeable future.[11]

All of the state's major regions have been growing rapidly. Los Angeles has added 2 million people in the past twenty years, while the San Francisco Bay Area has grown by 1.5 million residents. The regions outside of these two coastal metropolises have been growing even faster. The Central Valley—the vast inland home to the state's agricultural industry that is located between Redding and Bakersfield—has gained 2 million people since 1980. The major Southern California counties outside of Los Angeles—Orange, Riverside, San Bernardino, and San Diego—have picked up 3 million new residents. As a result of the rapid growth outside of the built-up coastal area, for the first time since the Gold Rush, more than half of the state's population is living outside of Los Angeles and the San Francisco Bay Area.

As is the case today, growth will continue to be more rapid outside of coastal regions than inside of Los Angeles and the San Francisco Bay

11. See population projections reported in Baldassare (2000) and Johnson (1999).

TABLE 2.8   CALIFORNIA'S
POPULATION GROWTH
(IN MILLIONS)

1980	23.7
1990	29.8
2000	33.9
2010 (prediction)	40.0
2020 (prediction)	45.5

SOURCE: Baldassare (2000); U.S. Census (2001).

Area. The only place left untouched by growth is in the largely rural, northern counties of the state. This means that sprawling land use patterns and all of its obvious consequences—loss of open space, traffic congestion, long commutes, a lack of affordable housing near work, and air pollution—are spread out over a large area and affect most Californians. It helps to explain why Californians in almost every corner of the state were worried about their state's and region's future.

Adding to the complexities of living in a state with growing numbers of people is the fact that this population increase is fuelled by a growing racial and ethnic diversity. (See Table 2-9.) Twenty years ago, the population of the state was two-thirds white. The 2000 Census revealed a 20-point drop in the white population—to 47 percent—making California a majority-minority state. As of the 2000 Census, one-third of the state's population, or nearly 11 million residents, was Latino. Almost 4 million residents were Asian. In fact, the state's population growth between 1990 and 2000 is accounted for by these two groups. The black population hardly grew at all, and the white population actually declined in absolute numbers—a function of declining births in this aging population group and an out-of-state migration up to the mid-1990s.

Although the state has become more diverse, even more profound racial and ethnic changes are on the way. Before the 2000 Census figures were released—revealing a decline in the white population percentage that exceeded most expectations—it was predicted that Asians and Latinos together would account for the majority of the state's population by 2020. Moreover, Latinos were expected to outnumber whites shortly thereafter. Based on what we now know from the 2000 Census, those two milestones are likely to be reached sooner.

TABLE 2.9   CALIFORNIA'S RACIAL AND ETHNIC MAKEUP

	White	Latino	Asian	Black	Other
1980	67%	19%	7%	7%	—
1990	57	26	10	7	—
2000	47	32	11	7	3%
2010 (prediction)	45	35	13	7	—
2020 (prediction)	40	39	14	7	—

SOURCE: Baldassare (2000); U.S. Census (2001).

What are the factors propelling the state's future trends of rapid population growth and racial and ethnic change? California's post–World War II growth was fueled by a migration of whites and blacks from other states, plus the births of the Baby Boom generation in the 1950s and 1960s. Since the 1980s, the state's major demographic forces have been immigration from Mexico and Asia and the high birth rates of this young immigrant population. An aging white population means that this group is hardly replacing itself, in terms of births versus deaths. In addition, some white retirees may be lured by lower living costs to leave the state. While there is not much in-migration from other states, California is a favorite destination for immigrants of all types from around the globe, including political refugees, the economically deprived, high-tech engineers, doctors, scientists, and wealthy entrepreneurs. It is the births to Latino and Asian residents, however, that account for most of the growth in the 1990s and most of what is projected for the future. While opening the international borders would swell the state's population, tightening restrictions would have little effect. This means that there is little that can be done to slow down the rates of growth and change. The state has no choice but to absorb what amounts to mostly newborn residents.

It would be difficult enough to cope with growth and change alone, but significant problems for the state's future lie in the emerging patterns of social and economic inequality. It turns out that all is not equal when it comes to socioeconomic resources and political participation. We can define California as a majority-minority state in demographic terms. However, this does not translate into economic privilege and political power being evenly distributed along racial and ethnic lines. Whites are the overwhelming majority among those with college degrees and living in the upper-income households. Although no longer in the majority statewide, they constitute most of the people who log on to the Internet, buy and sell stocks and mutual funds, own a home, and vote in the state's elections. Latinos and blacks are overrepresented in the lower income brackets and among those who never go to college. Latinos and Asians are overrepresented among those who do not cast votes in state elections. Some are not eligible to vote because of their noncitizen status, while others who are citizens are not registered to vote. Latinos and Asians also make up almost all of the new residents in the state, so unless their situation improves markedly, the state as a whole faces declines in an array of social indicators.

During these prosperous times, the gap in income between the rich and the poor was still growing (Reed, Glenn Haber, and Mameesh, 1996; Reed, 1999; Daly, Reed, and Royer, 2001). The low-income immigrant population, which is largely Latino, has not fared well relative to others. While the wealthy did splendidly in the good economy, the poor saw only modest improvements in their economic well-being. As a result, millions of Californians are making a bare living on low wages and have no health insurance, no college education, and poor job prospects in the high-paying end of a knowledge-based economy. Since all of the major regions of the state are seeing sharp increases in their Latino and Asian populations—Los Angeles, the rest of the Southern California region, the San Francisco Bay Area, and the Central Valley alike—these trends in inequality are pervasive statewide.

Government Performance: Weighed and Found Wanting

Faced with these challenges, Californians evidently found little to convince them that their state was in a good position to handle the growth and to alleviate the racial and ethnic inequalities that were surfacing. All indications were that California had fallen behind the curve in every facet of growth planning. There was a pervasive sense that the state was woefully unprepared for a challenging future. If anything had served as a warning of this predicament, it was the state's electricity crisis and the threat of rolling blackouts. But electricity problems were only a symptom of a much larger problem. California ranked near the bottom in state spending for infrastructure—the basic ingredients needed by communities, such as roads, water systems, sewers, bridges, jails, courts, libraries, and public buildings of all sorts. Some have estimated the tab to be around $90 billion for meeting the state's infrastructure needs of the next decade; others claim it is even higher. Simply put, the state government did not and does not have this kind of money and would have to go on a borrowing binge to get it.

School spending is another critical area where the state had failed to keep pace with population growth and changes. The state's public schools and its public colleges and universities offer the last, best hope for improving the future jobs, wages, and living conditions of the growing Latino and Asian populations. They offer an avenue to a better future for the new Californians. Yet California's spending per pupil was behind that of many other states, even after dedicating the government's budget surplus to this purpose. The jury was still out on whether education reforms had halted a downward slide in students' test scores. Nonetheless, the task at hand for the state's schools was monumental in nature, while the local and state resources at their disposal were modest by comparison.

In the late 1990s, California had the luxury of several back-to-back years of job growth and budget surpluses as it faced these challenging demographic trends. Still, the government was struggling to keep up with the changes and fell further behind in planning for the future. A great unknown was how well the state and local governments could perform under these circumstances while weathering a future economic storm.

Evidence from the recent past was not encouraging. During the deep recession of the early 1990s, the state's elected officials may have tried their best under difficult conditions, but the record would indicate that they were not able to perform well under crisis conditions.[12] The state government quickly ran up a huge budget deficit. It was forced to take back money from cash-strapped local governments in order to pay for the public schools. These state government activities placed county government in Los Angeles on the brink of fiscal meltdown, as it ran out of money to pay for the health care bills of a large, uninsured population. The Orange County government went bankrupt by making risky investments to solve the cash flow problems created by the state government's moves. Angry with the gross mismanagement of local funds and ever-distrustful of giving their government more money to work with, Orange County voters refused a half-cent sales tax to bail out their county government. Luckily, the county government was able to resort to a massive bond offering that ended the fiscal crisis.

12. The fiscal problems facing state and local governments during the 1990s recession are reported in Baldassare (1998) and Baldassare et al. (2000).

Throughout the state, the voters' mood turned sour and ungenerous, and they directed their frustration at illegal immigrants. In 1994, a citizens' initiative that called for turning illegal immigrants away from health care and public schools received the solid support of the electorate. The governor supported this initiative. Latinos were bitter about this experience. Many Latinos felt they were the targets of a political campaign that sought to blame immigrants for the state's fiscal and economic problems. This whole unpleasant episode ended when the state's economy began to improve in the mid-1990s and state and local fiscal circumstances turned rosy again.

But the state did not pass this test with flying colors, and this gave residents pause for thought about the ability of California to handle serious crises. The governor and state legislature, reluctant to raise taxes too much, made fiscal choices that proved to be harmful to local governments. The constraints on passing new taxes, which were imposed earlier by the voters, made it difficult for local governments to find new revenue sources to make up for the state government cuts. As the state continued to grow and change during tough economic times, the voters reacted by passing citizens' initiatives that cut off government aid to illegal immigrants and that ended affirmative action programs in state and local governments. Californians had no reason to feel assured that their government would be any better able to cope in the next downturn.

Did California government do less well in the 1990s than any other democratic government in the world? That is debatable. In all fairness, there were certain elements of its governance system—strict controls on state and local tax increases, specific rules about how state funds are allocated, stringent term limits for legislators, and a generous use of the initiative process by wealthy special interests—that seem to make for more difficult circumstances of policymaking for the governor and legislature. It might also be that Californians have higher expectations for what their state government needs to do to prepare for the future, because there is a general recognition that this is a big state that is growing rapidly and changing in its social composition. Places in a more steady state of growth may expect less from their government.

Is a lack of confidence in government during the 2000 elections a uniquely California phenomenon? Probably not. Californians in the past, as well as Americans as a whole and voters in other states during these prosperous times, also expressed distrust in government. Indeed, a lack of confidence in government has been a political constant in many Western nations for decades. California was a special case in that its residents were able to, and often did, express their preferences for government actions through the citizens' initiative process. Californians at this time were also in the special circumstance of recognizing that they needed the government to act and prepare for a future of rapid growth and change. Like others, they would struggle with this question: should they overcome their distrust and ask government to address the needs around them?

CONCLUSIONS AND IMPLICATIONS

There were many doomsayers who had given California up for dead in the early 1990s. They were proven wrong by the end of the decade. The Golden State did indeed survive the economic shocks of closing military bases, shrinking defense and aerospace industries, earthquakes, fires, and a violent episode of urban unrest in Los Angeles. By the mid-1990s, the state's high-tech, globally oriented economy was growing rapidly, and its residents were the beneficiaries of a healthy job market, rising incomes, a booming stock market, and extraordinary housing appreciation.

The federal and state governments' conditions also improved remarkably in parallel with the economy as the 1990s progressed. Washington had routinely run up large federal budget deficits in good times and bad times, but now the winding down of the Cold War and increasing employment resulted in growing federal budget surpluses. Closer to home, Californians watched their state government switch from fiscal austerity to significant budget surpluses, which could provide extra funding for schools, roads, and an array of neglected state and local programs. On a range of social issues, such as crime, chronic unemployment, and welfare, government appeared to be making headway in tackling the issues that had once seemed resistant to change.

The public's mood was buoyant and bordering on exuberant. Californians were overwhelmingly and consistently rating the current state of their state as healthy. They were optimistic about the direction of the state's economy and positive in their assessments of the overall quality of life. As for their own financial circumstances, most felt they were seeing improvement and expected better times ahead.

Yet despite all of the positive sentiment, the public's mood turned glum when the conversation turned toward the state's long-term future. Many Californians expected conditions in the state to become worse over the next several decades. Most residents worried about the prospects of living in a society where the beauty of the natural environment around them would deteriorate and economic inequalities would grow larger.

Why do Californians expect things to get worse? First, residents are conscious that their state is in the midst of rapid population growth that is changing California's social character and environmental landscape. They are convinced that their government is not up to the task of accommodating the growth and change that lies ahead. Pessimism is strongest amongst those Californians who are most distrustful and disappointed in government's performance. Still, many residents feel their government has done too little to prepare for the future and that some things need to be done by government to plan for growth and change. How the public weighs its belief in the need for government actions against its feelings of distrust in government—while making choices during the 2000 elections—is explored in the next few chapters.

CHAPTER 3

The Tax Revolt and the
Golden State

It would be hard to find a better testing ground for the staying power of the tax revolt and any related, underlying feelings of government distrust than California in an era of budget surplus. The Golden State is the birthplace of Proposition 13, the home of the Reagan Revolution, and the place where voters have routinely displayed their antipathy for taxes and politicians through the initiative process. For more than two decades, California has been the place where a unique brand of conservatism on fiscal issues and liberalism on personal freedom has prevailed across political party lines.

Would the good times experienced during the 2000 election reduce support for Proposition 13 and other measures designed to limit government's ability to raise taxes? Voters were feeling good about the economy and their own finances. Federal and state government coffers were overflowing with revenues from new jobs, income growth, and a hot stock market. There was apparently no end in sight for the bulging budget surpluses and no threats of federal or state tax increases on the horizon. The normal factors that strained government budgets—increased spending on the military, crime control, and welfare programs—all seemed to be in check for the time being. The only major fiscal concern of politicians seemed to be this one: how should we spend the surplus dollars that were being amassed by the federal and state governments?

The big unknown was how the voters would respond to this unique fiscal circumstance. On the one hand, they were blessed with huge federal and state budget surpluses that could free up money to spend on many government programs. This windfall coincided with a time in which the California public was nervous about problems that were clouding the state's future and were highlighting the need for more government funding. On the other hand, residents did not trust their governments with the money those governments now had. The temptation was to ask for the money back in the form of a tax refund. How these competing agendas were resolved in California voters' minds during the state's 2000 presidential election provides a fascinating insight into the tenacity of the tax revolt and its relationship with distrust of government.

THE TAX REVOLT: FISCAL CONSERVATISM AND VOTER DISTRUST

The public's commitment to the tax revolt has run deep in California. The effects of voter support for limiting taxes have been immense. Often, though, the causes and consequences of the antitax attitudes have been misunderstood. Some of the loudest and best-organized proponents of tax cuts are ideological conservatives who favor drastic reductions in government spending and a much more restricted role for government in addressing social problems. But that is a relatively small group compared with the high level of voter support often achieved in antitax initiatives and one that by no means reflects the broad and varied profile of tax revolt advocates that surfaces in public opinion surveys. Some have studied the public opinion surveys and concluded that many of the advocates of tax reductions also want government spending maintained or in some cases increased. This has led some scholars to describe the tax revolt in California and elsewhere in the nation as not much more than an effort by the public to get "something for nothing" by reducing their taxes (Citrin, 1979; Sears and Citrin, 1982), but there appears to be more than a naive self-interest at work in the tax revolt.[1]

---

1. This section relies on the findings from a number of political science studies on attitudes towards taxes and spending and distrust of government, including Alvarez and Brehm (1998); Beck, Rainey, and Traut (1990); Citrin (1979); Hansen (1998); Hawthorne and Jackson (1987); Lowery and Sigelman (1981); MacManus (1995); Roberts, White, and Bradley (1994); Scholz and Lubell (1998a, 1998b); Sears and Citrin (1982); and Shapiro and Young (1989).

Studies have focused on a wide range of political and economic factors that led people in California and other states to favor tax limits. Many have been disappointed in their efforts to find differences in support levels across broader demographic categories. Certainly, there has been evidence suggesting that public employees or people receiving government assistance are more opposed to tax cuts than others, but there has not been much in the way of demonstrable evidence of the characteristics that determine support for tax cuts. This has led some to conclude that there are many factors at work, which vary from state to state—such as the actual tax burdens, issues of tax equity, episodes of government inefficiency, and conflicts over how the tax revenues are distributed into public programs.

Much of the study of the tax revolt in the past two decades has been tied to what was seen as a chronic problem of "fiscal strain" in all levels of government. In other words, governments were under tight budget constraints to provide the funding for needed programs, because tax revenues were not growing as fast as service needs. To make matters worse, the public was at the same time calling for restraint on taxes and the same or higher levels of public services. Some observers concluded that the public would some day have to choose between tax increases and drastic service reductions. At that point, it would come to its senses and realize that it could not get something for nothing and it would abandon its unrealistic preferences. But that day of reckoning never came, at least in a way that most of the voting public would ever notice.

Who are these tax revolt supporters and what do they really want? They are a loosely knit political coalition who oppose any further broad increases in the tax burden at a given point in time. They might, on the other hand, favor limited tax increases for special purposes. Clark and Ferguson (1983) refer to them as "new fiscal populists," and others have called them "fiscal conservatives," which distinguishes them from ideological conservatives. There is evidence of solid middle-class support; thus, it is not simply a conflict over redistributing the wealth from rich to poor. Much of the support base is also evidently among suburban dwellers and many home owners, and it includes substantial numbers of middle-aged, professional, and well-educated voters, who are among the most likely to recognize what government does, and does not, do well.

We believe that the main factor in explaining the tax revolt is distrust in government. The timing of the two movements in public opinion is very coincidental—the first major drop in the public's confidence in government began shortly *before* Proposition 13 passed in California, and

antitax sentiments and distrust in government have been political con-
stants ever since in the United States, up to and including the 2000 election. These two phenomena also share a common demographic and political base—extending beyond the conservative electorate to include
large numbers of suburban, middle-class voters. Moreover, many who
favor the tax revolt can overcome their opposition to taxes only if there
are assurances that the money will be spent for specific purposes that
they deem necessary and if there are efforts to assure that the elected
officials will be held accountable for the way the new money is spent.
The conditions imposed on any new tax increases suggest that distrust
of government is a major factor.

Clearly, it is easy to see how a tax revolt could have broad popularity. Most of the public has been telling us that they are dissatisfied with
their government's ability to solve problems, unhappy with the record
of government efficiency in spending tax dollars, and displeased with
their government's responsiveness to the needs for services for people
like themselves. It is not hard to imagine, then, that many people would
think that it is possible to maintain spending on existing programs after
tax cuts and even improve the delivery of public services, since government is viewed as wasteful and ineffective with the money it has. Moreover, the experiences of the past two decades—as governments provided
services in a seemingly uninterrupted fashion after tax limits were imposed—would only reinforce the view that government can do more
with less.

In our analysis of this topic, we recognize that people often combine
antitax sentiment with prospending attitudes, because they harbor deep
feelings of distrust in government. We are not interested in uncovering
seemingly contradictory feelings toward taxes and spending. The effort
here is to establish the scope and content of distrust in government at this
particular time and to examine the implications for tax-and-spending attitudes. We are especially interested in reactions to the real trade-offs that
were offered by the budget surplus during the 2000 elections. People were
confronted with issues such as how much of a tax-cutting effort they
would like to see relative to how much they would prefer current and increased spending on specific programs.

Most studies of the tax revolt have focused on the dilemmas presented
by the combination of fiscal strain and the public's desire to limit taxes.
We know that people believe there is room for both tax limits and decent levels of government spending under these conditions. The circumstances in California at the turn of the century provided a unique op-

portunity to test the staying power of the tax revolt and distrust in government. We can learn through our public opinion surveys if people give much credit to their government for the budget surpluses and whether they are trustful of government in light of these new, positive fiscal circumstances. Earlier in the book, we discussed that the public was worried about the state's future and that many thought that actions are needed to address problems. At the same time, the public's fears about the future in part reflected its disappointment in the government's performance. In light of the budget surplus, we can see if people want a more expansive role to address concerns, or if many still maintain a cautious approach to allocating new money to government.

PROPOSITION 13 AND THE TAX REVOLT LEGACY

California took the national lead in the tax revolt. In June 1978, voters passed Proposition 13 by a wide margin. It has been described by many scholars and writers as one of the most significant political events in California's history (see Citrin, 1979; Lo, 1990; Schrag, 1998; Sears and Citrin, 1982). This citizens' initiative both reflected a prevalent point of view about government and affected how government would have to operate in a world with voter constraints. The proposition has implications on state and local fiscal issues and affects how voters treat their elected officials. It established long-term antitax and antigovernment movements in the state. Proposition 13 has become the "third rail" of California politics: no elected official or candidate for statewide office dares to touch it.

Proposition 13 was a citizens' initiative placed on the ballot by Howard Jarvis, an antitax activist from Los Angeles, and it passed by a wide margin. The initiative rolled back property tax rates and restricted the government's ability to increase local property taxes in the future. Current property assessments were rolled back to the lower levels of the 1975–1976 fiscal year. The property tax rate was limited to 1 percent of the sales price. Increases in property assessments were limited to 2 percent annually until the property was sold again. The new law also made it very difficult to pass new state and local taxes. A two-thirds vote from the state legislature was required to pass any new state taxes, and a two-thirds vote was required from local voters in order to pass local special taxes (see Baldassare, 1998; Legislative Analyst's Office, 1993, 1995).

The fiscal implications of Proposition 13 for California were far-reaching. There was initially a sharp drop in property tax collections, and a major cap was placed on the future growth of this significant local revenue source. The proposition placed the allocation of the property tax on state government, thereby causing local governments to become more dependent on state government to provide funding for their local services. Cities, counties, and schools had to turn to funding from the state government to compensate for the loss of both property tax funds and the ability to increase taxes. This dependence made it more complicated for local governments to make any long-term plans. It also meant that Proposition 13 had different impacts, depending on the state's economy and revenues. In good economic times, the state government could more easily allocate funds to local governments. In bad economic times, the state government might not have the wherewithal to meet the requests for local services. For example, the state government cut back on local funding during the recession of the 1990s, and this had serious consequences for local governments (Baldassare, 1998; Baldassare et al., 2000; Raymond, 1998; Shires, Ellwood, and Sprague, 1998; Shires, 1999; Silva and Barbour, 1999).

The political consequences of Proposition 13 were even more significant. Voters made it much more difficult for their state and local governments to raise taxes. Californians would also have a say in whether their local governments would be able to create any new special taxes. Perhaps as important, the passage of Proposition 13 sent a clear message to state and local elected officials that antitax sentiments and voter distrust in government had reached a critical stage. The political establishment of the state had opposed the citizens' initiative with dire warnings of the consequences, but the voters ignored their advice. Voters seemed to say that they were willing to take the risk of limiting government's ability to raise funds for government services. This would have a chilling effect on political candidates for state and local offices and already-elected officials who talked about raising state or local taxes. It would also invigorate the political careers of conservative candidates who could now find a message that cut across political allegiances. The idea of cutting taxes and limiting the size of government had gained popular appeal and had achieved political success.

Proposition 13 was the beginning, rather than the end, of a two-pronged effort by California voters to both restrict taxes and limit the political power of their elected officials. A year later, Californians voted to impose spending limits on state and local governments when they passed Proposition 4. In 1988, they started a trend of earmarking state spending and taxes for their favorite programs when they passed Proposition 98, an initiative that required the governor and state legislature to maintain a minimum state funding level for schools. In the 1990s, the voters turned against the state's political establishment, passing Proposition 140, which ended career politicians in the state legislature and constitutional offices by setting consecutive term limits, and passing Proposition 198, which threatened the political parties' control by creating an open primary system. California voters extended their reach into limiting spending and taxes in the 1990s, passing an initiative to restrict funding for illegal immigrants and bilingual education and passing an initiative that made it more difficult for local governments to raise fees and taxes not already affected by Proposition 13. For a twenty-year period, up through the 1998 elections, every indication was that the tax revolt was alive and well in California.

There have been many harsh critics of Proposition 13 from academic and policy circles, who have fretted over its negative consequence on local governments in California. Over the years, many blue-ribbon commissions have recommended ways to reform, limit, or turn back the constitutional tax reforms that were enacted by the voters in 1978 (Cain and Noll, 1995; California Constitution Revision Commission, 1996). But the public has given unwavering support to Proposition 13 through all of the second-guessing by the experts. In a poll taken at the time of the twenty-year anniversary of this proposition, the majority of Californians said they would vote "yes" on Proposition 13 again if it were on the ballot. Among its lasting positive effects, according to the voters, is the limiting of property taxes while forcing elected officials to find ways to reduce the costs of government rather than increasing taxes (DiCamillo and Field, 1998). As for its negative effects, a PPIC Statewide Survey conducted in 1998 found than only one in four Californians thought that Proposition 13 had done any harm. Moreover, while Californians may think there are elements of this initiative that have proven to be unfair, there is no agreement on how to reform it (Baldassare, 2000). In sum, there is no groundswell of support for making it easier for local governments to pass taxes.

FROM BUDGET BUST TO BOOM

It is a testimony to the strength of the tax revolt that it could persist in the plenty of the late 1990s. However, some of its persistence may be explained by the economic roller coaster Californians rode during that

TABLE 3.1   CALIFORNIA'S
BUDGET DEFICITS AND
SURPLUSES, 1990–2000
($ IN MILLIONS)

1990–1991	–1,715
1991–1992	–2,962
1992–1993	–2,831
1993–1994	–281
1994–1995	313
1995–1996	235
1996–1997	461
1997–1998	2,595
1998–1999	3,116
1999–2000	8,665
2000–2001	5,849

SOURCE: California Department of Finance (2001c).
NOTE: Deficits and surpluses are calculated based on total
resources available minus expenditures and reserve funds.

decade. (See Table 3-1.) It would be difficult to find a time of greater contrasts in fiscal conditions. The state government was in a deep financial hole early in the decade, forcing the state to divert its funding to local governments and its governor to back a tax increase. At the end of the decade, there was so much surplus cash on hand that the problem for state officials was how to spend it.

California's budget picture was dismal when Governor Pete Wilson entered office in 1990. The state was beginning its most serious recession since the Great Depression. A combination of plummeting tax revenues and skyrocketing costs of providing services to jobless residents and new immigrants was taking a toll on the state budget. In the first fiscal year in the decade, the state budget ran a deficit of $1.7 billion. Then, for the next two years, the deficit ballooned to nearly $3 billion per fiscal year. By 1993–1994, the state's budget deficit had dropped to $281 million. Thus, in the course of four fiscal years, the state's deficit amounted to almost $7.8 billion.

The state's revenues began to improve in the 1994–1995 fiscal year and showed the first surplus of the decade. There were relatively modest budget surpluses for three fiscal years in the mid-1990s. This was a time in which the economy was improving, and tax increases and spending restraints were in effect. It was in the last few years of the decade that the state's budget picture changed dramatically toward the positive. California had a $2.6-billion surplus in 1997–1998, and that increased to $3.1 billion in the following year. The surplus jumped to $8.7 billion in 1999–2000 and to $5.8 billion in 2000–2001. Thus, within a four-year period, the budget surplus totaled $20 billion—an astounding record for state government, made possible by new employment, income growth, and taxes collected on capital gains from a soaring stock market.

California's budget experienced tremendous growth during this decade of improving economic fortunes. The picture at the beginning of the decade was quite bleak. The 1990–1991 state budget was just over $51.4 billion and was little changed for the next four years, which coincided with the period of state budget deficits. In 1994–1995, the state budget was $54.6 billion, amounting to an increase of only about $3 billion from four years earlier (California Department of Finance, 2001c).

The state's fiscal circumstances changed at first slowly and then dramatically for the rest of the decade. The state's budget was growing by about $4 billion to $5 billion a year in the mid-1990s, as the budget surplus increased and the economy was improving the state's revenue flows. It is also important to note that the actions of the state's divided government—a Republican governor and Democratic legislature—were keeping a lid on spending increases. There was uncertainty about the duration and strength of the economic recovery, and this also made state officials cautious in their fiscal outlook. The end of the decade saw large year-to-year increases in state government spending. The state's budget reached $75 billion in 1998–1999, and a year later it grew by almost $10 billion. By the 2000–2001 budget, the state was spending over $100 billion a year, which was nearly twice the amount on record for the 1990–1991 state budget.

Californians also saw their federal government's fortunes change in the course of the 1990s. (See Table 3-2.) The federal government was running a budget deficit of between $200 billion and $300 billion per year for the first half of the decade, according to the Congressional Budget Office. The budget deficit dropped in 1995 and 1996 and was nearly eliminated in 1997. The budget actually ran a small surplus in 1998, much to the surprise of many Washington observers who had taken for granted that the federal government could not balance a budget. The following year, the federal budget surplus exceeded $100 billion, and then it reached $236 billion in 2000. Suddenly, there were estimates that the

TABLE 3.2   FEDERAL
GOVERNMENT BUDGET
DEFICITS AND SURPLUSES,
1990–2000 ($ IN
BILLIONS)

1990	–221
1991	–269
1992	–290
1993	–255
1994	–203
1995	–164
1996	–108
1997	–22
1998	69
1999	124
2000	236

SOURCE: Congressional Budget Office (2001).

federal government would have a budget surplus for several back-to-back years. The policy discussions were changing from how to reduce the federal deficit, including tax increases and spending cuts, to how to best spend the surplus, such as by income tax cuts and increased spending on social, health, and educational programs.

The fiscal conditions of the federal government were benefiting from two important changes in the federal budget. Between 1990 and 2000, revenues grew by nearly 100 percent, from $993 billion to $1.8 trillion. In the meantime, expenditures increased by only about 50 percent, from $1.1 trillion to $1.7 trillion. Foremost, there was considerable improvement in the tax revenues in the late 1990s. The government was taking in more money, while federal government spending was being held in check.

The end of the Cold War meant military expenditures were no longer increasing. The end of a recession also signaled a slowdown in government spending for welfare, health, and other public assistance programs. The Democratic president and Republican Congress were showing restraint in spending and were committed to reducing the size of the government bureaucracy. As a result, we were seeing relatively modest gains in government expenditures at a time when the federal revenue picture was significantly improving. Together, these factors provided for a healthy federal budget surplus, and the predictions in 2000 were that a budget surplus would continue for years (Congressional Budget Office, 2001). Of course, these rosy predictions proved to be shortsighted and wrong only a year later. The events of September 11 placed the federal government in the role of paying a big bill for a war on terror at home and abroad, while a weakened economy and job layoffs meant lower tax revenues for the federal government. Still, the continued prospects of a hefty budget surplus had been on people's minds in 2000.

THE PERSISTENT SPIRIT OF THE TAX REVOLT

As the state moved toward the 2000 election, these economic conditions led candidates and backers of some initiatives to wonder how the dynamics underlying voters' support of Proposition 13 might translate into policy preferences and voting decisions. Would attitudes toward government and taxes change in the light of more positive news about the budget? No one doubted that Californians would still be reluctant to raise their taxes, but the need to do so had evaporated as talk turned to continuing surpluses.

Residents were not at all shy with us when we asked them to voice their views about government in focus groups during the spring of 1999. Nor were they especially generous, even at a time when everything seemed to be going well in the state. "I lack trust in our government," said one respondent, while another added that the problem was that "government is too cloaked in secrecy." A third respondent simply said, "I don't trust them." We also uncovered a general perception among the public that elected officials are not responsive to its needs. One respondent put it simply, "Officials don't listen to us," while another added, "They need to be more responsive and ask us for inputs." There was a cynical view about politicians, best summarized by individuals who said, "Politicians fix only what gets them elected," and "Politicians only care about reelection."

Californians seem to reserve their most negative comments for taxes and their government's performance on fiscal issues. "We don't know where our tax money goes," claimed one respondent, while another observed, "I'm appalled by what comes out of my paycheck." There seemed to be a belief that fiscal inefficiency is rampant in public agencies. "Too many taxes. There's always another level of bureaucracy to handle the money." In fact, many have concluded that fiscal performance rather than a lack of funding stands in the way of solving problems. "They don't deserve more money unless they use it wisely," said one person, while another said, "It's not money—it's using it intelligently," and a third respondent agreed, "They need to better use the money they now have."

What California might do with the budget surplus would seem to present some serious conflict. On the one hand, returning the money to taxpayers in the form of tax cuts would be consistent with the tax revolt. On the other hand, using the surplus for spending on needed services during this time of plenty would not raise taxes, and it could address some problems that had surfaced. As it turned out, Californians' attitudes toward their tax burden and toward government kept the spirit of the tax revolt very much alive. These attitudes deeply influenced their priorities for spending the surplus and regarding the possible expansion of government.

Tax Burdens

On the subject of taxation, a majority of Californians thought their taxes were too high in almost every category of federal, state, and local taxes mentioned in our surveys (see Table 3-3). In general, the perception of paying too much in the way of taxes is part of an overall pattern of anti-tax sentiment that includes the underlying belief that government at all levels wastes the taxpayers' money. In the surveys, two in three Californians complained that their federal income taxes were "too high." This was considerably more than the number complaining that the state and local sales tax, the state income tax, and the local property tax were too high. The federal income tax was more likely than the state and local taxes to be perceived as "much too high." Among the more surprising findings was that the perceived burden of the local property tax was light compared with other state and local taxes. Proposition 13 reduced the local property tax rate and limited property tax increases, so this perception was, in effect, the voters affirming the tax policies they made into state law. Even among home owners, less than half said their local property taxes were too high, while only one in four said these local taxes were much too high.

The public's attitudes toward state and federal income taxes were fairly uniform across regions of the state and across racial and ethnic groups. However, there were very distinct partisan differences with respect to federal taxes. Republicans were much more likely than Democrats and independent voters to say that their federal income taxes were

TABLE 3.3   TAX BURDEN

*"Do you think that each of the following taxes is much too
high, somewhat too high, about right, or too low?"*

	Too High (total)	Much Too High	Somewhat Too High
Federal income tax	65%	35%	30%
State and local sales tax	53	24	29
State income tax	49	24	25
Local property tax	43	24	19

SOURCE: PPIC Statewide Survey (1999b), all adults.

too high. In fact, nearly half of Republicans said that federal income taxes were too high.

The state taxes that evoked the most negative response were related to automobile ownership and driving. Even after the recent fee reduction, six in ten residents said that the state vehicle license fee was too high, and four in ten believed it was much too high. A greater number—three in four residents—said the state gasoline tax was too high, with more than half stating it was much too high. The public's views on these two types of taxes were uniformly negative across regions, political groups, and socioeconomic groups.

Clearly, Californians were not happy with their tax burden and were especially unhappy about the amount of federal income tax they had to pay. In a survey a month before the November 2000 election, the majority of Californians said they felt they paid more than their fair share in taxes, four in ten said they paid about their fair share, and only 2 percent of all adults described themselves as paying less than their fair share. Still, there were sharp differences of opinion between Republicans and Democrats on how much tax money the federal government should be taking.[2]

Attitudes toward Government

Despite mankind's perennial resentment of taxes, one might expect that such a strong economy and large budget surpluses would reduce distrust

2. See PPIC Statewide Survey (2000g). The national survey question by National Public Radio (NPR), the Kaiser Family Foundation, and the Kennedy School in June 2000 had a similar response.

of government and dispose Californians more kindly toward elected officials. What we found was that this distrust persisted, and that few residents gave their elected officials a lot of credit for the economic boom.

A Continued Lack of Trust Only one in three Californians said they thought the government in Washington could be trusted "just about always" or "most of the time." Two in three said they trusted the federal government "only sometimes" or "never." This was one of the most consistent findings in our statewide surveys during this time period. We first recorded it in September 1998, and found almost identical results in January 2000 (see Table 3-4). Our results in California closely parallel those found in numerous national surveys since the 1970s, including those taken at the same time as ours.[3] A break from the long-standing national trend of distrust toward the federal government did not occur until well after the 2000 elections, as part of the American public's immediate response to the terrorist attacks of September 11, 2001, and the government's domestic and international war on terror.

Within California, overall trust in government does vary by partisanship, race and ethnicity, and region. Republicans and independent voters were significantly more likely than others to say they distrusted the federal government. Latinos tended to have a better opinion of the federal government than others did. Those living in Los Angeles were more likely than the rest of the state to say they always or mostly trusted the federal government. Still, overall trust was fairly low in all demographic and political groups.[4]

Perhaps even more impressive during an era of budget surpluses was that the vast majority of Californians (93%) still believed that the people in the federal government wasted at least some tax money, while al-

3. See, for example Citrin (1974); Craig (1996); Dionne (1992); Lipset and Schneider (1983); Miller (1974); Miller and Shanks (1996); Nye, Zelikow, and King (1997); Putnam (1995, 2000); Tolchin (1996); and Yankelovich (1983, 1991, 1999) on the national decline in public trust. Many scholars have linked declining trust to general skepticism about authority (Clark and Inglehart, 1998; Greenberg, 1995; Inglehart, 1998; Lipset, 1996; Samuelson, 1996; Sandel, 1996) or reactions to specific failures such as Watergate and Vietnam (Bok, 1996; Garment, 1991; Orren, 1997; Weisberg, 1996).

4. Multiple regressions were analyzed for this "overall federal trust" question, with age, education, income, gender, home ownership, region, political party, and race and ethnicity in the equation. The following B values and significance levels (in parentheses) are for the significant variables from the final equations with all variables, with positive correlations indicating more trust in government: Republicans $= -.51$ (.001), Independent Voters $= -.55$ (.001), Latino $= .76$ (.001), Los Angeles $= .42$ (.001).

TABLE 3.4   DISTRUST IN
FEDERAL GOVERNMENT

*"How much of the time do you think you can trust the government
in Washington to do what is right—just about always, most of the time,
some of the time, or never?"*

	Always	Mostly	Sometimes	Never	Don't Know
January 2000	7%	25%	62%	5%	1%
September 1998	5	28	63	4	0

*"Do you think the people in government waste a lot of the money we pay in
taxes, waste some of it, or don't waste much of it?"*

	A Lot	Some	Not Much	Don't Know
January 2000	58%	35%	5%	2%
September 1998	65	31	3	1

SOURCE: PPIC Statewide Survey (2000a), all adults.

most six in ten thought "a lot" of money was wasted. This is similar to
the national trend, in which almost all Americans (97%) thought there
was at least some waste in taxpayer money and six in ten felt there was
a lot of waste.[5] The percentage of Californians who believed that the
government wastes a lot of money was higher in the fall of 1998, but it
dropped only 7 points despite the surplus.

Public attitudes toward the federal government's fiscal performance
did vary by partisanship, ethnicity and race, and region, but not by much.
Republicans and independent voters held more critical views of their government's use of taxpayer funds. Once again, Latinos and Los Angeles
residents were less negative toward government.

A major factor in the public's attitudes toward the federal government
was its perception of the role of special interests. Two in three Californians believed that "government is pretty much run by a few big interests looking out for themselves," while three in ten saw government as
"run for the benefit of all of the people." Californians have not softened

5. See the report in February 2000 (PPIC Statewide Survey, 2000b), which also references the 1999 national survey by the Pew Research Center.

their views over time on the role big interests play in their government: A similar 70 percent of residents held this cynical view of government in September 1998. Most Americans believe that government is pretty much run by big interests, an opinion that has held steady in national polls over time. On this issue, Democrats and Republicans were not far apart, while independent voters held even more cynical views of government. While all groups expressed cynicism, those whose characteristics make them among the most likely to participate more frequently in elections and the political process—white, older, and college-educated adults—were even more negative.

Many forms of political alienation also surfaced in our interviews with Californians. For instance, only about four in ten residents believed that "most elected officials care what people like me think." Democrats and Republicans were about equally likely to think that elected officials cared about their opinions, and independent voters were even more negative. There were no differences in this perception across racial and ethnic groups or regions of the state. Californians were a little less alienated than Americans generally in a national survey taken in 1999. Still, most state residents had concluded that their elected officials were indifferent to their views.[6]

Californians were fairly cynical about government. Only one in ten believed that Washington pays a "good deal" of attention to what the people think when it decides what to do. Four in ten residents thought it pays only some attention. Half said the federal government pays "not much" attention to the people. In a recent national survey, a similar percentage of Americans also said that the federal government does not pay much attention to what the people think when it decides what to do (PPIC Statewide Survey, 2000g). In California, Democrats expressed only a little more faith in their government than Republicans did, and independents were even less likely to believe that the federal government is listening at least some of the time. We found little difference across racial and ethnic groups or regions.

In general, the pattern of distrust that we found at the federal government level persisted at the state level. (See Table 3-5.) Californians were somewhat more trusting of their state government than of the federal government and somewhat more positive in the era of big surpluses and a good economy than they had been earlier. But many were still

6. Several of the questions in this section, including this one, are repeated from the National Election Studies (1998). See also PPIC Statewide Survey (2000b).

TABLE 3.5   DISTRUST IN STATE GOVERNMENT

"How much of the time do you think you can trust the government in Sacramento to do what is right—just about always, most of the time, some of the time, or never?"

	Always	Mostly	Sometimes	Never	Don't Know
January 2001	7%	39%	50%	2%	2%
January 1999	4	33	60	2	1

"Do you think the people in state government waste a lot of the money we pay in taxes, waste some of it, or don't waste much of it?"

	A Lot	Some	Not Much	Don't Know
January 2001	47%	43%	8%	2%
January 1999	52	41	5	2

SOURCE: PPIC Statewide Survey (2001a), all adults.

highly distrustful of government, whatever the timing or specific levels that were described.

In a survey conducted right after the 2000 election, fewer than half of Californians said they trusted their state government just about always or most of the time. Slightly more than half said they trusted the state government only sometimes or never. The public was more likely to trust its state government than it did the federal government and was more likely to trust the state government than it did in the fall of 1998. Still, the public's views of state government were not very positive during those good economic times. A slim majority of Democratic voters trusted their Democratic-controlled state government to do what was right, while only four in ten Republican voters and independent voters held this view.

Ninety percent of the state's residents believed that the state government wastes at least some of their money. Nearly half believed that the state government wastes a lot of money. Californians were more likely to say that the federal government rather than the state government wastes a lot of money. The proportion of residents who said that the state government wastes money had declined slightly since the fall of 1998, indicating that the lack of fiscal trust in state government remained as dominant a theme in 2000 as it was two years earlier. Even a large number of Democrats felt the state government wastes a lot of money, while independent voters and Republicans were even more likely to have a negative opinion of the fiscal performance of their state government.

By a two-to-one margin, Californians believed that their state government was run by a few big interests. Only three in ten said the state government was run for the benefit of all the people, while one in ten were uncertain. Here, we see no evidence that Californians were more trusting at the state level or had changed their attitudes over time. The percentage of Californians who said big interests run the government in Washington and Sacramento was similar. The results in the 1998 survey were similar. Democrats and Republicans were equally likely to believe that the state government is not run for the benefit of all the people, and independent voters were even more cynical.

While many Californians believed their federal and state governments are not trustworthy, we might expect a better view of the local level. However, most Californians held similarly negative views of their local governments when it came to their fiscal performance: three in ten said their local governments wasted all or most of their tax dollars, and six in ten said some of it is wasted. Republicans and independent voters were less trusting in their local governments' fiscal performance, but there were no racial and ethnic or regional variations.[7] In this case, a more proximate, local government did not breed more trust than a more distant, state government.

Local governments have had the reputation of gaining the public's confidence in ways that state and federal government are incapable of doing. But we did not see evidence of high trust in local government in California. Many residents reported that they were not at all satisfied with the way their local governments handled issues such as housing, traffic, and schools. In sum, local governments in California—closely tied to state finances since the passage of Proposition 13—were not immune from the lack of confidence in government (PPIC Statewide Survey, 1999a).

Government Gets Little Credit for the Economic Prosperity   Rightly or wrongly, most people have a dim view of politicians' performance in office when the economy is going badly. In the early 1990s, the approval ratings for federal and state elected officials were in negative territory, reflecting that the people were unhappy with the economy's poor per-

7. See PPIC Statewide Survey (1999b), reporting findings from September 1999.

TABLE 3.6   CREDIT FOR THE ECONOMY
AND BUDGET SURPLUS

"How much credit do you think the Clinton Administration deserves for California's economic conditions today—a lot, some, very little, or none?"

	All Adults	Democrats	Republicans	Other Voters
A lot	26%	38%	11%	23%
Some	40	46	27	43
Very little	20	10	32	26
None	12	4	28	6
Don't know	2	2	2	2

"How much credit do you think Governor Davis and the legislature deserve for the state budget surplus this year—a lot, some, very little, or none?"

	All Adults	Democrats	Republicans	Other Voters
A lot	12%	16%	8%	10%
Some	47	51	42	45
Very little	24	21	31	27
None	10	5	15	13
Don't know	7	7	4	5

SOURCE: PPIC Statewide Survey (1999b, 2000a), all adults.

formance and their state and federal governments' budget deficits. (See Table 3-6.)

Beginning in the late 1990s, with an expanding economy and budget surpluses, one might have expected that the public would give its elected officials some credit for the change. However, only one in four Californians gave the Clinton administration "a lot" of credit for the state's economic conditions in late 1999. Four in ten gave the president some credit, while one in three said Clinton deserved little or no credit for the economy in California. There was a strong partisan bias to these responses, as one would expect, with most Republicans giving the Democratic president little or no credit for the economy. It was surprising that, even among Democratic voters, fewer than four in ten were willing to say that the Clinton administration deserved a lot of credit for the economy.

State officials did not fare much better. Only 13 percent of residents said the governor and legislature deserved a lot of credit for California's economic conditions in early 2000, while one in three felt they deserved very little or no credit at all. Half of Republicans, four in ten independent voters, and three in ten Democrats gave the Democratic governor and Democratic-controlled legislature very little or no credit for good economic times.

Governor Gray Davis had a large state budget surplus to work with every year since he entered office in January 1999. The public did not view these plentiful circumstances as having much to do with his fiscal decisions. Twelve percent of Californians gave the governor and state legislature "a lot" of credit for the state budget surplus in early 2000, while one in three said they deserved very little or no credit at all. Few Democrats gave Davis and the legislature significant credit for the surplus. Nearly half of Republicans and four in ten independent voters gave them very little or no credit.

The approval ratings of the highest elected officials improved with the positive mood generated by the strong economy. But this trend should not be confused with an increased tendency to trust public officials. Rather, these good job ratings are strongly correlated with positive attitudes toward the economy. Similar trends are found amongst Californians in earlier times and also with regularity elsewhere in the nation.

President Bill Clinton's approval ratings are a good case in point. The president's job performance ratings were consistently positive from the fall of 1999 up to a month before the November 2000 election. About six in ten Californians said the president was doing an excellent or good job in office. In contrast, about one in four said he was doing only a fair job. At most during this time period, only one in five residents rated his performance as poor. The positive ratings given by six in ten Californians to the president were virtually unchanged from what we had recorded in the fall of 1998. All through this time period, there were also positive feelings about the economy. Predictably, there were strong differences in approval ratings across party lines, with most Democrats and a majority of independent voters saying that Bill Clinton was doing an excellent or good job in office, while only about one in four Republicans had a positive opinion.

What is most fascinating about Clinton's high approval ratings is that they were in the aftermath of a congressional impeachment and Senate trial. The accusations of lying under oath about a sexual encounter with a White House intern, and the calls for his removal from office for these actions, did not seem to shake the public's approval of the president's performance in office. In fact, the ratings that were generated for the president in the postimpeachment period were no different from what we saw in the fall of 1998: about six in ten Californians gave the president either excellent or good ratings.

What explains the seeming contradiction of a public that dislikes and distrusts government but gives particular government officials high ratings? After all, someone is doing the governing that the public distrusts. The explanation would seem to be that perceptions of the state of the state strongly influence the public's perceptions of officials' performance in office—even though they give those officials little credit for control over the economy. In the late 1990s, as described in Chapter 2, about two in three Californians felt the state was headed in the right direction and three in four felt the economy was in good shape. Of those who felt the state was headed in the right direction, most felt the president was doing an excellent or good job in office, while those who felt the state was headed in the wrong direction overwhelmingly rated Clinton's performance as sub par. In sum, the president could take little solace in high approval ratings. They rise and fall with the economy. As other presidents have learned—before and after Clinton—approval ratings can also rise during wars and national emergencies.

Similar to the president's ratings, the ratings of Governor Davis were remarkably steady during this time period. On average, half of the public said the governor was doing an excellent or good job in office, one in three rated his performance as fair, and one in ten said he was doing a poor job. The Democratic governor's ratings did vary across political parties, but not as sharply as we had noticed with the presidential approval scores.[8] The governor's ratings were higher in regions of the state and among racial and ethnic groups that were more Democratic than Republican. Still, ratings were fairly positive and poor scores were rare across demographic groups and regions.

Once again, though, these approval ratings for a high public official are closely tied to the public's overall perceptions about current conditions in the state. In early 2000, two in three Californians felt the state was headed in the right direction. Of these residents with a positive out-

8. We changed the rating scales for the governor and California legislature from "excellent, good, fair, or poor" to "approve or disapprove" in the fall 2000 surveys. The governor's approval rating was at 66 percent in September 2000 and 60 percent in October 2000, while the legislature's approval rating was at 56 percent in September 2000 (PPIC Statewide Survey, 2000f, 2000g).

look, most gave the governor either excellent or good marks for his performance in office. Of the relatively few who said the state was headed in the wrong direction, they overwhelmingly rated Davis as doing a fair or poor job in office. A year later, Davis's approval ratings would fall dramatically when the mood turned sour over the electricity crisis, as had also been the case with his predecessor, Governor Pete Wilson.

Further evidence that the approval ratings of the president and governor should not be mistaken as a warming trend toward public officials is in the ratings given to the federal and state legislative branches at this time. The ratings of the U.S. Congress were much less glowing than they were for the president. About four in ten Californians said the U.S. Congress was doing an excellent or good job. Half thought the federal legislative branch was doing only a fair job, while about one in seven believed it was doing a poor job. More important, these opinions changed very little over time: at no point between September 1999 and October 2000 did more than four in ten Californians give positive ratings to the performance of the U.S. House of Representatives. Even though the Republicans controlled both the Senate and House, we did not find partisan differences. Democrats and Republicans gave similar evaluations of the U.S. Congress, while independent voters gave even lower ratings.[9]

Similarly, the public's ratings of the California legislature were not nearly as positive as they were for the governor. About one in three gave excellent or good grades to the legislature for its job performance. Four in ten rated it as fair, while one in ten said the California legislature was doing a poor job. At no time between September 1999 and August 2000 did we see more than four in ten residents give positive ratings. The Democrats controlled the state legislature, and we did find partisan differences in ratings: Democrats were a little more generous than were Republicans or independent voters in giving out excellent or good grades. There was little variation across regions, while racial and ethnic differences tended to parallel differences in party registration: specifically, Latinos gave higher approval ratings to the legislature than did whites.

In sum, Californians did not give their state and federal elected officials a great deal of credit for the rosy budget picture and strong economy. Most seemed to be saying that the government was benefiting from factors outside of their control. While the approval ratings of high-

9. As further indication of approval for higher elected officials, 59 percent approved and 29 percent disapproved of the job performance of U.S. Senator Dianne Feinstein in a January 2000 survey (PPIC Statewide Survey, 2000a).

ranking individuals in office were impressive, this trend reflects the public's good mood because of the state of the economy rather than a new appreciation for all elected officials. For instance, state and federal governing bodies did not enjoy a similar bounce in public approval ratings from the perceptions that things were going well in the state. Moreover, we found that most Californians maintained their distrust of government even while giving their approval to those who held positions in high office.

ATTITUDES ON SPENDING
AND INFLUENCE OF GOVERNMENT

Attitudes toward taxes and government evidently affected the public's preferences for what should be done with the budget surpluses and, to some degree, for how much influence government should have on residents' lives.

When asked about the appropriate use of the federal budget surplus, Californians were evenly divided on the issue but deeply split along partisan lines (see Table 3-7). Forty-eight percent told us that the federal budget surplus should be used to cut taxes, while 47 percent thought that it should be used to pay for social programs. Americans as a whole were, at the time, also equally likely to say they preferred cutting taxes to increasing funding for social programs. Beneath this statistical deadlock, political party divisions reflected strong differences in ideology about taxes and government: Two in three Republicans in California strongly favored tax cuts over increased spending, six in ten Democrats wanted the surplus to be dedicated to increased spending rather than tax cuts, and independent voters were evenly divided on how to use the surplus.[10] These findings indicate that antitax sentiments in California still had considerable strength.

We tapped into the power of antitax sentiments in another, similar question about how to use the federal budget surplus (see Table 3-8). We asked people if they would like to see the surplus funds used for an across-the-board tax cut, reducing the national debt, or for improving

10. Multiple regressions were analyzed for this "tax cut versus spending" question, with age, education, income, gender, home ownership, region, political party, and race and ethnicity in the equation. The following B values and significance levels (in parentheses) are for the significant variables from the final equations with all variables, with positive correlations indicating support for cutting taxes: Republicans = 1.1 $(.001)$, Democrats = $-.34$ $(.02)$, Education = $-.13$ $(.02)$, Income = $.11$ $(.004)$.

TABLE 3.7   CUT TAXES OR
INCREASE SPENDING?

"The federal surplus should be used to ... "

	All Adults	Democrats	Republicans	Other Voters
Cut taxes	48%	35%	68%	49%
Pay for social programs	47	59	28	46
Both (volunteered)	2	2	3	2
Don't know	3	4	1	3

SOURCE: PPIC Statewide Survey (2000a).

funding for needed government programs. The preferred option was cutting taxes, the choice selected by four in ten Californians, followed by one in three who said they wanted to use the surplus to reduce the national debt. When given these three choices, only one in four favored improving funding for unspecified, "needed" government programs. Again, the partisan differences are striking: half of Republicans and four in ten independent voters favored a tax cut. Democrats were most likely to say the surplus should be used to reduce the national debt. So underlying concerns about the habits of excess government spending do seem to severely limit support for using the surplus for needed spending.

In the presidential debates, Al Gore and George Bush made a point of distinguishing between their plans for spending the surplus on tax cuts: Gore emphasized that his plan targeted the middle-class and lower-income families for tax cuts, while Bush stressed that his plan would cut taxes for everyone. When asked to choose between these two options in a survey taken weeks before the November election, Californians were evenly divided, with about half supporting each option. Californians gave a little more support for an across-the-board tax cut and less support for targeted tax cuts than Americans as a whole had in a national survey conducted earlier in the year.

Party registration correlated with preferences for tax cut proposals: seven in ten Republicans supported cutting taxes for people in all income brackets, while two in three Democrats favored targeted tax cuts that would exclude upper-income people; independent voters were evenly split on these two proposals. As might be expected, support for across-the-board tax cuts increased with income and was more prevalent among those who felt that they were paying more than their fair share of taxes.

TABLE 3.8   OPTIONS FOR USING THE FEDERAL
BUDGET SURPLUS

"For which of the following would you like to see the surplus funds used?"

	All Adults	Democrats	Republicans	Other Voters
Tax cut	40%	29%	50%	39%
Reduce national debt	33	36	36	34
Improve program funding	22	29	10	23
Other (volunteered)	2	3	3	2
Don't know	3	3	1	2

SOURCE: PPIC Statewide Survey (2000f).

Once again, though, the issue of taxes seemed to bring out the fiscally conservative attitudes of state voters.[11]

However, other questions in the course of the 2000 election point out the importance voters placed on maintaining certain kinds of federal government programs while cutting taxes with the federal surplus. We once broached the tax-and-spending issue while President Clinton was haggling with the Republican leaders in Congress over the size of a federal income tax cut. It was surprising to me that even though most Californians complained that their federal income taxes were too high, and nearly half favored a tax cut, they gave little support to the big federal tax cut proposed by Congress. Only three in ten residents favored using the federal budget surplus to pay for a large tax cut of about $800 billion over the next ten years. In contrast, seven in ten residents would prefer a smaller tax cut and more spending on Medicare, education, the environment, and other federal programs as proposed by the president. Certainly, the list of government programs resonated with some of the top issues identified by voters.

Republicans only narrowly favored the bigger tax cut, while Democrats and independent voters were supportive of a smaller tax cut coupled with funding for these programs. There was little support in any demographic group or region of the state for the bigger federal tax cut. The smaller tax cut was favored over the larger tax cut, even among

11. See PPIC Statewide Survey (2000g) findings from October 2000, which included a comparison with a national survey by the Pew Research Center in April 2000.

those Californians who thought that their federal income taxes were much too high. In fact, more than eight in ten of those who thought that federal taxes were too high wanted the smaller tax cut. This tells us that most Californians saw a valuable role for spending on government programs and that they wanted at least some of the federal surplus saved for this purpose (see PPIC Statewide Survey, 1999b).

During the 2000 elections, we asked Californians a number of questions about the nation's Social Security system. Clearly, this is the kind of government spending issue that many Californians worry about and think of as directly affecting their futures. Thus, they may be more positive toward spending for this purpose. A majority of the state's residents had serious doubts about how well the Social Security system will perform in the future. In fact, Californians were more likely than Americans as a whole to believe that the system will not provide their earned benefits when they retire. Younger residents were particularly pessimistic about the future of Social Security.

Given these concerns, it is not surprising that Californians placed a higher priority on strengthening Social Security than on cutting taxes. By a two-to-one margin, they said the next president should focus on saving Social Security. There were, once again, strong partisan differences: half of Republicans would rather have a tax cut, while eight in ten Democrats and two in three independent voters wanted the next president to make strengthening Social Security a priority. In all, though, many people across political parties, demographic groups, and regions were more interested in Social Security than a tax cut. Again, this suggests Californians see an important role only for government spending on programs that matter a great deal to themselves now and that will in the future.

These attitudes are analogous to their attitudes toward government influence in their lives. President Clinton concluded early in the 1990s that "the era of big government" was over. But was it? His statement reflected the reality of budget deficits and a public that was turned off by any suggestion of increasing taxes. However, the preference for bigger or smaller government would undergo further scrutiny in the new circumstance of large budget surpluses. Indeed, all of the discussions about what to do with surplus government funds raised a central issue for a distrustful public: How much do people want the government to be a part of their lives—above and beyond its present influence? Would the public still opt for a leaner and less active government, given the problems that remained unsolved? Or would it reconsider at this juncture having a larger government, even in light of its distrust of elected officials? We explored this topic during the 2000 election in California.

To put the question of preference for size of government in perspective, consider how Californians perceived government's current influence on their lives. While people may not like government or what it does, we found that few Californians defined it as irrelevant. Most Californians (79%), like most U.S. adults (79%), believed that the federal government had at least some impact on their daily lives.[12] Four in ten state residents said the federal government had a lot of influence, four in ten said it had some influence, and one in six said it had just a little influence. Only 4 percent said Washington had no impact on them at all. Surprisingly, there were no partisan differences in responses. We found only slight variations in responses to this survey question across racial and ethnic groups, geographic regions, or demographic categories.

As for state government, Californians viewed its importance about the same. Most of the state's residents saw the decisions made in Sacramento as highly relevant. Nearly eight in ten Californians said the state government had at least some influence on their daily lives. Four in ten said it had a lot of influence, four in ten said it had some, and one in six said it had just a little influence. Only 5 percent of Californians said that what goes on in Sacramento had no influence on their daily lives. The percentage of Californians who thought the state government had at least some impact on them is thus similar to those who saw the federal government as having at least some impact. Again, there was agreement across partisan lines. Considering that there was disagreement about how good a job the government was doing, there was remarkable agreement across regions and racial and ethnic groups that Sacramento has personal relevance.[13]

The feeling that the government had a big personal influence did not translate into an overwhelming desire for a larger and more active government. Whether Californians believed the federal government had a lot of, some, just a little, or no effect on their lives was irrelevant. All of these groups expressed the same preference, by a similar margin, for a smaller government with fewer services over a larger government with many services (see Table 3-9).[14] In all, more than half of Californians

---

12. See PPIC Statewide Survey (2000g), which included a comparison with a national survey by NPR/Kaiser Family Foundation/Kennedy School in June 2000.
13. See PPIC Statewide Survey (2001a) in January 2001.
14. See PPIC Statewide Survey (2000g), which included a comparison with a national survey by ABC News/*Washington Post* in October 2000.

TABLE 3.9   PREFERRED SIZE OF GOVERNMENT

"Would you say you favor smaller government with fewer services or larger government with many services?"

	All Adults	Democrats	Republicans	Other Voters
Smaller government	54%	37%	78%	63%
Larger government	39	54	17	34
Don't know	7	9	5	3

SOURCE: PPIC Statewide Survey (2000g).

said they would prefer a smaller government, while less than four in ten wanted a larger government with more services.

There was a partisan divide on this issue: a slight majority of Democrats wanted a larger government with many services, while eight in ten Republicans and two in three independent voters (63%) wanted a smaller government with fewer services. The concept of a smaller government had some appeal even among Democrats in liberal areas of the state such as the San Francisco Bay Area and among demographic groups whose socioeconomic conditions place them in need of government programs, such as Latinos and lower-income residents. It is important to note, though, that we did not ask residents which specific programs were unnecessary and could be cut in creating a smaller government. Undoubtedly, many may have resisted the concept of a smaller government that excluded the programs they viewed as most valuable.[15]

There seemed to be a direct tie-in between preferring a smaller government and the public's distrustful attitudes toward government spending and taxes. The people who believed that government can only sometimes be trusted and that government is run for the benefits of a few big interests were most inclined to support smaller government. Those who thought that government had a mediocre track record in solving problems and who felt that they were paying more than their fair share in taxes were the most likely to opt for a smaller government. In other words, the

15. Multiple regressions were analyzed for this "small versus large government" question, with age, education, income, gender, home ownership, region, political party, and race and ethnicity in the equation. The following B values and significance levels (in parentheses) are for the significant variables from the final equations with all variables, with positive correlations indicating a preference for smaller government: Republicans = 1.2 (.001), Independent Voters = .55 (.001), Democrats = −.42 (.01), Whites = .46 (.03), Age = .25 (.001), Income = .15 (.001), Women = −.56 (.001).

preference for a larger role for government has limited public support because of a fairly widespread belief that the current government is not performing at adequate levels of effectiveness, responsiveness, or efficiency. Clearly, while Californians were aware of problems and of government's importance, the tax revolt still had relevance in the era of surpluses.

CONCLUSIONS AND IMPLICATIONS

We said at the beginning of the chapter that the fiscal and economic conditions were favorable for increasing trust in government in 2000. This was an ideal time to revisit the mix of antitax sentiments, prospending preferences, and distrust in government that has played a forceful role in policymaking. On closer examination, California does not really offer a hospitable political climate for setting aside the tax revolt. One reason is that the popularity of Proposition 13 is deeply ingrained in the state's political fabric. Voters passed this tax-limitation initiative by a wide margin in the late 1970s, and it remains widely supported in public opinion polls today. The message behind Proposition 13—that voters are not pleased by the way their governments go about the tax-and-spending business—is one that the state's elected officials correctly fear is still a relevant and threatening force at the ballot box. So most Democrats and Republicans running in statewide elections would be reluctant to lead the charge toward increasing spending and loosening up the voters' restrictions on raising taxes.

Moreover, Californians simply do not trust their elected office holders and governments with their money. Most do not give a lot of credit to federal and state elected officials for the favorable economy and budget surplus. The approval ratings mirror feelings about the current economy rather than confidence in public officials. The public continues to lack confidence in their ability to spend the taxpayers' money wisely and to effectively solve problems in a way that is responsive to the public's will. There is no deep partisan divide when it comes to a basic lack of trust in government and no evidence that the recent good times have shifted opinions in a major way. It is very difficult for Californians to come to grips with supporting a more active and larger government when they are not that comfortable with the government they now have. As a result, the state's residents are less than enthusiastic about plans to expand the scope and size of their governments, even though budget surpluses offer "free money."

Yet most Californians recognize the important role of government in their daily lives. Very few describe their state or federal government as irrelevant. As a result, Californians are fairly decided in their views that critical government programs ought to have the funds they need to operate effectively. This is why most would prefer a smaller tax cut that preserves the federal government's funding to a larger tax cut that might jeopardize programs that can affect their lives. A good case in point is Social Security, which many Californians fear will not be able to meet their expectations for retirement. Many other examples exist in a state the voters perceive as unprepared for its future.

Because of the ambivalence that Californians have toward government's role in their lives, and perhaps also because of a lack of belief and confidence in what politicians have to say about the issues, neither of the presidential candidates in the 2000 campaign seemed to have a special advantage on this issue of taxes and spending the surplus. On the general issues of using the federal surplus for tax cuts versus spending increases, the public was evenly split and was deeply divided along the lines of partisan loyalties. The Reaganesque calls for large tax cuts by George W. Bush were highly popular among conservative Republicans, but they received mixed to negative reviews from Democrats and independent voters. The New Democrat calls by Al Gore for using the government surplus to expand government had a strong appeal among liberal Democrats, but they received mixed to negative reviews from Republicans and independent voters.

Californians sent very clear signals on taxes and government spending in an era of budget surpluses and a strong economy, and they also expressed serious concerns about the state's planning for the future. The message we received from voters during an exhaustive series of public opinion surveys was that spending and taxes is an issue that politicians must handle with special care. While Californians are reluctant to give a green light for overall increased spending, they are equally unlikely to throw their weight behind support for reducing taxes at the expense of their favored programs. In these good times, Californians moved beyond ideology to specific programs. They are willing to admit that there are special circumstances when government programs should become better funded and more active. However, they still need firm assurances that the government they distrust will spend their money on what they view as important to them.

CHAPTER 4

Schools, Schools, and Schools

"My first priority as you know—in fact my first, second, and third priority—is education."[1] Gray Davis uttered this quotable statement soon after he was sworn in as governor of the state of California in early 1999. However, it could just as easily have come out of the mouth of any average citizen in the state at the time. "Fix the schools" was the message that candidate Davis heard time and again from the voters as he traveled the campaign trail. As he settled into his first year in office, the governor and California legislature turned their attention to what the state government could do to improve a woefully underfunded and chronically underachieving kindergarten-through-twelfth-grade (K–12) public school system. At that time, of course, the state's large budget surplus offered the opportunity to make additional financial commitments to schools without asking the voters to contribute any more than they already had to the solution.

In the months prior to the 2000 elections, Californians were quick to turn to the subject of the public schools when they were asked about their top concerns. There was no topic that residents seemed to know more about or were more eager to discuss with others. In our focus

1. Governor Gray Davis "State of the State Address," January 6, 1999 (Davis, 1999). I was helped by discussions with Gary Hart, who provided background information on proposals as former education secretary to Governor Davis. Jon Sonstelie offered suggestions, interpretation, and data for this chapter on state and national trends in spending per pupil, pupils-per-teacher ratios, and student test scores.

groups, there was a widespread belief that California's schools were not what they used to be. "The school systems are going downhill," lamented one respondent. For parents of public school children, this problem had a greater sense of urgency. "Schools must improve. I want my son to pass his competency test," said a parent of a high school–age child.

This raises an important question. Through the late 1990s and the 2000 presidential election, the public schools enjoyed an undisputed top ranking as the issue most in need of attention. What is interesting to note is that the single focus on schools developed at this moment in time among policymakers at all levels and among the public in all regions and walks of life. What drove this consensus of concern?

THE NEW POLITICAL CULTURE:
EXPLAINING THE PUBLIC'S FOCUS ON SCHOOLS

The idea that California's public schools had problems was not a new concept. There was widespread recognition for years that the state's school system was in serious trouble and that other states were doing a much better job of educating their children (see Schrag, 1998, 2000a; Sonstelie, Brunner, and Ardon, 2000). Nor was the concern about the state's schools based only on narrow self-interest by parents with children in the schools. Most adults do not have children in the public schools, and some of those who do say their schools are functioning quite well. People with and without school children were equally upset about what they viewed as the sorry state of education.

The fact that public schools received so much attention points once again to the importance of the concepts of postmaterialist values and the New Political Culture for our understanding of the California context (see Inglehart, 1998; Clark and Hoffman-Martinot, 1998). When people experience prosperity, their concerns drift away from the basic material needs of food, shelter, safety, and work. In other words, other national and state problems were in check for the time being. From the early 1980s to mid-1990s, Californians had a lot of other issues on their minds. At the federal level, they were worried about the Cold War and rising budget deficits. Closer to home, there were fears about crime, joblessness and a weak economy, and the fiscal impacts of legal and illegal immigration on state and local governments. But the late 1990s saw a sharp decline in the salience of all these issues. As noted earlier, there was a sense that peace and prosperity could be taken for granted; the crime rate was dropping, and federal and state governments were amassing budget surpluses. With basic needs taken care of, the public and law-makers could focus on other pressing issues—such as the quality of education.

Be that as it may, another reality may help explain why the public fo-cused on education as the top issue at this particular juncture of the state's history: The schools literally reflected the state's recent experiences of demographic change and its uncertain future. The student body had become increasingly immigrant, Latino, and nonwhite over time. The state's schools are where the new immigrants and the children of immi-grants need to go to learn the basic skills to succeed in American soci-ety. The schools are also where the next generation of California's work-force must pick up the complex tools needed to succeed in the high-tech and knowledge-based economy. If the schools fail, then California will fail in its transition to a more diverse, information-age society. So it is likely that fears about what the future holds for this state also drove Cal-ifornians' desires to see their schools improve. Will there be a growing gap between the rich and the poor, and a society divided into "haves" and "have nots"? The answer largely depends on how well our schools perform in the coming years. Efforts to improve the schools would thus provide a better, more stable future for all living in the state. Nonethe-less, even the capacity to think about long-term issues reflects the devel-opment of postmaterialist values; otherwise, the public would have to focus on immediate needs.

A failing public school system offered Californians a Gordian chal-lenge: Was their concern for education, with all its implications for the well-being of the state, enough to overcome their distrust of government and to reconsider the tenets of the tax revolt? How would the public re-spond to statements that public schools will need much more money—from the state's taxpayers—to operate more effectively? Would distrust make the public unwilling to throw more money at this problem, espe-cially since limits on spending set by distrustful voters were what created the cash shortfall for schools in the first place? Or would the failure of schools be the kind of issue that would override their distrust? What kinds of assurances would the public need to support an infusion of new funds for the schools?

These questions are salient because distrust in government is a major component of the postmaterialist values that we referred to previously. There is supposedly a healthy skepticism toward the problem-solving abilities of large bureaucracies and a marked desire to address important issues through citizens' efforts at the local level that goes along with this particular worldview. So the basic ideas of providing more resources for the state government and expending more effort toward improving a large bureaucratic organization such as the state's public school system are not ideas that naturally flow out of the beliefs of members of the New Political Culture. It is, thus, not at all a given that Californians would express a strong willingness to give more of their money to schools, even though they defined this as their top issue at the time.

Once again, the state's good economic times and large budget surplus provided an opportunity to explore the public's willingness to expand the role of government without increasing taxes. But would the public need some assurances that the taxpayers' money was being spent for useful purposes? How far would people be willing to go with school reforms?

All of these questions were implicitly addressed in the context of the 2000 elections. The elections offered many opportunities to gauge public perceptions and policy preferences from different vantage points. The presidential candidates were aware of the public's interests in this topic, and they focused their time and energies on their ideas for school reform and spending in their debates and campaign stump speeches. Three education initiatives on the ballot in the March primary and November election—school vouchers and two efforts to lower the hurdle for passing local school bonds—attracted intense media attention and heavy spending on television advertising. The governor's continuing efforts to focus the state's energies on improving the schools—more funding, teacher training, student testing, and accountability—and the early evidence of his education reforms also attracted close scrutiny.

SCHOOLS' REPORT CARD

Once upon a time, California's K–12 public schools were among the best in the nation. By the late 1990s, it became widely known that the state's rankings on a variety of measures, such as per-pupil spending, pupils per teacher, and student performance on test scores, had tumbled in comparison with other states. Many factors appear to have contributed to California's fall from grace in the educational arena, especially when we consider that the decline appears to have started in the late 1970s. Some factors were a result of the distrustful voters themselves, who tightened restrictions on passing taxes for local school funding and changed the way that school spending took place in California. Other factors had to do with court decisions that changed the patterns of local school spending. The governor and state legislature had an indirect role, through implementing these voter and court-initiated policies and thus determining the available state funding for public schools.

Two events in the 1970s had a dramatic effect on the way that school funds are allocated in the state. In 1971, the *Serrano v. Priest* court decision required the state to act to equalize school funding across local school districts. A judicial ruling that could have implied more and equal funding for local public schools, meant in practice less and equal funding for the state's school districts. In 1978, the voters passed the Proposition 13 citizens' initiative, resulting in new legislation that required the state legislature to take over responsibility for allocating the reduced base of local property tax revenues. The state legislature thus took on the role of distributing most of the funds going to local schools (Legislative Analyst's Office, 1999b), and it provided state funding sources so that local school districts would avoid the immediate consequences of losing local property tax revenues. But from then on, local schools could also lose ground in the state's annual budget battles. What appeared to happen is that school spending fell behind from the 1980s to mid-1990s, at the very same time of the local-to-state transition.

Rather than increasing the funding in low-spending school districts, the state government's efforts resulted in reducing funding for high-spending districts. Certainly, this was not the intention of the governor and state legislature, since it was a response to voter actions and court rulings. It was the unintended consequence of the state's role as the agent that would redistribute local property tax revenues and also take the leadership role of insuring an equitable system of school finance, while trying to balance schools against other state priorities. Between 1970 and 1997, per-pupil spending in California fell more than 15 percent relative to the rest of the country (Sonstelie, Brunner, and Ardon, 2000). While there are problems with these comparative scores, California's ranking was anywhere from thirty-first through thirty-sixth out of the fifty states in the mid-1990s, based on the National Center for Education Statistics (Legislative Analyst's Office, 2000b). Obviously, the state's spending fell behind the national average for a sustained period of time.

California students also lost ground in their academic performance since the late 1970s. The state had ranked near the top relative to other states, but that seemed to change. For instance, based on the National Assessment of Education Progress (NAEP) tests of eighth graders, California ranked thirty-fifth of thirty-eight states in reading proficiency in 1998 (Legislative Analyst's Office, 2000a). There have been many reasons given for this decline in student test scores, including the relatively low spending per pupil, a growing student-to-teacher ratio, a decline in teacher quality, and the changing demographics of the state (see Sonstelie, Brunner, and Ardon, 2000; Betts, Rueben, and Danenberg, 2000). In fact, the large percentage of immigrant students in California whose native language is not English would seem to account for a relative decline in test scores. But apparently, the changing demographics alone do not explain the entire student test score gap, although clearly this change is a contributing factor. Sonstelie, Brunner, and Ardon (2000) argue that the timing of the student test score decline is coincidental with the change from a local finance system to the state finance system. The decline in student performance might have been related to how much money was spent and to how it was divided and distributed by the state at the local level.

As the state went through a recession in the early 1990s, school funding suffered. After all, K–12 school spending is the largest budget item for the state (Legislative Analyst's Office, 2000a). But when the economy recovered in the mid-1990s, the state began to invest more money in the K–12 public schools. This is evident in Table 4-1, which compares real spending per pupil in California with that in the rest of the United States over the ten-year period from 1989 to 1998. Spending fell in California from 1989 to 1995, and then it improved between 1995 and 1998. Overall, though, California's spending per pupil was basically unchanged during this ten-year period, while there was an increase for the rest of the nation. Moreover, California was behind the rest of the nation in per-pupil spending every year, and the gap was bigger in 1997–1998 than in 1988–1989.

California's student population was growing at the same time that the relative school spending was falling in the 1990s. This had consequences for one measure of the quality of education—the number of pupils per teacher. On average, the pupils-per-teacher ratio in California exceeded the level achieved in the rest of the nation by about 5 to 7 students for every year between 1989 and 1999 (see Table 4-2). It is notable that the national figures are fairly steady, while the California ratio of students to teachers increased between 1989 and 1995 and then declined between 1995 and 1998. In recent years, the state government has mandated smaller class sizes in the lower elementary grades, and this state policy change, along with increased spending, accounts for the improvement.

TABLE 4.1 REAL SPENDING
PER PUPIL, 1989–1998

	California	U.S. (except California)
1989–1990	$5,733	$5,938
1990–1991	5,549	5,970
1991–1992	5,429	5,939
1992–1993	5,230	5,942
1993–1994	5,220	5,986
1994–1995	5,159	6,054
1995–1996	5,167	6,064
1996–1997	5,440	6,097
1997–1998	5,789	6,179

SOURCE: Sonstelie, Brunner, and Ardon (2000).
NOTE: Adjusted for inflation.

Still, California's pupils-per-teacher ratio declined by just one student during this time period.

Student test scores in California have also lagged behind the rest of the nation for every year since 1990. Specifically, in verbal and math Scholastic Assessment Tests (SATs), the student scores in the rest of the United States steadily improved every year from 1990 to 2000. In California, student test scores showed little change in the early 1990s, and then there were significant improvements in the late 1990s. In sum, the student performance measures followed the same pattern found for spending per pupil and teachers per pupil: troubles during the state's recession, and improvements during the recent upswing in the economy (California Department of Education, 2000).

With the state having a large budget surplus to work with and a new governor who made better schools a campaign promise, the state government became much more active in promoting school improvements after 1998. Governor Davis called the state legislature into special session early in 1999 and passed a series of bills that established a public school accountability program and other education reforms (Legislative Analyst's Office, 1999a). This legislative package included an academic performance index for each school, based on student test scores; rewards for schools where student test scores showed high achievement or significant improvement; interventions for schools where student test

TABLE 4.2   PUPILS PER
TEACHER, 1989–1999

	California	U.S. (except California)
1989–1990	22.44	16.68
1990–1991	22.79	16.63
1991–1992	22.88	16.73
1992–1993	24.04	16.77
1993–1994	24.02	16.71
1994–1995	24.03	16.63
1995–1996	23.98	16.60
1996–1997	22.86	16.51
1997–1998	21.61	16.29
1998–1999	21.54	16.10

SOURCE: Sonstelie, Brunner, and Ardon (2000).

scores showed low performance; peer review for teachers; special attention to elementary school reading; and a high school exit exam. The next
year, legislation was passed that focused on efforts to attract and retain
teachers and to improve student achievement (Office of the Secretary of
Education, 2000).

A strong economy, solid state and local revenues, and the huge budget
surplus allowed the state government to increase funding to K–12 public schools in recent years. The state's nearly 6 million K–12 public school
students were automatic beneficiaries of a larger state budget through
increased funding from the Proposition 98 allocations—the spending formula passed by voters that required that a certain proportion of the state
budget go to K–12 schools. Additionally, they received one-time spending increases made possible by a budget surplus and increases in other
local, state, and federal funding. The increase in K–12 Proposition 98
spending was approximately $2 billion per year—increasing from $31.6
billion in 1998–1999 to $33.8 billion in 1999–2000 to $35.8 billion in
2000–2001. School funding from all sources increased from $40.1 bil-
lion in 1998–1999 to $44.1 billion in 1999–2000 to $46.7 billion in
2000–2001. State spending for local public schools increased by 28 percent between the bad times of the 1994–1995 budget and the good times
of the 2000–2001 budget (Legislative Analyst's Office, 2000b). By 2000,
California had made up lost spending ground, although its K–12 schools

PUBLIC OPINION BEFORE AND DURING THE 2000 ELECTION

Californians named "schools" as their most important issue with impressive consistency from the closing months of the 1998 gubernatorial election to the final days of the 2000 presidential election. These trends were evident in a series of public opinion surveys asking residents in different ways to rank the public policy issues in the state.

Toward the end of the November 1998 gubernatorial election, we asked Californians what one issue they would most like to hear the candidates for statewide office talk about in the remaining weeks of the campaign. Three in ten named schools, while no other topic was mentioned by a large percentage of the residents. Crime, jobs and the economy, taxes, the state budget, and poverty were each mentioned by more than 2 percent but less than 9 percent of the survey's respondents. The issues of abortion, gun control, the death penalty, and the environment had all been common topics on the television commercials and debates leading up to the gubernatorial election. However, few residents said these were the issues they wanted the candidates to talk about. Schools led all other topics in every region and in all racial and ethnic groups.

A month after the 1998 election was over, when asked to name the one issue they would like to see Governor-elect Davis and the state legislature work on in 1999, more than one-third of Californians singled out schools and education. Again, fewer than 10 percent mentioned other issues, including crime, immigration, jobs and the economy, poverty, and taxes. The schools were the top issue in every region. There were no differences between Republicans and Democrats or race and ethnic groups in the desire for the governor and legislature to work on K–12 public schools.

In the fall of 1999, despite the flurry of legislation and increased funding for education during the governor's first half-year in office, Californians still ranked schools as by far the most important public policy issue facing the state (PPIC Statewide Survey, 1999b). The same was true at the end of 1999. At both times, there was consensus across all the regions that education was the top issue facing the state, with no differences by age, gender, income, or race and ethnicity. Democrats and Republicans alike named schools as the number one state problem. (See Table 4-4.)

When the presidential campaign was the focus, one would consider that topics other than education might emerge as the leading issues for discussion. The candidates were focused on national issues, such as cam-

were still behind the rest of the nation in most measures of school success and well below the public's high expectations. Future progress was uncertain, since the gains could be credited to a good economy providing surplus funds, rather than new, dependable sources of funding.

THE VOTERS AND EDUCATION INITIATIVES, 1978–1998

California voters have become accustomed to weighing in on the state's public policies rather than leaving all of the decisions to the governor and state legislature. Decisionmaking about schools was no different. In the previous section, I alluded to the negative effects of Proposition 13 in the discussion of how California school funding had failed to keep pace with the nation. On a number of occasions, California voters have been asked to make important policy decisions about their schools. The choices voters have made to pass or defeat citizens' initiatives and state bond measures have had profound effects on public schools. More often than not, voter distrust in government has played a major part in the decisions the California public has made about school funding and education reforms.

Proposition 13 passed in June 1978, and it negatively affected local public school funding in two important ways. Local school districts would have more trouble passing local tax increases because of a two-thirds vote requirement. Moreover, the fact that the state government became the single biggest revenue source—accounting for about two-thirds of public school funding—meant that school funding is held hostage to the ups and downs in state revenues. In good years, the state can be generous with schools and other state programs, but in times of recession, school funding could lose ground to other pressing programs, such as health care and public assistance. Indeed, this is the pattern that we outlined for school funding in the 1990s.

A lack of certainty about school funding was one of the reasons that Proposition 98, a citizens' initiative, was placed on the ballot a decade later. This was an effort to establish a minimum funding level for K–12 public schools in the state's annual budget process. The voters passed Proposition 98 in November 1988, setting in motion a formula based on general fund revenues, state population, personal income, and other factors in determining the minimum dollar amount for schools (Legislative Analyst's Office, 2000b). A major reason that Proposition 98 passed was that it represented a popular concept to distrustful voters—

earmarking funds specifically for their favorite programs and taking fiscal decisions out of the hands of elected officials. Moreover, Proposition 98 did not call for more taxes, but rather a different way of allocating existing tax dollars.

Still, the state fell behind in its school spending despite the Proposition 98 guarantees. Minimum spending levels were apparently not enough to meet the state's needs, nor were the additional funds from the budget surplus. In the meantime, frustration grew with the low student test scores. Another ten years passed, and the voters then faced a flurry of state propositions seeking to fund and reform the schools.

There were many public and private interests who were not satisfied with the pace of school progress and reform. They would exercise their right to place measures on the ballot for the public's consideration in the 1998 primary and general elections. Voters' reactions to these proposals were telling of the mood for reforms and the willingness to spend money in times of prosperity, demographic change, and distrust. (See Table 4-3.)

In the June 1998 primary, voters were confronted with two very different propositions. Proposition 223 would prohibit school districts from spending more than 5 percent of their funds for administration and instructional supervision, beginning in 1999–2000. Clearly, this initiative took a direct aim at the perception that public schools included bloated and wasteful bureaucracies. This measure failed by a relatively narrow margin (45% to 55%). It faced a well-funded opposition by the education establishment, which defined it as an unworkable initiative. Nonetheless, this vote indicated that many Californians believed that too much money was spent on things other than the students.

Proposition 227, the English Language in Public Schools initiative placed on the ballot by Republican activist Ron Unz, required all public instruction to be conducted in English. This initiative passed by a wide margin (61% to 39%). Proposition 227 tapped into a growing public sentiment especially among white voters that bilingual education programs were a failure and that the public schools needed to take a different approach to improving student achievement among immigrant and non-English-speaking students. Obviously, the vote reflected major frustrations about the progress toward improving schools.

On the November 1998 ballot, voters confronted two propositions, and these propositions had almost opposite outcomes. The legislature placed a $9.2 billion state bond measure on the ballot to provide funds

TABLE 4.3   STATE PROPOSITIONS ON EDUCATION ISSUES, 1978–1998

Proposition 13	Local property tax limitation	June 1978	Passed
Proposition 98	Minimum school funding	November 1988	Passed
Proposition 223	School spending reforms	June 1998	Failed
Proposition 227	Bilingual education	June 1998	Passed
Proposition 1a	$9.2 billion school bonds	November 1998	Passed
Proposition 8	Class size/Teacher reforms	November 1998	Failed

SOURCE: Baldassare (1998, 2000); California Secretary of State (1998a, 1998b).

for building and repairing school facilities. This was the largest school bond measure in the state's history. Proposition 1a was billed in the ballot title and summary as a bond act for class-size reduction, which referred to one of the most popular school reforms at the time—an effort to reduce class sizes in the lower elementary grades. This state proposition faced little opposition and passed by a large majority (62% to 38%). This indicated that voters were willing to borrow large sums of money to improve their schools. Since state bonds are paid through the general funds, and not new taxes, Proposition 1a did not send any message about how the public was feeling about increasing their taxes for schools.

Proposition 8, appearing on the same ballot, was a citizens' initiative that would have created permanent funding for the popular class-size reduction in the lower elementary grades. This proposition also called for education reforms that were viewed unfavorably by the state's teachers unions but positively by outgoing Governor Pete Wilson. The following reforms were included: creating parent-teacher councils, credentialing teachers, using student performance data in teacher evaluations, suspending students immediately for drug possession, and creating an Office of Chief Inspector of Public Schools to evaluate school quality. Interestingly, it was the creation of the new chief inspector position, which became the subject of an advertising campaign against the initiative, that again pointed to the fact that voters were concerned about their school funds being spent on bureaucracy rather than students. Proposition 8 failed by a margin (37% to 63%) that was even larger than the victory margin for Proposition 1a.

TABLE 4.4   MOST IMPORTANT
STATE ISSUE

*"Which one issue facing California today
is the most important for the Governor and
State Legislature to work on in... "*

	1999	2000
Schools, education	36%	28%
Crime, gangs	7	7
Immigration (legal and illegal)	7	5
Jobs, the economy	5	5
Taxes	4	4
Health care	3	5

SOURCE: PPIC Statewide Survey (1999a, 2000a).

paign finance reform, tax cuts, Social Security, national defense, Medicare, and health care. Moreover, schools are more of a state and local issue, since the federal government has a more limited role in the K–12 public school arena. Still, Californians seemed to be looking for an "education" president.

Early in 2000, the voters told us they most wanted to hear the candidates for president talk about schools before the March primary.[2] During the national party convention season in the summer of 2000, what did people want the convention to tell them about a presidential candidate? Similarly, it was the candidate's views on education.[3] The presidential candidates, Bush and Gore, were set to face off in a series of debates during the fall. When asked which one issue they would most like to hear the candidates talk about during the debates, education was the favored choice among Californians.[4] In the final weeks before the November election, we asked California voters what they were most interested in hearing the presidential candidates talk about on the campaign trail. Of all the possible issues, schools were again the top choice, followed by foreign policy and national defense, health care and health maintenance organization (HMO) reform, Social Security, Medicare, and taxes.[5]

2. See PPIC Statewide Survey (2000b) in February 2000.
3. See PPIC Statewide Survey (2000e) in August 2000.
4. See PPIC Statewide Survey (2000f) in September 2000.
5. See PPIC Statewide Survey (2000g) in October 2000.

In a variety of survey questions leading up to the 2000 elections, large proportions in all demographic and political groups and across all regions rated schools as their number one issue. This was true for questions that focused on both national and state politics.[6]

To put the concern about education in perspective, we compared it with concern about another continuing issue—crime. In January 2000, eight in ten Californians said that the quality of education in K–12 public schools was a problem, with more than half saying it was a "big" problem. At this time, the state's residents were even more likely to say the schools were a problem than they were a month before the June primary in 1998. Compare that with public concern about crime. Californians were becoming less worried about crime at the time that they were increasingly concerned about their schools. Half said that crime was a big problem in the January 2000 survey, a steep drop from the two in three residents holding this view in May 1998.

Only two in ten said that the schools had improved in the past few years, while four in ten actually thought the quality of education in California had gotten worse. In contrast, Californians were much more likely to say that crime rates had been improving than to perceive that the quality of schools was improving: four in ten residents believed that crime rates were declining.[7]

These perceptions of school problems varied somewhat across regions and demographic groups. For instance, parents with public school children were less likely to say that schools were a big problem and that the quality of education had gotten worse. However, the state's schools were viewed by most in a negative light among all groups.

We also learned something about how concerned Californians were about their schools by asking them how closely they followed news stories on this topic. Californians are not known for being highly engaged in policy issues (Baldassare, 2000), but they were fixated on the schools. In a series of questions in the course of the election cycle, we found uniformly high levels of interest in schools. Half of Californians said they closely followed news stories about student test scores for public schools

6. Multiple regressions were analyzed for the "most important problem" question in February 2000, with age, education, income, gender, region, political party, liberal-conservative orientation, children in public schools, and race and ethnicity in the equation. The following B values and significance levels (in parentheses) are for the significant variables from the final equations with all variables, with positive correlations indicating mention of schools as the top issue: Age $= -.16$ (.001), Education $= .23$ (.001), Children in Public School $= .54$ (.001), Income $= -.11$ (.02).

7. See PPIC Statewide Survey (2000a) in January 2000.

in August 2000; to place this number in perspective, four in ten residents were closely following the news about the state budget being passed and signed into law, and seven in ten were following the presidential elections. In October 2000, six in ten residents were closely following news about student test scores that were released, and a similar number were following news about the school vouchers initiative; at that time, eight in ten were closely following the news about the closing stretch of the presidential campaign.[8]

What the Public Thought Was Wrong with Schools

As for what was specifically wrong with the state's schools, there seemed to be a great deal of recognition of the very same issues that the experts were mentioning. Near the top of the list were deep concerns about the lack of resources of all kinds. In focus groups, the talk about school problems soon turned to a discussion of the lack of money. There was recognition that California had fallen behind in the quest for better schools and a number of ideas about how money should be spent to improve the state's public schools. "Let's be number one in comparison to other states, and spend more money on schools and teachers," said one of our participants. Another respondent added, "Schools need more materials, teachers, and money for books." "We can't build enough schools," said another participant in our groups. In all, we heard a surprisingly high level of willingness to spend more money on schools from residents of a state usually quick to judge government institutions as having enough funds.

One of the favored purposes for increased funding was teachers' salaries. In focus groups, there was a strong belief that teachers were underpaid and were working under difficult circumstances. "Good teachers need to be paid more, and they need to have smaller class sizes," said one respondent. "Good teachers leave for better pay, and we can't fire the bad teachers," added another focus group participant. "Teachers can't afford to live in the area [where they teach], and we have to subsidize housing for them," observed another respondent, concerning local circumstances. What is interesting to note here was a willingness to pay higher salaries to public employees—that is, the teachers—in a state that is not known for having especially generous attitudes toward those working for state and local governments. Teachers were not perceived as lazy

8. See PPIC Statewide Survey (2000e, 2000g) in August and October 2000.

public servants but, instead, as victims of a government bureaucracy un-appreciative of their value and importance to society.

Similar to the focus groups, in a public opinion survey in late 1998, residents recited a laundry list of school woes. The quality of teachers, lack of state funds, crowded classrooms, and lack of parental involve-ment were the top reasons given when residents were asked why the pub-lic schools were not performing as well as they could. It seems that most of these reasons for the schools' failures were relevant a year later. When asked what the most important factors were for success and failure in California's K–12 public schools, a similar list emerged: teachers' expe-rience and education topped the list, followed by issues such as class size and student family background. The belief that the teacher's experience and education was the most important ingredient for success and failure was even higher among those who had children in public schools.

How much did Californians really know about school funding? We found out by quizzing them about the low ranking the state receives for school funding relative to other states (see Table 4-5). We found that Cal-ifornians are keenly aware that their state is not overly generous to its pub-lic schools. Half of the state's residents knew that their state was ranked below average in per-pupil spending compared with other states. Demon-stration of this knowledge had actually increased slightly over time, largely as a result of fewer people thinking that their state was not average in its school spending habits. By February 2000, only one in four residents be-lieved that California was spending an average amount on per-pupil spend-ing, while one in six thought that it was spending more than other states.[9]

Moreover, despite many efforts over the years to equalize school re-sources, most residents believed that inequality was placing some schools at a greater disadvantage. Eight in ten Californians believed that schools in lower-income areas of the state did not have the same amount of re-sources—including good teachers—as schools in wealthier areas. At least three in four parents with school children, and residents in all regions of the state, held this view. The perception that schools in poorer neigh-borhoods were worse off than others was held across all income, age, racial and ethnic, and education groups. Moreover, seven in ten residents believed that the school districts with the lowest student test scores should be getting more resources than other school districts. The pref-erence to give more resources to lower-performing schools was found in all regions, across racial and ethnic groups, and for those with and with-

9. See PPIC Statewide Survey (2000b) in February 2000.

TABLE 4.5   CALIFORNIA'S
SCHOOL SPENDING

*"Where do you think California ranks in
spending per pupil compared to other states?"*

	April 1998	February 2000
Below average	47%	51%
Average	28	24
Above average	14	16
Don't know	11	9

SOURCE: PPIC Statewide Survey (2000b).

out children in the public schools. Evidently, Californians believed that one problem was chronically underachieving schools that were poorly serving students in lower-income areas.[10]

Californians pointed to problems in the school system in general and in lower-income areas in particular, but were they pleased with their own schools? The possibility existed that they may have been complaining about schools in an abstract way and that in reality their own local schools were just fine. Such was not the case. Californians graded their local schools closer to a "curve," rather than bunching their rankings in the top categories, offering yet another indication that schools really were perceived as problematic. When asked to rate the quality of local public schools, four in ten Californians gave their local schools more than mediocre grades: one in ten residents gave an A grade and three in ten gave a B grade to their own schools. Six in ten gave grades lower than a B or no grade at all: three in ten said C, two in ten say D or F, and about 10 percent were not sure. Perhaps not everyone had enough experience to accurately assess their local public schools, so what did the actual local consumers think? Grades of A or B were given by only half of parents with children in local public schools. Fewer than four in ten residents in the San Francisco Bay Area and Los Angeles gave positive ratings. Almost half of Asians and Latinos gave their local schools excellent or good ratings, while only four in ten whites and one in four blacks gave their schools A or B grades. Clearly, most Californians were not all that impressed by what their local schools had to offer.[11]

10. See PPIC Statewide Survey (2000b) in February 2000.
11. See PPIC Statewide Survey (2000d) in August 2000.

In another view of the specific problems associated with the schools, Californians were asked if the education reforms that the state government had set in motion were making any major difference. Largely, residents still said that there was much room for improvement. In a survey taken in early 2001, half of Californians were still saying that the quality of education in K–12 public schools was a big problem. Only three in ten believed that the quality of education had improved in the schools, while four in ten thought it had stayed the same, and two in ten actually thought it had gotten worse. As for the effectiveness of the specific state policies, four in ten residents thought that reducing class sizes in the lower grades of elementary schools had made a major difference—which was a policy begun in former governor Pete Wilson's administration and continued when Governor Davis entered office. However, only one in six residents felt that increases in per-pupil spending in the state had made a big difference, and only one in eight residents thought that the use of test scores to rank schools and reward their performance had a significant impact on K–12 public schools. Even among parents with children in the public schools, only half felt that class-size reduction had a major positive effect, while two in ten believed that increased spending and the use of student test scores were making a big difference in efforts to improve the schools.[12]

As they approached the 2000 elections, most Californians were of the mind that their public schools were seriously off on the wrong track. Many residents viewed their own schools as mediocre at best, and most believed that schools in lower-income areas were not getting the resources they needed to succeed. They viewed the problems they face as multifaceted and complex, they perceived the solutions to-date as inadequate, and they believed that more needed to be done. But were they willing to increase tax dollars for schools, or would distrust and vestiges of the tax revolt prevent them from doing so?

Public Distrust Extended to School Spending and Tax Increases

In recent times, as we noted, the state's voters have not been that generous with school funding. In good economic times, voters might be inclined to give the green light to bonds, but feelings about taxes and spending are always tempered by distrust. This raises crucial questions: Are residents willing to significantly increase spending for schools, so

12. See PPIC Statewide Survey (2001a) in January 2001.

that the funding can be more comparable to the rest of the nation? Under what conditions are voters willing themselves to pay more taxes for better schools?

The fact that the public wants school improvement does not rule out the possibility that the public is too critical of the schools to favor increased funding. In fact, in our focus groups, there were many calls for education reforms to take place either before or in the course of increasing the funding that schools should receive—including testing and standards, public and private school choices, and accountability for how the money is spent. Moreover, many people are reluctant to see their taxes increased, even though they might think that the schools need more money. They would prefer to see the money taken from some other programs that they consider less important. "School standards must be higher," remarked one focus group participant. "No higher taxes for better schools. We throw money at them. Accountability first," added another respondent. In these remarks, there is a not-so-subtle suggestion that certain conditions should be met before the schools are given any new funding.

Californians ranked K–12 public education spending as a top priority after the 1998 statewide election. Eight in ten residents said that spending on public schools should be a high priority when the state has limited funds due to budget deficits. By comparison, six in ten residents said that public health and welfare and public colleges and universities deserve a high priority for state funding, while only one in four residents ranked the state's prisons and the corrections budget as equally important. Schools received the highest rankings across all demographic, political, and regional groups. Moreover, the importance that the public places on K–12 education funding had remained constant in recent years: a similar eight in ten gave schools the highest priority for funding in a statewide survey of voters that I conducted in the summer of 1994.[13]

Despite the fact that the voters passed a $6 billion state education bond measure in November 1998, and that the governor and state legislature significantly increased spending for schools in 1999, the public's perception of a shortfall in state funding for schools remained. Two in three Californians thought that their local public schools were not getting enough funding in a survey in the fall of 1999 (see Table 4-6). Two in ten residents thought the state had given just enough money, and only

---

13. See PPIC Statewide Survey (1999a) in December 1998, including reference to 1994 survey.

TABLE 4.6   LOCAL
SCHOOL FUNDING

*"Do you think the current level of state funding for
your local public schools is more than enough,
just enough, or not enough?"*

	September 1999	August 2000
More than enough	10%	10%
Just enough	21	23
Not enough	65	62
Don't know	4	5

SOURCE: PPIC Statewide Survey (1999b, 2000e).

one in ten thought the state had given too much money to the schools.
The perception of a lack of adequate funding for schools was widely held
in all political groups, demographic groups, regions of the state, and
racial and ethnic groups. These results are nearly identical to the number of state residents who said there was not enough funding for public
schools in the fall of 1998.

A year later, in summer 2000, two in three Californians were still saying that their local public schools were not getting enough money from
the state government. Three in ten thought their own schools had either
just enough or more than enough state funding. The public's perception
of a lack of state funding persisted despite the significant increases in
school spending allocated by the governor and state legislature from a
state budget awash in surplus funds. There were significant differences
in these perceptions across political and demographic groups.[14]

While residents might like the concept of giving their schools more
state funds, they are not as keen on the idea when they are asked to provide more tax dollars from their wallets. When residents were informed
in our February 2000 survey that their state ranked around fortieth in
the nation in school spending, three in four people said they would sup-

14. Multiple regressions were analyzed for the "local school funding" question in
August 2000, with age, education, income, gender, region, political party, liberal-
conservative orientation, children in public schools, and race and ethnicity in the equation. The following B values and significance levels (in parentheses) are for the
significant variables from the final equations with all variables, with positive correlations indicating a perception that there is not enough local school funding: Age = −.12
(.001), Democrats = .64 (.001), San Francisco Bay Area = .49 (.001), Children in Public School = .29 (.001), Conservatives = −.20 (.001).

port an initiative that would require the state to reach the national average in five years. However, Californians were not nearly as enthused about increased spending for schools when they heard how much it might cost. Public support dropped by about 20 points when people were told that an estimated $4 billion tax increase would be needed to bring the state up to the national average in per-pupil spending.

California voters are more inclined to support raising new money for their schools by borrowing funds than raising taxes. Slightly fewer than two in three voters said they would vote for local school construction bonds if they appeared on the March primary ballot. Three in ten said they would vote "no." Public support for passing school bonds was strong across all demographic and political groups and regions of the state. Most voters—again a little under two in three—said they would vote in favor of local school construction bonds if they were on the November general election ballot. Once again, opponents outnumbered supporters across all regions, political groups, and racial and ethnic groups. However, in both cases, the level of support falls just short of the two-thirds vote required by the state constitution to pass local school bonds. The fact that local school bonds enjoy such strong support, yet fall below the "super-majority" vote requirement of the state, is one of the reasons that the proponents of school funding wanted to place an initiative on the ballot in 2000 that would change the vote needed to pass local school bonds to a simple-majority (50%) vote. However, we found that not all of those who may want to pass local school bonds would necessarily favor changing the state law and make it easier to pass all local school bonds.

One factor that limited the public's generosity toward increased school funding, either in the form of borrowing or more tax dollars, was that many people had serious misgivings about the fiscal management of their local school districts. (See Table 4-7.) Only one in seven voters had a lot of confidence that their local school district officials were spending money wisely. One in three said they had some confidence in local fiscal management. Nearly half reported that they did not have much confidence that their local school district officials were spending money wisely. Confidence was low in all political groups, across regions of the state, and in all racial and ethnic groups. The distrust in local school officials was but one of many issues that might shift support as the pros and cons of the simple-majority initiative were publicly debated. Another issue that voters might focus on was the possibility that easing local vote requirements for passing school bonds could result in higher local property taxes to pay for the increased borrow-

TABLE 4.7   VOTER
DISTRUST AND LOCAL
SCHOOL SPENDING

"Do you have a lot of confidence, some confidence,
or not much confidence that your local school
district officials are spending money wisely?"

A lot	15%
Some	34
Not much	47
Don't know	4

"Overall, do you think that the two-thirds vote
requirement for passing local school bonds has been
a good thing or a bad thing for your local schools?"

Good thing	53%
Bad thing	32
No difference	4
Don't know	11

SOURCE: PPIC Statewide Survey (1999b, 2000a).

ing, and our earlier surveys suggested that this could turn many voters off of passing local school bonds.[15]

Perhaps fueled by the perception that their local governments were wasteful in spending the taxpayers' money, the majority of California voters believed that a supermajority vote requirement for passing local school bonds was a good thing for their local schools. In fact, only one in three voters thought the two-thirds vote requirement was a bad thing. While Republicans were more likely than Democrats or independent voters to see the two-thirds vote as positive for their local schools, those who said that a supermajority vote was bad for their school districts were in the minority in all political groups. This positive perception of constraints on passing local school bonds is shared across regions of the state, racial and ethnic groups, and demographic categories.

Indeed, the feeling that a two-thirds vote was a good thing grew when the prospect of making it easier to increase taxes was also raised. By an even wider two-to-one margin, voters felt that the Proposition-13 im-

15. See PPIC Statewide Survey (1999b) conducted in September 1999.

posed requirement of at least a two-thirds vote to raise local property taxes was a good thing rather than a bad thing. At least a majority in all political groups, regions of the state, and racial and ethnic groups saw the supermajority vote for raising local property taxes in a positive light. Moreover, the deep loyalty to Proposition 13 reasserted itself when voters were asked about the general idea of changing the vote requirements to pass local special taxes. Seven in ten voters opposed the idea of allowing local special taxes to pass with a simple-majority vote.[16]

To the extent that making it easier to pass local school bonds was perceived as also making it easier to pass local property taxes, the idea of changing the supermajority vote requirement for school bonds would run into serious opposition. This case was relatively easy for antitax forces to make in the course of the campaign, given that local school bonds are generally paid from the proceeds generated by an increase in the local property taxes. In other words, efforts to change the laws governing local school bonds were controversial, reflecting the depth of the antitax sentiment: Many residents perceived that the schools were in need of funds, but many were still unwilling to make it easier for voters to pass tax increases in their communities.

ELECTION 2000: THREE EDUCATION INITIATIVES FACE VOTER DISTRUST

In March and November 2000, the voters would confront three education initiatives. Two would make it easier for school districts to raise more money through passing local school bonds, and one would set up a school voucher system. Their outcomes tell us a great deal about how feelings of government distrust were expressed, even in times of plenty, despite a strong outcry by the public to improve the schools.

Local School Bonds Initiative in March 2000: A Narrow Loss

Encouraged by the prospects of working with a less stingy electorate in good economic times, and buoyed by the finding that the voters thought their local schools needed much more cash than the state was providing, school fiscal reform advocates placed a citizens' initiative on the March

---

16. See PPIC Statewide Survey (2000a) in January 2000.

2000 ballot that would make it possible to pass local school construction bonds with a simple-majority vote instead of a two-thirds vote. This
measure—which was labeled Proposition 26, "the school facilities,
bonds, majority vote" initiative—had significant help from Silicon Valley millionaires Reed Hastings and John Doerr, who were willing to fund
the campaign. The California teachers' unions were also supportive of
this effort to increase school funding, even though business leaders led
the charge. The opponents of changing the vote requirement for local
school bonds included the antitax establishment, such as the Howard
Jarvis Association.[17]

Proposition 26 narrowly failed in March 2000. It was revived in a
slightly altered form as Proposition 39 and narrowly passed in November 2000. The reasons for these two close outcomes say a lot about the
consequences of voter distrust on the prospects of increasing school funding and raising taxes, even in a best-case scenario.

At first sight, public support for the simple majority was overwhelming. Often in California, though, support can quickly evaporate
once the fiscal issues are exposed. Three in four voters were in favor of
changing the requirement for passing local school bonds from two-
thirds to a simple-majority vote when we first raised this issue in September 1999. Voters across party lines were strongly in favor of this
change. Eight in ten voters with children in the public schools wanted
this fiscal reform. The priority voters gave to improving the public
schools was less in evidence when we next asked about Proposition 26
in December 1999. Two in three voters were in favor of this education
initiative, reflecting a significant drop in support after the initiative was
named and the ballot description provided a bit more information. Still,
a solid majority favored it. There was at least a majority support across
all voter registration groups, and eight in ten Latinos and six in ten
whites favored Proposition 26.[18]

One month later, voters were read the most up-to-date ballot summary
and title for Proposition 26. Public support dropped by 20 points, and
there was a tie between those who supported and opposed this measure.
Why the sudden change? The ballot measure was now called the "school
facilities, local majority vote, bonds, taxes" initiative. Specifically, it now
included the word *taxes*. The summary also mentioned these facts: property taxes could go higher with a majority vote instead of a two-thirds

17. See list of contributors developed by the California Voter Foundation (2001).
18. See PPIC Statewide Surveys (1999b, 1999d) in September and December 1999.

vote, and the fiscal costs to local school districts within a decade could potentially be in the hundreds of millions of dollars a year statewide. As a result of these changes, the tax implications and fiscal costs were out in the open. With this, support fell. A narrow majority of Democrats, just under half of the independent voters, and only one in three Republicans now supported Proposition 26 and its simple-majority vote for local school bonds. Only in the liberal-Democratic stronghold of the San Francisco Bay Area did a majority of voters support this measure. Latinos were narrowly in favor, while six in ten whites were opposed. Without much of an opposition campaign, matched by significant funds and organization by the supporters, the wording for Proposition 26 placed the election in serious jeopardy.

A few weeks before the primary election, our February 2000 survey showed that the fate of Proposition 26 was still uncertain, even as the proponents were spending significant amounts of money on television advertisements to make their arguments. When voters were read the summary and title of Proposition 26, as many said "yes" as said "no," while one in ten voters were undecided. A bare majority of Democrats supported the measure, Republicans were strongly opposed, and independent voters were leaning against it. No region of the state showed a majority in support of Proposition 26. Latinos were inclined to vote in favor of this measure, but whites were not. Clearly, many voters were not convinced that they wanted to change the local vote requirement and make it easier to pass local school bonds. The results were unchanged from a month earlier.[19]

Proposition 26 lost in the March 2000 primary by 49 percent to 51 percent. The "no" vote outnumbered the "yes" vote by less than 200,000 of the over 7.2 million votes that were cast in this election (California Secretary of State, 2000b). The initiative failed for a number of reasons. The *Los Angeles Times* exit poll (2000a) in Table 4-8 offers some clues. Simply put, the state's antitax and voter distrust forces were once again at work. While Democrats voted for Proposition 26 by a two-to-one margin, Republicans were strongly opposed to making it easier to pass

19. Multiple regressions were analyzed for the "Proposition 26" question in February 2000, with age, education, income, gender, region, political party, liberal-conservative orientation, children in public schools, and race and ethnicity in the equation. The following B values and significance levels (in parentheses) are for the significant variables from the final equations with all variables, with positive correlations indicating a "yes" vote: Latino $= .43$ (.001), Age $= -.21$ (.001), Income $= -.11$ (.01), Conservative $= -.17$ (.001), Children in Public School $= .27$ (.001). See PPIC Statewide Surveys (2000a, 2000b) in January and February 2000, and see also Jeffe (2000a).

TABLE 4.8   EDUCATION INITIATIVES ON
THE 2000 BALLOTS: VOTING TRENDS
ACROSS GROUPS
(% "YES")

	Prop. 26 (50% vote)	Prop. 39 (55% vote)	Prop. 38 (vouchers)
All Voters	49	53	29
Men	47	50	36
Women	51	54	39
Democrats	67	66	18
Republicans	30	35	50
Independents/Others	48	48	35
White	48	50	33
Latino	61	60	29
Black	62	60	31
Asian	46	57	42
Los Angeles County	50	57	27
San Francisco Bay Area	62	59	25
Other Southern California	46	48	34
Central Valley	n/a	49	32

SOURCE: *Los Angeles Times* exit polls (2000a, 2000b); PPIC Just the Facts (2000b).

local school bonds. Independent voters went narrowly against the measure. Moreover, whites and Asians voted narrowly against Proposition 26, which negated the support it received from six in ten blacks and Latinos. Men opposed the measure, while women only narrowly supported it. Lastly, the simple-majority vote initiative was favored by six in ten San Francisco Bay Area residents, yet only half in Los Angeles County supported it, and fewer than half of the voters in the rest of the state voted in favor of Proposition 26.

The message from the March primary was that voters who were concerned about tax increases and excessive spending were strong enough to turn away the prospects of making it easier for local schools to borrow more money. This was not, strictly speaking, a tax measure, but a fiscal reform that would make it easier to pass local bonds that could have tax implications. For the proponents of this school fiscal reform, this suggested that a second try with a reformulated proposal was in order. The general electorate was, after all, supposed to be larger and

more representative of the state voter profile; that is, the voters were supposed to be more Democratic, younger, and more liberal than the March
primary electorate. But they would need more than a new electorate to
win: they would need to develop a campaign that emphasized a voter
distrust theme and perhaps to create a certain amount of confusion to
get past these distrustful voters.

Local School Bonds Initiative in November 2000: A Narrow Win

In the November election, voters were asked to vote on the issue of local
school bond requirements once again through Proposition 39. It was
dubbed the "son of Proposition 26" initiative. The school fiscal reform proponents collected the signatures needed to place the revised measure on the
ballot, with the aid of million-dollar-plus contributions, once again, from
Silicon Valley businessmen John Doerr and Reed Hastings (California Voter
Foundation, 2001). The campaign and outcome for Proposition 39 is telling
in many respects. It is a clear indication that the voters' concern that propositions are written by proponents in ways that lead to confusion about what
they are supporting has validity, even for noble causes such as schools. Some
voters thought they were supporting tighter restrictions, rather than easing
requirements to pass local school bonds. The public confusion surrounding Proposition 39 seemed to convince enough distrustful voters to vote
"yes," tipping the election outcome. So did an emphasis on elements of the
proposal that sounded themes of voter distrust.

Proposition 39 was different in a number of important respects from
its earlier version. The vote-requirement change was altered from a simple majority to a 55 percent vote needed to pass local school bonds. (See
Table 4-9.) Right away, this change could only help the antitax sentiment: the "55 percent" could be read by a public unaware of the two-
thirds vote as a tougher standard than a majority vote. The ballot title
included the term *accountability requirements,* and the measure included
annual performance and financial audits on the use of the school bonds.
Also noteworthy was that the ballot label (as it appeared on the ballot
mailed to voters' homes) made no mention of the current two-thirds majority needed to pass local school bonds nor of the fact that under some
circumstances this measure could make it easier to increase local property taxes. For those who were unfamiliar with the past history, Proposition 39 could be read as a fiscally conservative initiative that was requiring a more stringent, 55 percent vote.

TABLE 4.9   VOTER DISTRUST
AND THE 55% MAJORITY VOTE
FOR LOCAL SCHOOL BONDS

Proposition 39 authorizes accountability requirements for local school bonds:	
Would vote "yes"	57%
Would vote "no"	32
Don't know	11

Proposition 39 raises taxes with 55% vote rather than the current two-thirds vote:	
Would vote "yes"	41%
Would vote "no"	48
Don't know	11

Proposition 39's perceived impact on passing local school bonds:	
Would make it easier	38%
Would make it more difficult	15
Would make no difference	30
Don't know	17

SOURCE: PPIC Statewide Survey (2000f, 2000g), likely voters.

The importance of the wording of Proposition 39—what was said and not said in the ballot title, label, and summary—could not be underestimated in this election. We read voters the full ballot title and summary as provided on the California secretary of state's Web site in August and found that a majority opposed the proposition and only one in three were in favor. The description included the prospects of tax increases, the current two-thirds vote requirement, and the anticipation of hundreds of millions of dollars in increased debts. Democrats and San Francisco Bay Area residents were evenly divided, while other voter groups and regions showed strong opposition. One of the problems facing Proposition 39 at this time was resentment about being asked to revote on an issue. Almost half said they had an unfavorable view of reconsidering an issue that was narrowly defeated in March 2000. Of those holding this negative view of a revote, eight in ten said they would vote "no." But even among those who did not mind being asked to vote again on local school bond requirements, three in ten said they would vote "no" on Proposition 39. It is likely that the latter group was troubled by references in the ballot summary to easier tax hikes and higher debts.[20]

Only one month later, when voters were read only the ballot title and label that were publicly released by the California secretary of state in September 2000, a near majority was in favor of Proposition 39, while about one in three was opposed. Well before the campaign was in full swing, it suddenly seemed feasible that the effort to make it possible to pass local school bonds with a 55 percent majority vote might succeed—largely, it appeared, because of what was not said. The ballot label made no mention of the two-thirds majority vote and the possibility of making it easier to increase property taxes. Given the wording of the ballot label, which was read verbatim in this survey, Democrats were strongly in favor of this proposition, and a narrow majority of independent voters supported it, while a near majority of Republicans were opposed.

To gauge the effect of facts about the initiative that were not explained in the short ballot labels, we asked two follow-up questions that might be considered the pro and con arguments for the state's fiscally conservative voters in our survey. The changes were dramatic. Support declined from half of the voters to four in ten when survey respondents were told that property taxes to pay for local school bonds could pass with a 55 percent vote instead of a two-thirds vote. However, support increased from half of the voters to six in ten when the accountability requirements of Proposition 39, including financial audits and annual fiscal performance reviews, were more fully explained. These results suggest that the fate of the measure hinged on how well the supporters of Proposition 39 kept the voters from all of the facts and how well the opponents focused public attention on the tax-related details of the measure.[21]

A few weeks before the election, a bare majority of voters said they would vote "yes" on Proposition 39. The results were nearly identical to the survey a month before, when voters were also read the ballot title and ballot label, with its limited details on the change in vote requirements and its tax implications. The slight majority support was achieved by getting overwhelming support from Democrats and a small majority of support from independent voters, while keeping the opposition to a small majority among Republicans. Perhaps most important, there was considerable confusion about the perceived effects of Proposition 39.

20. See PPIC Statewide Survey (2000e) in August 2000.
21. See PPIC Statewide Survey (2000f) in September 2000 and Dionne (2000).

Fewer than four in ten voters thought the measure would make it easier to pass local school bonds. One in six actually thought this measure would make it more difficult to pass local school bonds; one in six were not sure. Three in ten thought it would make no difference, and, importantly, most of those voters said they would vote in favor of Proposition 39. Another one in three voters either were not sure or thought the proposition made it more difficult to pass bonds. Many voters did not realize that Proposition 39 would actually lower the requirement from a supermajority to a 55 percent vote, and this apparently helped the proposition. The minority (38%) who recognized the true facts were the strong supporters of the measure, but it was the large number of voters who said "yes" while not knowing that they were making it easier to pass school bonds that cast the decisive votes.[22]

Proposition 39 passed by a relatively narrow margin—53 percent to 47 percent. The "yes" votes outnumbered the "no" votes by about 675,000, among the 10.2 million votes cast for and against this state initiative (California Secretary of State, 2000c).

When we contrast the *Los Angeles Times* exit polls (2000a, 2000b) on Proposition 26 and Proposition 39 in Table 4-8, we see how the slim loss in March turned into a narrow victory in November. Support increased among both men and women by three points, but the change for men meant the narrowest majority now supported easing the requirement on passing local school bonds. The only change in voting trends by political party registration was a 5-point increase among Republicans, who still strongly opposed the change in the vote requirement, although now by a narrower margin. White support for Proposition 39 increased by two points, thus creating a slight majority among the largest voter group, while Asians also increased their support. Latinos and blacks continued to strongly support this measure. As for changes across regions, the most notable shift was a 7-point increase in support among the voters in Los Angeles. Support remained strong in the San Francisco Bay Area, while less than a majority of voters supported Proposition 39 elsewhere in the state.

22. Multiple regressions were analyzed for the "Impacts of Proposition 39" question in October 2000, with age, education, income, gender, region, political party, liberal-conservative orientation, children in public schools, and race and ethnicity in the equation. The following B values and significance levels (in parentheses) are for the significant variables from the final equations with all variables, with positive correlations indicating a belief that Proposition 39 will make it easier to pass bonds: Latino = .41 (.001), Education = .14 (.001), Children in Public School = .36 (.001). See PPIC Statewide Survey (2000g) in October 2000.

The fact that California voters changed the two-thirds vote requirement to pass local school bonds could be viewed as an historic moment.
While this state law was enacted over a hundred years ago to prevent
local governments from borrowing beyond their means, the concept of
the supermajority vote requirement is best remembered as an important
cornerstone of the Proposition 13 local tax limitations enacted in the late
1970s. In effect, the voters turned their backs on the tax revolt, or at
least made an exception with regard to their local schools. However, to
place this change in the supermajority vote requirement in perspective,
all of the facts should be considered. First, it took two tries to make this
change during one of the best of economic times, and, as it was, this issue
was decided by only a narrow win. Moreover, there is evidence to suggest that this vote reflected confusion rather than a change of heart about
tax limitations. Finally, the campaign emphasized creating restrictions
rather then increasing funding. Many people may have thought they were
tightening the restrictions when they supported a 55 percent majority
vote with accountability requirements. Without the voter confusion and
distrust themes, in all likelihood the supermajority vote for local school
bonds would have withstood this test and would still be the law in California today.

School Vouchers Initiative in November 2000: A Landslide Defeat

A different perspective that was part of the political dialogue on schools
in the 2000 election was increasing "choice"—the right of parents to se-
lect which schools their children will attend—through a school voucher
program. This idea was discussed by presidential candidate George W.
Bush and formulated in an initiative on the November ballot. In our focus
groups, one respondent summed up the antiestablishment view of the
role of vouchers this way: "Teachers say, 'If choice happens, we'll lose
our best students.' What does this say about the quality of our schools?"
Clearly, vouchers appealed to those who felt the public school system was
broken and could not be fixed. Ironically, given its fundamental roots in
the public's distrust of government and its fiscally conservative base, the
costs of the school vouchers program to taxpayers would be its undoing.

The idea of having a school vouchers program is not novel. In fact,
the state's voters had overwhelmingly rejected a school vouchers initiative in a special election in 1993. What was unique about the school
vouchers initiative in 2000 was that a wealthy Silicon Valley business-
man would be the guiding force behind it throughout the ballot process.

Tim Draper spent about $27 million in an effort to convince voters that the school vouchers initiative should pass (California Voter Foundation, 2001). In doing so, the school voucher movement gained national attention and the debate over parental choice was given new life. The proposition failed miserably at the polls. The reasons for its dismissal are highly instructive of the way Californians think about their public schools and state education reforms.

The basic concept behind having school vouchers is a simple one. Schools are funded with taxpayer money, and currently the money goes only to support public school systems. Instead, why not give the taxpayers a choice as to how the school money should be spent? This would involve giving parents of school children a voucher that could be used to pay for any public, private, or religious school they chose. This way, parents rather than the government would make the decision as to where the money allocated for their children's education was actually spent. They might choose a public school inside their neighborhood or a public school elsewhere, or they might opt to take the money that the government has allocated to them to a private or parochial school.

Public support for school vouchers may come from various motivations—including self-interest, altruism, or ideology. Not all who favor vouchers will directly and financially benefit from them. Of course, parents who currently send their children to private schools might want to see the government pick up at least part of the tab. Then, there are religious groups who would like to see their parochial schools receiving more funding and their enrollments flourishing. Others may feel that low-income parents should be provided with a government subsidy so that they can send their children to a better school than what might otherwise be available locally. There are also the fiscal conservatives who believe that vouchers give taxpayers the right to choose how their government money is spent. There are some who believe that the "free market" economy is the best way to stimulate school reform. The latter group believes that competition for school children will cause the public school system to try harder to improve and that without this incentive, they will not make changes. The latest incarnation of school vouchers was grounded in this thinking in business terms about education reform.

Opposition to school vouchers comes from many sources expressing a variety of ideas—including the public, experts, and the K–12 education establishment. Some believe that the government should not subsidize the wealthy who are already sending their children to private schools. Others think that the separation of church and state should exclude the government from supporting tuition at religious schools. There are some who argue that the loss of government funds to private and religious schools from an already underfunded K–12 public school system will do great damage to the public schools. Even among the parents who send their children to existing private schools, some think that the voucher program may create unwanted government interference. Others think that vouchers will not offer enough money for lower-income parents, who are most in need of increased school choices. Some think that vouchers will spawn low-quality private schools that exploit those who live in poor neighborhoods. Finally, some fear that the cost, size, and complexity of a voucher program could overwhelm the state bureaucracy and ultimately cause more harm than good.

The citizens' initiative that was placed on the November 2000 ballot was a sweeping measure that would have radically altered the state's public education system. Voucher programs that were targeted to inner city areas or low-income parents were becoming more popular on the national scene. One of the presidential candidates, Republican Governor George W. Bush, had talked about limited voucher plans as one of many efforts to encourage improvements in student performance. But in California, the initiative's supporters dismissed the notion of a more limited voucher program. They were looking for a way to reform the entire school system, not just some of it. Proposition 38 called for annual state payments of at least $4,000 for every pupil in the state, amounting to annual cost estimates of between $1 billion and $2 billion. The interest was in creating a wholesale change in school choice, rather than in modest education reforms.

We first asked Californians about their general reaction to the concept of school vouchers in a survey conducted right after the November 1998 election. The response reflected an issue that appeared to be highly divisive, politically partisan, and ideologically driven. It was also obvious that school vouchers did not have a groundswell of public support: about half of California voters said they were in favor of a voucher system that would allow the use of public funds to help parents to pay for sending their children to private or parochial schools, while more than four in ten were opposed. A slight majority of Democrats were against creating a voucher system, while a slight majority of independent voters were in favor of it. Two in three Republicans supported this school reform proposal, indicating its conservative base. The division of public support was mirrored almost exactly in responses to a question about the expected effects of school vouchers: A slim majority thought a voucher system would make public schools better by creating competition, while four in ten voters thought a voucher system would make public schools worse because the loss of students would result in a decrease in public funds.[23]

A year later, we repeated a question about school vouchers that had been asked in a national survey. We again found a mixed response, as we had in our earlier survey and as was evident in the nationwide poll. A slim majority of Californians believed that "government funding should be limited to children who attend public schools," while just under half thought the government should give parents more educational choices by providing them with tax-supported vouchers to pay for private or religious schools. Six in ten Democrats favored limiting government funding to public schools, while six in ten Republicans wanted school vouchers; independent voters were evenly divided on this issue. Once again, there was a lack of overwhelming support for school vouchers.

As noted previously, we found voters to be evenly divided on Proposition 38 when we first began to ask about the initiative. This was before there was much advertising or media attention, so we were once again basically measuring reactions to the concept. We read the ballot title and summary, which mentioned state payments of $4,000 per pupil, fiscal effects in the hundreds of millions of dollars, and the potential for billions of dollars in long-term savings. The summary also mentioned the additional requirement that the state would have to guarantee a new minimum of per-pupil spending that would be no less than the national average. As we had seen earlier, a majority of Democrats were opposed to vouchers, while a majority of Republicans were in favor, and independent voters were evenly divided.

The reason that school vouchers were receiving a high level of initial support seemed to have more to do with attitudes toward the public schools than knowledge of how a school voucher program would work. Our surveys leading up to the November 2000 elections indicated that voters were disillusioned with the public schools. For many, this may have signaled a need to shake up the system. For instance, only one in four felt the public schools had been showing any improvement in the past few years. Fewer than one in five said they were very satisfied with the way their local government was handling the public schools. As for

23. See PPIC Statewide Survey (1999b) in September 1999.

the quality of education in their own local public schools, few Californians were giving them top grades. Of those who gave their schools a C or less, the majority favored the vouchers initiative.

A major issue that limited the amount of public support for the school voucher initiative at this point was a lack of belief that this particular reform would make a positive difference. About one in three voters said the quality of their local public schools would improve if the voucher initiative passed, but just about as many thought quality would decline; one in four said that it would make no difference if this initiative passed. Predictably, those who thought the quality of their schools would improve if Proposition 38 passed were strongly in favor of this initiative, while other voters were not enthusiastic about the prospects of radically changing the way that the government allocated funds to schools. Was there any sense of urgency about the need to pass Proposition 38? Apparently not, since as many voters thought the quality of their schools would decline as thought it would improve if the initiative did not pass.[24]

As more became known about the school vouchers initiative, support diminished and opposition grew. A majority opposed the initiative by the early fall, while only about one in three favored it, and about one in ten voters were still undecided. Two in three Democrats and a slim majority of independent voters were now opposing the school vouchers initiative, while Republican support was just shy of a majority. We could not find majority support for this state proposition in any region or among whites or Latinos. These results did not look favorable, especially since the antivouchers campaign had just begun.

A major factor that was driving opposition to school vouchers was a lack of confidence that their implementation would end up helping the public schools. Only one in three felt that it would help the public school system in California if the proposition passed, while six in ten thought it would not help. A similar number of voters expressed doubts that Proposition 38 would be of much assistance to students with the lowest test scores. Overwhelmingly, people holding these negative perceptions said they would vote against Proposition 38. In sum, many voters had very little reason to support this initiative since they were not convinced that it would be a solution to the public school's problems.

What had changed public opinion in so short a time? The "yes" campaign had begun running their advertisements, and the "no" campaign had not, so one would have assumed that this would have favored the

---

24. See PPIC Statewide Survey (2000e) in August 2000.

proponents of school vouchers. The fact that support had slipped while proinitiative advertisements were on the air was, indeed, a welcome sign for the opponents who were gearing up to defeat the initiative.

One event that seemed to contribute to the decline in support was a change that was made in the ballot wording between our August and September surveys. Specifically, the fiscal impacts that were mentioned in the ballot summary went from hundreds of millions of dollars in August to between $1 billion and $2 billion in September. In all likelihood, this moved some cost-conscious conservative voters from support to opposition of Proposition 38. In all, our results suggest that the more people learned about the costs to taxpayers, the less they liked school vouchers. Instead of building its support on voter distrust of government, the school voucher initiative was coming up against resistance by those who did not want higher taxes and spending for California's schools.

In our final preelection survey, a solid majority of voters were opposing Proposition 38. The results were similar to the survey taken one month earlier, but support was slipping while opposition was growing. Two in three Democrats and a solid majority of independent voters were opposed, while a majority of Republicans favored it. We could not find majority support in any region or across racial and ethnic groups.

Despite a flurry of television commercials by the proponents and opponents of Proposition 38—by the end of the campaign, each side would report a bankroll of about $30 million—only one in four voters felt they had learned a lot about how a voucher system would actually work in the state. Importantly, two in three who said they knew a lot about how it would work said they would vote "no" on the proposition. Apparently, what they took away from the antivouchers commercials was that this was an education reform that would cost a great deal of money without offering improvements. Most telling, the "no" campaign stressed the fact that the school voucher system would not provide accountability for spending taxpayer money on schools. Thus, it relied partly on the theme of distrust to win. Perceptions of vouchers' impacts did not improve at all as a result of heavy advertising by the provouchers side: six in ten voters said the school vouchers initiative would not help the public schools if it passed, and most who held this negative view had decided to vote against Proposition 38.[25]

25. Multiple regressions were analyzed for the "Proposition 38 Impacts" question in October 2000, with age, education, income, gender, region, political party, liberal-conservative orientation, children in public schools, and race and ethnicity in the equation. The following B values and significance levels (in parentheses) are for the significant variables from the

Proposition 38 fared much worse in the November election than anyone had anticipated, given the $30 million campaign budget in support of school vouchers. The measure lost by a 29 percent to 71 percent vote, which amounted to a margin of defeat of over 4.3 million votes of the 10.5 million votes cast in the election. The *Los Angeles Times* exit poll (2000b) provides an indication of the overwhelming rejection that this measure received across genders, racial and ethnic groups, and regions of the state. The only group that gave Proposition 38 a bare majority of support was Republican voters—while Democrats and other voters were strongly opposed. What is interesting is that opposition transcended the typical liberal and conservative dimensions: The measure lost by a landslide in the Central Valley and the San Francisco Bay Area and among both white and black voters. Even a sizable number of dependably conservative Republicans voted against this version of the school vouchers program.

How did a reform proposal that received mixed reviews in concept become so unpopular when voters were confronted with the prospect of real change? One reason was that Californians who were looking for ways to improve their public school system were not convinced that this particular initiative would help them attain their ultimate goal. Certainly, many people were convinced that their public schools were not as good as they should be, but few were willing to take the chance that this initiative might actually make them worse. However, there was also an added element of voter distrust toward increasing government spending and the accompanying threat of higher taxes. In all likelihood, the potential of billions of dollars in costs entailed by giving out $4,000 in school vouchers to each pupil in the state was more than most voters could stomach. Once again, this demonstrates that many people were not willing to pay the price for school reforms that they supported in concept. Every effort to increase school funding in California will face tough scrutiny, despite the public's concerns about education.

CONCLUSIONS AND IMPLICATIONS

There was no issue that concerned the state's residents more than education in the years between the 1998 gubernatorial election and the 2000

---

final equations with all variables. Positive correlations indicate a view that Proposition 38 will help the schools improve: Age = $-.11$ (.001), Education = $-.14$ (.001), Conservative = .36 (.001). See PPIC Statewide Survey (2000f, 2000g) in September and October 2000.

presidential election. There were many reasons for the fixed focus on improving K–12 public schools. First, there was a growing body of evidence that California's school system had fallen from its status of being among the best to among the worst in the nation. Peter Schrag (1998, 2000a) refers to this trend as the "Mississippification" of California's schools. Next, as the literature on postmaterialist values and the New Political Culture suggest, the presence of peace and prosperity and the absence of rising crime rates allowed the public and politicians to focus on other issues. The public schools also offered the best hope for raising the living standards and job prospects of a growing Latino and immigrant population, thereby avoiding the prospect of growing social and economic inequality.

There are many reasons for the decline in California's schools. Among the contributing factors was Proposition 13, which transferred the primary responsibility for funding from the local to the state government, thus limiting the local governments' ability to raise additional funds for their schools. In good economic times, the schools would be treated generously in the state budget process. But in bad economic times, like the early 1990s, budget shortfalls meant schools would suffer along with other state programs. As the state recovered from the worst recession since the Great Depression, the governor and state legislature committed money and reform efforts to improve the state's schools. In this time of economic plenty and state budget surpluses, the funding for schools received top priority. There had been noticeable improvements in schools, but apparently not enough to convince voters that their schools were now in good shape.

Californians told us in our surveys at many times, and in many different ways, that they had become very concerned about the condition of the public schools. They named schools and education as the top issue for the governor and state legislature to work on, as the most important issue facing the state, and as the one issue they most wanted to hear about during the 2000 presidential campaign. They said that education was an issue that worried them a great deal and increasingly so over time. Most had not perceived much in the way of real progress. There was a lot of consensus across regions and political and demographic groups that something needed to be done to improve the state's public school system.

Were Californians willing to commit their own money to improve the schools? This is a critical issue since, after all, it was the public's lack of generosity toward local taxes, manifested in citizens' initiatives such as Proposition 13, that was part of the problem. The voters passed an initiative to set a minimum level of public school funding within the state budget process in 1988, and they overwhelmingly supported a record state bond issue to build and repair schools in 1998. In both cases, voters showed that they supported allocating existing state funds in a manner that favored the schools, but they did not give us any indication in the surveys that they would be willing to pay higher taxes to support increased school spending. Our surveys leading up to the 2000 elections showed that Californians were keenly aware that the state had fallen behind in school funding relative to other states and that their local public schools needed more funds from the state than they were receiving. However, Californians demonstrated time and again a basic lack of trust in local school officials and state government officials, which dampened their enthusiasm when it came to paying more for improving schools out of their own pockets.

Three education initiatives on the statewide ballots enabled us to examine how the public resolved its basic conflict between a lack of confidence in government institutions and the recognition that the schools needed more money. Two initiatives called for making it easier to pass local school bonds by ending the century-old two-thirds majority vote requirement. They showed that voters were evenly split on a tax-and-spending issue involving the one problem they cared most about— the quality of their schools. The measure failed narrowly in the March primary, when voters were asked to change the requirement for passage of a local school bond from a two-thirds to a simple-majority vote. However, the measure passed narrowly in the November election, when the wording of the proposition was changed. Voters were confronted with a ballot summary describing a 55 percent vote requirement with accountability requirements for spending the local school bond funds and no mention on the ballot label of ending the two-thirds vote requirement. According to our surveys, to some voters this new initiative sounded like it made it more difficult for local governments to raise taxes. Whether intentional or not, overcoming public opposition to making it easier to pass local school bonds, in the end, required at least some voter confusion and messages that soothed deep feelings of distrust.

Several conclusions can be drawn from our close examination of the school vouchers initiative on the November ballot. Californians were divided on the general concept of allowing more choice in how public funding was spent on schools and were deeply split along partisan lines. About as many favored as opposed the idea of giving parents a tax-supported voucher to pay for public, private, or religious schools.

Voters' attitudes toward school vouchers turned very negative when they were confronted with the specific proposals for paying for a school vouchers program and when they began to weigh the program's potential consequences on the public school system. In California, the school vouchers initiative lost ground once voters decided that this reform would not help the schools or the children who were most in need of better schools. Voters may have been unhappy with the way the government was running their schools, but they were unwilling to pay for expensive experiments that might interfere with the goal of improving schools.

The three education initiatives in one year offered fresh proof that voter distrust in government was alive and well in California. The voters may have been eager for the governor and state legislature to improve the schools, but they still wanted to have a major say in school reform and funding decisions. Undoubtedly, California voters will have more opportunities to vote on school reform efforts in upcoming elections, especially if they become disappointed in trends in student test scores or if improvements in their local schools do not live up to the expectations of New Economy business leaders.

Growth and Environmentalism

It is hard to imagine a better context for environmentalism to flourish than California in the year 2000. Conditions created the so-called perfect storm that the antigrowth activists dream of and the prodevelopment forces fear the most. Three factors had come into play: a long period of prosperity that made many people take their jobs and the economy for granted; a strong period of population increases putting pressure on local land use and the state's environment; and regional growth-related problems taking a toll on residents' perceptions of traffic, pollution, and other key quality of life indicators.

The resurgence of consumer confidence, job growth, and budget surpluses in the mid-1990s provided the foundation for growth concerns and proenvironmental attitudes to find expression.[1] Both growth concerns and environmentalism are among the key components of the postmaterialist values and the New Political Culture discussed in earlier chapters. There is considerable evidence that proenvironmental attitudes and antigrowth sentiments exert themselves when people are feeling economically secure. Some scholars trace the roots of environmentalism to postindustrial, Western societies where residents have made the transition from worrying about their material needs to expressing concerns about the quality of their lives. In California, such quality of life issues

1. See Baldassare (1986, 1992); Glickfeld and Levine (1990); Baldassare and Wilson (1996); Fulton et al. (2000); and Lewis and Neiman (2001).

are crucial to an array of people and interests competing for New Economy jobs and workers. California's wealth and strong economy at the turn of the new century thus offered an ideal setting for a new environmentalism to flourish that went beyond local or so-called NIMBY (i.e., Not In My Back Yard) issues to regional, state, national, and global environmental concerns.[2]

Conditions also have to be right to fuel the public's interest in growth issues. There have to be real experiences with population increases and development projects for the topic to gain any traction in the public arena. Certainly, there was plenty of action on the growth front in California during the 1990s. The state gained 4 million more residents in this decade, on top of having added 6 million people during the 1980s. There was population growth in all but a few remote rural counties of the state. Moreover, this was the kind of growth that was being noticed not only locally but also in the broad geographic regions where people commuted on a daily basis or visited for leisure purposes. It was having a visible impact on vanishing wildernesses, open space, and farmlands, and it was tied to environmental problems such as endangered species, air pollution, toxic contamination, and beach closures due to pollution runoff into the ocean. In other words, there were actual growth and environmental issues for the public to see.

Where Californians are most likely to experience the impacts of a strong economy and population growth is in the local communities they live in and the regions where they travel daily and commute to work. Past studies have shown that it is the perception of rapid local growth and its related impacts on the region's quality of life—such as traffic congestion, smoggy air, unsightly sprawl, and a lack of affordable housing—that can push people into a growth-control mentality.[3] There were many regions in the state where residents experienced the feelings of traffic gridlock, too much growth, and an overheated economy. Perhaps the conditions were most obvious in the San Francisco Bay Area, because of Silicon Valley and all of the New Economy activities, and less apparent in the Central Valley, where the economy was lagging. Still, other regions, such as Orange County, the Inland Em-

    2. See Clark and Hoffman-Martinot (1998) and especially Clark and Inglehart (1998) and Inglehart (1998).
    3. See studies on local growth attitudes such as Baldassare (1986, 1992, 1994b); Baldassare and Wilson (1995, 1996); Dowall (1984); Lewis (1996); Palen (1995); Teaford (1997); Logan and Molotch (1987); and Neiman and Loveridge (1981).

pire, and San Diego County were also overwhelmed with traffic and growth-related issues.[4]

In this chapter, we observe Californians' renewed interest in environmental politics in times of plenty and the powerful surge of interest in local growth control in the course of the 2000 elections. We see how the politics of government distrust influenced policy preferences regarding growth and environment and we see what the public wanted from government in the realm of growth and environment regulations.

PERCEPTIONS OF LOCAL GROWTH

In our focus groups, many people said the trends in local growth were disturbing. One of the concerns that surfaced was traffic, a serious problem made worse by an inadequate transportation system. "They're building more and more without improving roads," said one respondent, in reference to the joint shortcomings of the public sector and private developers. Another participant added, "Not enough infrastructure to cope with the influx of population," and another echoed that perception in saying, "The growth is outstripping the infrastructure." A common conclusion was that the state had lost ground in its efforts to keep up with growth. One respondent said, "In the 1950s, we did a lot of infrastructure, but the bridges have started falling apart." The frustration that many felt toward their commutes was best expressed in this statement, "You can't have a quality of life while you're sitting in your car."

As for planning for the future, everyone seemed to agree that more needed to be done than was being done by their local governments. "Planning is after-the-fact crisis management. There is no long-range planning," explained one focus group member, when asked to rate the government's current efforts on growth issues. "Long-term planning at the local, regional, and state levels. How can we accommodate this new population? We've got to get ready," explained another focus group member, when asked what the government should be doing today to prepare for the future. To what extent, though, was the public willing to allow its elected officials to control the process?

Indeed, local population growth has been a persistent complaint in California for decades—not surprisingly, since most parts of the state have seen a rapid increase in population. In fact, most cities and counties registered

4. See *Special Survey on San Diego County* (PPIC Statewide Survey, 2000d) and *Orange County Annual Survey* (Baldassare and Katz, 2000).

population gains in recent decades. We found the public highly aware and concerned about growth in our June 2000 survey. Both perceptions and preferences for solutions varied in interesting ways across regions of the state. The regional differences reflected varying strength of the economy in combination with population growth and development pressures.

Most Californians (81%) believed that their local population had been growing in recent years. (See Table 5-1.) Six in ten believed it had been growing rapidly. Very few thought there had been no growth, and almost no one reported that the local population had been declining.

People in all regions, community types, and demographic groups perceived that the population of their city or community had been increasing. However, the perception of rapid population growth was more common in the Central Valley and San Francisco Bay Area than elsewhere. Perceptions of growth were less common in Los Angeles than in the rest of Southern California. Across community types, people living in the large cities and suburbs more often cited rapid population growth in their surroundings than those who resided in small cities and rural areas. There were no differences across racial and ethnic groups in the perceptions of rapid community growth.

As for the future, most expected their current locales to continue to expand in population. Eight in ten Californians expected their city or community to grow in the next ten years, and the majority expected them to grow rapidly. Only one in six expected the population to remain stable, while hardly anyone predicted a loss of local population. More than half of the residents in all of the regions of the state outside of Los Angeles were expecting the local population to grow rapidly. Moreover, the majority in every type of community—large city, suburb, small city, and rural area—was expecting rapid increases in population over the next decade. There were no differences across demographic groups.

Residents' perceptions of current and future population growth seemed to have little influence on their satisfaction with community. Three in four rated their current localities as excellent or good places to live, so they seemingly were quite satisfied with the quality of life their communities were providing. Moreover, only three in ten residents thought the government regulations aimed at controlling growth in their city or community were not strict enough. Half of Californians said their area's growth regulations were about right, one in ten believed they were too strict, and one in ten was not sure.

Still, if faced with a choice at the ballot box, six in ten Californians said they would vote "yes" on a local initiative that would slow down

TABLE 5.1   PERCEPTIONS OF LOCAL POPULATION GROWTH

"In the past few years, do you think the population of your city or community has been ... "	
Growing rapidly	58%
Growing slowly	23
Staying the same	15
Declining	1
Don't know	3

"In the next ten years, do you think the population of your city or community will ... "	
Grow rapidly	54%
Grow slowly	26
Stay the same	17
Decline	1
Don't know	2

SOURCE: PPIC Statewide Survey (2000c).

the pace of development in their city or community, even if this meant less economic growth. About one in three said he or she would vote against a local growth control initiative. Across regions, support for local growth controls was strongest in the San Francisco Bay Area. Across community types, support for growth controls was highest among those who lived in the suburbs. Opposition to slow-growth initiatives was strongest in the Central Valley, where the economy was weakest. However, a majority supported slowing down the pace of development. In fact, majorities in all regions and types of communities said they would vote "yes" on a local growth control initiative.

Local perceptions of growth and growth policies play a role in the public's willingness to support a local growth control initiative. Among those who believed that local population had been growing rapidly in recent years, two in three residents said they would support a local growth control initiative. (See Table 5-2.) A similarly high level of support was registered among those who expected their local areas to grow rapidly over the next decade. Seven in ten of those who thought that the growth regulations of their local governments were not strict enough

TABLE 5.2   POLICIES REGARDING
LOCAL POPULATION GROWTH

*"If an election were held today, would you vote yes or
no on a local initiative that would slow down the pace of
development in your city or community, even if this
meant having less economic growth?"*

	All Adults	San Francisco Bay Area	Central Valley
Favor	58%	65%	52%
Oppose	37	29	44
Don't know	5	6	6

*"If an election were held today, would you vote yes or
no on a local bond measure that would allow local government
to buy undeveloped land and keep it free from development,
even if this meant paying higher taxes?"*

	All Adults	San Francisco Bay Area	Central Valley
Favor	43%	51%	38%
Oppose	52	44	57
Don't know	5	5	5

SOURCE: PPIC Statewide Survey (2000c).

said they would support a local initiative to slow the pace of development. Even among those who thought current government efforts to regulate local growth were about right expressed concern, with a majority
saying they would vote "yes" on a local growth control initiative.

Interestingly, there were differences related to levels of affluence and
economic security. For instance, upper-income residents and college graduates were more likely than lower-income residents and the non–college
educated to support growth control initiatives, even if it meant having
less economic growth. Following this trend, whites were more likely than
Latinos to support a slow-growth initiative. There were no differences
in support for local growth controls among Democrats, Republicans,
and independent voters. Women were more likely than men to support
growth controls.[5]

5. Multiple regressions were analyzed for the "local growth controls" question in June
2000, with age, education, income, gender, region, political party, and race and ethnicity
in the equation. The following *B* values and significance levels (in parentheses) are for the

In line with their strong support for slowing down the pace of development, most Californians also liked the idea of shielding open space from local development. Six in ten residents said they favored using public funds to buy undeveloped land to keep it free from residential and commercial development. In fact, Californians were more likely than Americans in general to support this land use policy.[6]

Once again, public support for growth control policies grew out of perceptions of local population growth and was related to feelings of economic security. Most who thought that local growth had been rapid and would continue so in the future wanted to see their governments buying up undeveloped land. San Francisco Bay Area residents were the most supportive of this idea. Although the majority of residents in all of the major regions of the state were in favor of using taxpayer money to buy undeveloped land, those living in the Central Valley were the least enthusiastic about this proposal. Although support was strong across demographic groups, there were differences related to socioeconomic standing. Whites, upper-income residents, and college graduates were more likely than Latinos, lower-income residents, and the non–college educated to want the government to purchase open space to keep it free from development. More Democrats than Republicans and independent voters were in favor of this policy, but again, a majority in each voter group favored this idea.

Public support was overwhelming when it came to using other people's money to fund the purchase of open space. Seven in ten Californians were in favor of the idea of nonprofit organizations allocating their money to buy undeveloped land to keep it free from residential and commercial development. Only one in four residents opposed this idea. The involvement of the David and Lucile Packard Foundation and other nonprofit organizations in such land purchases in the state had attracted attention in the news around the time of the survey, and this involvement was apparently viewed favorably.

The differences across political groups disappear when taxpayer money is not involved in purchasing open space: more than seven in ten Democrats, Republicans, and independent voters were in favor of non-

significant variables from the final equations with all variables. Positive correlations indicate support for local growth controls: San Francisco Bay Area = .44 (.004), Whites = .44 (.001), and Women = .31 (.001).

6. The results of a national survey conducted by Yankelovich Partners in 1999 and reported in the PPIC Statewide Survey (2000c): 44 percent in favor, 49 percent opposed, and 7 percent don't know.

profit organizations assuming this role. Strong majorities in every region supported this idea; however, the differences noted earlier relating to economic insecurity still persisted, even with this highly popular concept, perhaps reflecting apprehension of withholding land from residential and commercial development that might otherwise contribute to jobs and economic growth. Eight in ten residents in the San Francisco Bay Area were in favor of the proposal, compared with two in three residents in the Central Valley. While support for the use of nonprofit funding was strong across all demographic groups, there were important differences: Whites liked this idea better than Latinos did, those with higher incomes were more positively inclined than those in the lower-income groups, and college graduates were much more in favor of using nonprofit funds to buy undeveloped land than were those with no college education.

However, when asked if they would approve a local bond measure to buy land to preserve it from development, support fell back. The majority of Californians said they would vote "no" if a local bond measure meant they would pay higher property taxes, even though the majority of state residents also said they were in favor of using taxpayer funds for this same purpose. A narrow majority of Democrats supported the idea of a local bond measure to purchase open space, while the majority of other voters opposed it. A slight majority of San Francisco Bay Area residents were willing to pay higher property taxes to keep land free from development, but majorities in the state's other major regions were against it. Support increased with affluence and education, but only a small majority of the wealthiest and most educated residents said they would support a local bond measure to purchase open space. Considering that such a "special tax" would require a two-thirds majority under the Proposition 13 tax limitations, public support fell far short of the threshold. Apparently, the funding that most of the public had in mind for keeping land free of development was to come at no additional cost to taxpayers like themselves. In all, voter distrust had profound implications for local growth policies—public support for increasing taxes to allow local governments to buy open space was quite weak, while citizens liked the idea of moving local land use decisions from elected officials to the ballot box.

LOCAL GROWTH INITIATIVES

Californians were destined to address their growth and environmental concerns through the local initiative process. Traffic congestion, high housing costs, the loss of open space, and a host of other growth-related environmental issues are local concerns. In California, the state government has little influence over specific growth, land use, and development issues. In a handful of states, state governments have taken a more active role in addressing such concerns at the local level (see Baldassare et al., 1996). Since Californians have the option of acting directly on public policy issues through the citizens' initiative process—and are in the habit of doing so in statewide elections—there is a strong tendency among residents to bypass their local elected officials and set their own course for local growth and development. Finally, population growth and pressure for development in most cities and counties in the state offer ample opportunities for local growth control initiatives.

In California, residents are rarely satisfied with leaving important issues in the hands of their elected representatives. Voters often prefer to turn to citizens' initiatives to make public policies because of their impatience with the speed of the legislative process and their distrust of the decisions that politicians make (Baldassare, 2000). The topic of growth is one of those issues that has generated a great deal of interest in local initiatives. It has even spawned the concept of *ballot box planning*, referring to the idea that voters want a direct say in how their localities are developed. The sense of political alienation that drives people to the initiative process was evident in these comments that we heard in focus groups: "Officials don't listen to us" and, even more to the point, "The public has spoken out, but county supervisors don't listen." There is also a sense of political empowerment through the local initiative process, best articulated by these statements, "I'd like it if we could vote on everything, so that they don't make decisions for us," and "The people have the power to change things." In the arena of local growth, Californians have an impressive track record for taking matters into their own hands.

Since there is heightened interest in controlling growth and development in good economic times, it would seem that conditions during the 2000 California elections would provide a banner year for local growth control initiatives. Indeed, California led every other state in the nation with respect to growth control measures on the ballot in November 2000. A national study prepared for the Brookings Institution found that thirty-eight states had local and state measures on the November 2000 ballot pertaining to growth issues. The vast majority of these measures were on local ballots. These measures dealt with a wide variety of growth issues. While about half were concerned with open space, natural resources, and recreation, one in four was concerned with infrastructure investments and the remainder with economic development, governance, and growth management and regulations. Most of the measures passed, although measures to preserve open space were much more popular than those seeking to place restrictions on development.

While the study did not analyze specific types of growth measures at the state level, certain conclusions can be drawn about the western region where California is situated. The most ballot activity at both the state and local levels was in the western states. The reasons for the higher level of ballot activity in the western states include local population growth pressures and the common use of citizens' initiatives to set public policies and make local policy decisions in these states.

As noted previously, California had more growth control measures on the ballot than any other state. The location of these California measures certainly fit the profile of growth-related ballot initiatives being most prevalent in fast-growing, affluent suburban localities. Of the 78 growth-related measures on the ballot, 76 were local and two were statewide. Almost nine in ten measures involved suburban jurisdictions. In fact, there was only one measure that involved a rural area, and only nine measures were on the ballot in central cities. Eight out of ten measures were at the city level, while two out of ten involved counties. The Brookings study's authors point to two specific issues that have led to California's frequent use of ballot box planning: a political climate of "initiative activism" since Proposition 13 and court rulings that affirm voters' rights to use initiatives to amend general plans and to make land use decisions (Myers and Puentes, 2001:8, 9).

California was also the leading state for *local* growth measures in November 2000. Using a narrower definition of growth measures than the Brookings national study, Fulton et al. (2000) counted 671 ballot measures on local land use issues between 1986 and 2000 in California. They reported 78 local ballot measures in the California primary and general election in 2000, with 61 appearing in the November election alone. Their trend analysis shows that the 2000 elections had the largest number of local growth measures since 1990, when there were a record-setting 99 local land use measures on the ballot. Only on one other occasion in the fifteen-year period of their study were there more growth measures on the ballot—in 1988, there were 93 ballot measures.

What do the years 1988, 1990, and 2000 have in common? Fulton et al. conclude that local land use measures are most popular in good economic times, while they fall out of favor and are used more rarely during economic recessions (see also Glickfeld, Levine, and Fulton, 1996). Of course, development projects would tend to increase in good times and decline in recessions. The authors report a steep drop in the appearance of local growth measures during California's deep recession in the early 1990s. There were fewer than 50 measures on the ballot for every year from 1991 through 1995. Then, there was an increase in the use of local land use measures when the economy was recovering in 1996, followed by a significant escalation in the appearance of these types of ballot measures during the very strong economy from 1998 through 2000. For instance, there were 149 local land use measures on California ballots in 1998, 1999, and 2000. During these three years, the slow-growth initiatives experienced victories in about six in ten instances. In the 2000 election cycle, six in ten of the local land use measures resulted in a "yes" majority for slow-growth measures or a "no" majority for progrowth measures.

There are some important trends in local growth measures during the 2000 elections. There were twice as many slow-growth measures as prodevelopment measures. However, the supporters of growth limits were equally likely to come out ahead, no matter who proposed the measure (Walters, 2000c). Suffice it to say that large sums of money spent by developers did not insure a victory for those who wanted more growth. A good example of the phenomenon that "money can't buy success" was in Orange County, where the growth control measures were on local ballots in November 2000. In each of three cities, coalitions of local developers outspent antigrowth citizens' groups by large margins. However, the slow-growth side won by a landslide in Newport Beach and lost—but only by narrow margins—in Brea and San Clemente (Mehta, 2000).

The vast majority of local growth measures in 2000, as in the recent past, were very specific in nature. Typically, they were concerned with changes in general plans or zoning that would or would not permit a certain development to proceed. Examples included a plan to build a 3,000-unit, senior-only community in Sacramento, which was defeated, and a plan to build a golf course and hotels in Monterey, which passed. Other local measures sought to limit the number of housing permits in the city of Tracy and the number of new dwellings allowed in the city of Healdsburg. Both of these efforts to slow development were passed by the voters (Gaudette, 2000; Nickles, 2000).

While such initiatives are still only a fraction of all local growth measures, there has been a trend toward placing on the ballot growth control initiatives that create growth boundaries and then require that the local voters make all future land use decisions. Such initiatives have recently proven to be quite popular with the voters and a source of problems for local elected officials and developers. While there have been only 37 such measures since 1990, two in three have appeared on the ballot since 1998 and about one in three of such measures was presented on the 2000 ballot. (See Table 5-3.) Over time, the pass rate for these local growth control measures has been extremely high (Fulton et al., 2000). One of the first of such measures passed in Ventura County in the mid-1990s, effectively taking away the ability to approve major projects from the county board of supervisors and placing the decisionmaking in the hands of county voters. Recent examples include an Orange County measure that passed in March 2000 that would require a two-thirds vote requirement to approve major public works projects such as airports. In November 2000, a measure passed in Alameda County that created a growth boundary that could only be changed by a public vote (DelVecchio, 2000; Pena, 2000; Vorderbrueggen, 2000). Both measures stopped development that had been approved by local governments, and they insured that similar plans could not go forward without another vote. The Orange County measure was challenged in court by the prodevelopment forces and overturned by a judge who described the measure as "unconstitutionally vague." The slow-growth groups have vowed to go back to the voters with another initiative (Pasco and James, 2000).

The normal trends for local growth ballot measures were evident in 2000. Cities and counties that are suburban in nature and are experiencing growth pressures are among the most likely sites for growth conflicts. Moreover, those places where residents feel more economically secure and, at the same time, inconvenienced by traffic congestion and other by-products of population and job growth were the best candidates for measures designed to limit growth. Local ballot measures appear to flourish in cities and communities with higher proportions of home owners and white, highly educated, and affluent residents. However, there are no trends linking ballot measures for slow growth more particularly with Republicans or with Democrats. The public's efforts to mobilize against growth problems appear to be truly nonpartisan in nature and neither conservative nor liberal. Walters (2000c) describes the typical slow-growth places as "older suburbs that are not experiencing high levels of population growth but are seeing traffic congestion and job-related commercial development. And in most cases, anti-growth forces win."

TABLE 5.3   GROWTH REVOLT
AT THE BALLOT BOX:
CALIFORNIA TRENDS OVER TIME

	Total Ballot Measures	Slow-Growth Victories
1990	99	59%
1991	20	70
1992	46	57
1993	19	71
1994	27	33
1995	12	55
1996	55	51
1997	15	40
1998	45	55
1999	26	58
2000	78	58

SOURCE: Fulton et al. (2000: 8).
NOTE: *Slow-growth victories* refers to combined total of "yes" majority for slow growth measures and "no" majority for pro growth measures.

There are consistent regional patterns in the appearance of local growth measures and their support by slow-growth voters. The urban coastal regions have had a much more active history of slow-growth and progrowth measures since the mid-1980s than the inland regions of the state have had. In particular, the San Francisco Bay Area and Los Angeles and San Diego Counties have been where most of the action has been centered (Fulton et al., 2000). In November 2000, almost three in four of the local growth ballot measures in the state were located in the San Francisco Bay Area and the million-plus population counties of the Southern California region, including Los Angeles, Orange, Riverside, San Bernardino, and San Diego. Three in four of the measures in these two regions resulted in victories for the slow-growth forces. There were very few local growth control measures in the Central Valley, and only three measures passed in this vast region. While there were a dozen measures in the remainder of the state, which is mostly low-density and rural in nature, most of those slow-growth measures failed.

The regional patterns reflect the underlying tendencies behind the most recent surge in support for local growth controls in California. A general optimism about prosperity is a necessary precondition for the public's desire to limit growth. Residents are more willing to take the economic risks associated with controlling development in environments where job increases have brought traffic congestion and growth-related problems. While attitudes about environmental regulations are often dictated by partisan differences and political ideology, the public's support for growth controls is largely an apolitical statement about a desire to maintain or improve the local quality of life. So, while all of California basked in the glow of economic good times, there tends to be a sharp distinction in the amount of support between regions with more or less economic security and growth pressures, as evidenced by the trends in the San Francisco Bay Area and Central Valley. Moreover, public support also depends on the growth experiences and economic well-being of residents and their local communities, which is why affluent suburban residents are more prone to vote against development.

COMPLAINTS ABOUT REGIONAL PROBLEMS

Californians may have a home address in a city or community, but functionally, most live in a broad geographic region where they work, shop, relax, and socialize. California is a large state made up of several regions of one million or more residents each—for example, the San Francisco Bay Area, Los Angeles, the Central Valley, San Diego, Orange County, and the Inland Empire. Nearly nine in ten residents live in these major regions. Most of the state's regions have experienced population growth over the past few decades. While Californians' approach to growth and environmental interests might seem parochial, most are keenly aware of the important role that the region plays in their local quality of life.

Although increased traffic is the most visible and commonly experienced phenomenon related to regional growth and development, people in our focus groups also noted that the broader environment they lived in was in a state of transition and was largely going from bad to worse. "Air and water are very important and threatened by continued growth," said one focus group participant. Another respondent added this concern, "They're cutting down the forests to build houses." That there were important lifestyle considerations involved with these environmental changes was evident in the following comments: "Water and open space are important—life is becoming too stressful without play areas," and, "I'm worried about the quality of life in California, like open spaces."

Responses in the June 2000 survey indicated how Californians were seeing their regions at the time and which policies they favored to preserve the quality of life in their regions.[7] Most Californians were at least somewhat happy with the overall conditions in their regions. Nearly nine in ten residents said the quality of life in their region was going well, with three in ten saying things were going "very well." For the most part, residents in all of the major regions and most demographic groups had positive impressions of their region's quality of life. Those living outside of Los Angeles, and more affluent residents, were more likely to say things were going very well.

Yet the state's residents readily admitted that their respective regions had a variety of growth-related problems. Traffic congestion was by far the most troublesome by-product of regional growth, but there were other issues. Three in four Californians said that traffic congestion was a problem in their region, and two in three residents said that both air pollution and population growth and development were at least somewhat of a problem. Nearly half rated traffic congestion in their region as a "big problem," and three in ten ranked growth and development and air pollution as significant issues.

There were major differences in perceptions of regional problems across the state, indicating that growth-related issues took unique forms. San Francisco Bay Area residents were by far the most concerned with traffic congestion, with three in four individuals citing this issue as a big problem (see Table 5-4). By contrast, fewer than half in Los Angeles and the rest of Southern California, and only two in ten residents in the Central Valley, cited traffic congestion as a big problem in their region. Nearly half of San Francisco Bay Area residents also said growth and development was a big problem for their region, while less than one in four residents of the other regions gave this rating to growth issues. Air pollution was viewed as most troublesome in Los Angeles, where four in ten residents rated it as a big problem, compared with one in four residents in the other major regions.

We found that these particular growth-related problems were even more common in the built-up areas of the state's regions. About six in ten residents who said they lived in large cities and suburbs cited traffic congestion as a big problem. Population growth and development was seen as a big problem by about one-third of those who lived in big cities and suburbs, while air pollution was considered a big problem by four in ten residents. By contrast, major complaints about traffic, growth and development, and air pollution were all less common in smaller cities

7. See Baldassare (2000) and PPIC Statewide Survey (2000c).

TABLE 5.4   REGIONAL
PROBLEMS IN CALIFORNIA

"How much of a problem is ___ in your region today?"			
	All Adults	San Francisco Bay Area	Central Valley
Traffic Congestion			
Big problem	44%	74%	21%
Somewhat of a problem	32	18	37
Not a problem	24	8	42
Growth and Development			
Big problem	27	47	17
Somewhat of a problem	39	34	36
Not a problem	34	19	47

SOURCE: PPIC Statewide Survey (2000c).

and communities. Demographic factors also influenced perceptions of growth-related problems. Whites, the college educated, and upper-income residents were more likely to cite problems with growth and development than were Latinos, the non–college educated, and lower-income residents. However, there were no demographic differences in perceptions of air pollution.

This is not to say that these were the only growth-related problems or that regions outside of Los Angeles and the San Francisco Bay Area did not have serious growth issues. For instance, in a special survey of the Central Valley, we found that two in three residents cited the loss of farms and agriculture as a problem confronting their region. This perception of increasing urban sprawl and suburbanization was a more pronounced problem in this fast-growing and newly developing region than either traffic congestion or growth and development. In fact, the mention of the loss of farms was more common in the San Joaquin region, which is experiencing pressures of growth, than elsewhere in the Central Valley. The lifelong residents of the Central Valley were more likely than those who have recently moved to this area to rate the loss of farmlands as a big problem facing their region.[8]

8. See PPIC Statewide Survey (1999c) on the Central Valley in November 1999.

When asked about the future of their region, almost everyone expected the population to increase. Across the state, six in ten residents predicted rapid growth in population over the next decade, while one in four expected a slow rate of growth. Only one in six residents thought their region would remain the same size or diminish in population. People who were living outside of Los Angeles—the most populous region in the state today—were the most likely to believe that their regions would grow rapidly. In fact, many of the state's demographers predict that growth will slow in Los Angeles and the San Francisco Bay Area and that there will be more rapid growth in the rest of Southern California and the Central Valley than elsewhere in the coming decades (see Baldassare, 2000).

Looking ahead to their region's quality of life in the future, relatively few residents were expecting improvement. Only three in ten expected their region to be a better place to live in 2010. About one in three thought their region would become a worse place to live, and another one in three expected little change. San Francisco Bay Area residents were the most likely to think that their region would deteriorate in the future, in line with their high level of complaints about traffic and growth at the time and their belief that the region would continue to see rapid population growth. Indeed, the expectation of rapid growth was related to people's perceptions of regional problems. Those who considered growth, traffic, and air pollution as big problems were more likely than others to say their region would grow rapidly in the future. Even more important, the perception of rapid growth in the future was linked to feelings of pessimism about the future. Nearly half of those who expected their region to grow rapidly in the next ten years also said that their region would be a worse place to live in 2010.

Faced with the prospect of continued population growth, most Californians believed that various proposals aimed at limiting growth and development could improve the quality of life in the future. For instance, three in four residents said the following policy ideas would be effective if implemented over the next ten years: establishing growth boundaries around cities, beyond which new development would not be permitted; encouraging the development of job centers near existing housing to reduce commute times for workers; and restricting development in order to preserve wetlands, rivers, and environmentally sensitive areas. The number of people who thought these ideas would be "very effective" in improving the quality of life ranged between three in ten and four in ten residents.

There were no differences across regions of the state in attitudes toward creating growth boundaries or encouraging job centers to develop near existing housing. However, Central Valley residents were less likely than others to want to place environmental restrictions on development. In a separate survey of Central Valley residents in November 1999, we found that residents of that particular region rated another policy proposal as the most effective way to improve the quality of life in their region: protect farm and agricultural lands from development. This preference is consistent with the high concern this region showed for the loss of farmlands, as well as the belief of seven in ten residents that their region would grow rapidly. These trends point to the fact that identification of growth-related problems and preferences for growth policies vary according to the type of growth and development experienced in various regions. Those living outside of the heavily built-up areas—notably the Central Valley and the Southern California suburbs—face different issues and favor different solutions than those in the San Francisco Bay Area and Los Angeles.

Californians' views about future population growth and the future of their regions are strongly shaping their desire to try various land use policies as solutions. Those who expected their region to grow rapidly in the next ten years were the most likely to think that establishing growth boundaries, encouraging job centers near housing, and restricting development in environmentally sensitive areas would be very effective in improving the quality of life in their region. Those who expected their region to be a worse place to live in the future were more likely than others to say that growth boundaries and restricted development would be very effective ways to improve their quality of life. Still, most did not believe that limiting and redirecting growth would be very effective ways to deal with increasing population and a deteriorating quality of life. Most Californians in this time of prosperity seemed resigned to the fact that there was little the government could do to help.

THE STATE'S ENVIRONMENTAL PROBLEMS

Around the turn of the century, the state's residents expressed a fair amount of concern about the environmental issues facing California. To some degree, their worries varied by region and demographic circumstances. But, in general, the experiences of growth-related problems, urbanization of the land, and increasing population seem to have led the public to focus on a number of environmental quality issues.

In our focus groups, many people extrapolated from the local growth and regional problems and assumed that living conditions in the state would be much, much worse in the future. That they perceived government as unprepared to handle the changes that lie ahead added to their concerns. "We're going to be packed in like sardines," was one of several dire predictions for California in the new millennium. "If we don't have leadership to deal with these issues, we'll be one big parking lot," stated another participant. "We've got millions coming in, and we have to get more creative," added another. Once again, the public's concerns went beyond the immediate issues of growth and development in their regions to broader environmental concerns involving the state. Some feared the loss of "clean air, clear water, and beautiful grass for picnics," while others looked to the finite nature of the environment and worried that "minerals and resources will shrink as we grow and consume." The strong desire for environmental preservation was evident in this comment from one focus group member, "My grandkids should not have to live where there are no natural resources."

In the June 2000 survey, we asked residents to name the most important environmental issue facing California. The top concern by far voiced in this open-ended question was air pollution, volunteered as a response by one in three residents. One in eight considered population growth and development to be the most important problem. Other issues, mentioned by fewer than one in ten residents, included water pollution, pollution in general, traffic congestion, and the water supply. Importantly, most Californians had some environmental concern, even if a majority could not agree on what it was. Fewer than one in ten could not identify any environmental issue.

There was a great deal of consistency across groups and regions in naming air pollution as the state's top issue. Air pollution was named as the most important issue in all major regions of the state, across racial and ethnic groups, among men and women alike, by home owners and renters, and in all age, income, education, and political groups. There were large differences across groups and regions in mention of growth and development and traffic congestion as the state's biggest environmental issues. San Francisco Bay Area residents were more likely than those living in other regions to mention growth and traffic. Suburban residents were more likely than those living in large cities or smaller places to name growth and development as the most serious problem. Mention of growth and development also increased with age, education, and income.

Californians may have been most likely to name air pollution as the biggest problem in the state, but they were also concerned about other environmental quality issues. Nearly half of the state's residents said that soil and water contamination from toxic substances was a big problem, and about the same number believed that water pollution from urban and agricultural runoff was a serious issue in the state (see Table 5-5). Four in ten residents felt that suburban development harming wildlife habitats and endangered species was a big problem in California. What is also noteworthy is that at least eight in ten residents believed that these three issues were at least somewhat of a problem in the state, and relatively few saw no problem at all with toxic contamination, urban and agricultural runoff, and suburban development harming wildlife habitats and endangered species.

Once again, there were sharp distinctions in environmental attitudes across geographic regions and demographic groups. San Francisco Bay Area residents were the most likely of all to rate toxic substances in the soil and groundwater as big problems in the state. Central Valley residents expressed the least worry of all the regions about urban and agricultural runoff causing water pollution and about suburban development harming wildlife habitats and endangered species. While there were no differences across socioeconomic groups, women were more worried than men about suburban development harming wildlife habitats and endangered species, while younger adults worried more than older adults about pollution from agricultural and urban runoff. There were also important political differences, with Republicans less likely than others to express concern about toxic contamination of land and water, pollution from runoff, and suburban development.

Californians also had concerns about environmental issues that went beyond the general problems and into the specific issues that were affecting the state's regions. About half said that ocean and beach pollution along the coast, as well as growth and pollution damaging the forests in the Sierra Nevada, were big problems in California. More than one in three also rated as big problems the issue of urban sprawl taking over farmlands in the Central Valley and the issue of logging old-growth redwoods in Northern California. At least eight in ten residents rated all four of these regionally based environmental issues as at least somewhat

TABLE 5.5 PERCEPTIONS OF ENVIRONMENTAL
PROBLEMS IN THE STATE

"How much of a problem is __ in California today?"

	All Adults	San Francisco Bay Area	Central Valley
Toxics in Soil/Water			
Big problem	48%	57%	45%
Some problem	32	28	37
Not a problem	8	6	10
Don't know	12	9	8
Urban Runoff Pollution			
Big problem	47	49	34
Some problem	37	38	44
Not a problem	12	9	18
Don't know	4	4	4
Growth Harming Habitats			
Big problem	39	43	27
Some problem	40	41	45
Not a problem	18	13	25
Don't know	3	3	3

SOURCE: PPIC Statewide Survey (2000c).

of a problem. These overall trends indicate that many members of the public who were not living in the particular region that was experiencing an environmental problem were still deeply concerned about the issue.

However, there were some striking regional differences in perceptions of these problems, indicating differences in direct exposure to the issues. Two in three residents in Los Angeles and the rest of Southern California cited ocean and beach pollution along the coast as big problems, compared with fewer than four in ten residents in the rest of the state. Half of those living in the Central Valley and the San Francisco Bay Area believed that urban sprawl taking over farmlands in the Central Valley was a significant issue, while only about one in three elsewhere expressed deep concern. Los Angeles residents were more worried than others about pollution damaging the Sierra forests, and San Francisco Bay Area residents were more likely than others to say that the logging of redwoods in Northern California was a big problem.

Most Californians seemed to be keenly aware of the state's environmental issues and even expressed serious concern about specific problems. A more salient question is whether they saw environmental issues as posing a threat to their own lives, which would be consistent with the postmaterialist values we would expect to see. In fact, seven in ten residents said that the environmental problems in the state did pose a threat to their own health and well-being. One in four said that environmental problems were a very serious threat, half rated the threat as somewhat serious, and only three in ten residents thought the threat of environmental problems not too serious.

When asked about the consequences of environmental problems for individuals' health and well-being, the patterns of regional and demographic variations differed from what we saw for other environmental attitudes. Some people felt more exposed to environmental problems than others. Specifically, lower-income residents, people living in Los Angeles, younger adults, and Latinos were among the most likely to believe that environmental problems posed a significant threat to their own lives. A smaller proportion of residents who were older, upper-income, white, and lived outside of Los Angeles worried "a great deal" about the personal consequences of the state's environmental problems. There were also partisan differences. Republicans expressed less concern than Democrats and independent voters about the threat of environmental problems in their own personal lives. Nonetheless, it is important to note that there were substantial majorities in all regions of the state and across all demographic and political groups who thought that environmental problems had at least somewhat of an effect on their personal well-being.

A REPORT CARD ON THE STATE'S HANDLING
OF ENVIRONMENTAL ISSUES

How were the actions of state elected officials and state government evaluated in light of the public's perceptions of environmental problems and their concerns about the real implications of environmental problems for their well-being? In sum, Californians did not have a lot of information on this topic. Still, they were not that impressed with what they saw their most visible state elected officials doing in this particular arena, compared with others. Also, while the public was generally reluctant to see the government get more involved in other issues, largely because of a lack of trust, many Californians felt their state government could and ought to be doing more and a better job on the environment.

When asked to rate the job performance of their governor, Gray Davis, overall throughout 2000, most Californians were pleased with the job he was doing. On a range of specific issues such as crime, the budget and taxes, and schools, more Californians approved than disapproved of the job done by Governor Davis. Such glowing reviews would be expected, given the strength of optimism people had expressed toward the state. However, these positive sentiments did not carry over to the governor's handling of environmental issues. In the June 2000 survey, when asked how the governor was handling such issues, only about one in three residents approved of his performance. By contrast, in the same survey, half said they approved of the job he was doing in handling economic issues.

In every region and demographic group, the governor's ratings on handling the economy were much higher than his performance ratings on environmental issues. In every region of the state, fewer than four in ten residents were pleased with the way the governor was handling environmental issues. About four in ten Democrats and about three in ten Republicans and other voters offered positive ratings. By contrast, evaluations of his job performance with respect to the economy were much more partisan: Six in ten Democrats and three in ten Republicans and other voters approved of the job he was doing. The public clearly had issues outside the overall "state of the state" in mind, which they generally felt was quite good, when evaluating the job the governor was doing with environmental issues. The job ratings on the environment revolved around their concerns with the state of the environment.

Overall, Californians were not all that impressed with their state government's efforts in the environmental arena, either. As Table 5–6 indicates, half believed that the government was not doing enough, one in three thought the government was doing just enough, and one in ten residents saw the government as doing more than enough to protect the environment. While there were no differences by education and income or across racial and ethnic groups, the feeling that the state government was not doing enough was most common among younger adults and men. The perception that state government was inadequate in the environmental policy arena was most prevalent in Los Angeles and the San Francisco Bay Area and the least prevalent in the Central Valley. In accord

TABLE 5.6   STATE GOVERNMENT
RATINGS ON ENVIRONMENTAL ISSUES

"Do you approve or disapprove of the way
Governor Davis is handling environmental issues in California?"

	All Adults	Democrats	Republicans	Other Voters
Approve	36%	42%	30%	41%
Disapprove	28	27	33	38
Don't know	36	31	37	21

"Do you think the state government is doing more than enough, just enough,
or not enough to protect the environment in California?"

	All Adults	Democrats	Republicans	Other Voters
More than enough	9%	6%	13%	9%
Just enough	37	36	42	34
Not enough	50	55	40	53
Don't know	4	3	5	4

SOURCE: PPIC Statewide Survey (2000c).

with regional trends, Democrats and independent voters most often felt the government should do more to protect the environment, while Republicans believed the government was already doing enough.[9] Of course, calls for a more active role for government and a willingness to raise taxes to support environmental policies are tempered by distrust.

SUPPORT FOR ENVIRONMENTAL POLICIES AND SPENDING

Many Californians expressed support for proenvironmental policies that went well beyond the local, regional, and state contexts. Moreover, res-

---

9. Multiple regressions were analyzed for the "state government environmental ratings" question in June 2000, with age, education, income, gender, region, political party, and race and ethnicity in the equation. The following B values and significance levels (in parentheses) are for the significant variables from the final equations with all variables. Positive correlations indicate a perception that the state government is not doing enough: Republicans = $-.55$ (.001), Los Angeles = $.44$ (.001), Age = $-.11$ (.02), and Women = .59 (.001).

idents consistently favored the environment when asked to consider a trade-off between having a strong economy and protecting the quality of their natural environment. All of this provides further evidence of postmaterialist values in prosperous times. There were, however, important differences along regional, party, and demographic lines that reflect variations in economic security and ideologies about government involvement. Moreover, many people stopped short of giving up a tax refund to support the environment.

For state residents who are usually reluctant to have the government involved in their lives and who are generally distrustful of their state and local elected officials Californians were surprisingly eager to have the government play more of a role in growth issues. "We need strong environmental leadership on a state level to protect our resources," explained one group participant. As for what the government should be doing, environmental protection was a major priority: "We all want a clean environment," observed one individual. Others pointed to the need to preserve what is left of the natural environment, as reflected in the following comments, "Let's save our trees that are already there and build around them," "If we can't purchase more, we should at least preserve what we have," and "Government must preserve as much as possible for future generations." A few residents articulated a desire to think about planning for growth in a different way, such as the one who said, "Let's find a way for housing people that makes sense, that does not aggravate the system or clog roads." For the most part, though, planning concepts such as "smart growth" or "sustainable development" were not yet part of the public's vocabulary. Instead, it focused on traffic and preserving the environment.

In our June 2000 survey, on one of the most controversial issues in environmental policy, there was a fairly strong consensus. A solid majority of six in ten residents believed that the evidence is already here to warrant action addressing global warming. One in three Californians thought that more research was necessary to establish global climate change, while fewer than one in ten residents thought that concern about global warming at this time was unnecessary. Indeed, Californians were even more likely than the nation as a whole to feel that actions should be taken to address global climate change.[10]

---

10. In a Hart and Teeter survey in 1999, 51 percent of Americans said they wanted action on global climate change. See PPIC Statewide Survey (2000c).

Still, the public was divided on the issue of global warming along partisan lines and demographic groups. Two in three Democrats and independent voters favored the government taking some action on global climate change, compared with just under half of Republicans. Following these party differences, those living in Los Angeles and the San Francisco Bay Area were more inclined to support government action than those who resided in the rest of the state. Public support for more government involvement in global warming issues increased with higher income and college education, and younger adults were more likely than older adults to believe there was enough evidence of global climate change for the government to take some action.

The issue of global warming may offer some evidence that the public is willing to sacrifice economic growth in favor of environmental quality. Other survey responses offer even more direct evidence of this trend. When asked to choose which statement came closest to their views, six in ten residents said that "stricter environmental laws and regulations are worth the cost," while only one in three agreed with the statement, "Stricter environmental laws cost too many jobs." Most Californians in all demographic groups said that stricter environmental regulations were worth the cost, but there were important differences across groups. Two in three Democrats and independent voters said they agreed with the proenvironmental policy position, compared with about half of Republicans. Upper-income residents were more likely than lower-income residents, whites more likely than Latinos, and younger adults more likely than older adults to believe that stricter environmental regulations are worthwhile. Nearly half of Central Valley residents—a higher percentage than elsewhere in the state—said that stricter environmental laws cost too many jobs. This rather united front probably reflects the combined roles of a more conservative ideology, less affluence, and the perceived negative consequences of environmental regulations on agricultural regions. By contrast, only three in ten San Francisco Bay Area residents took the position that environmental laws cost too many jobs— a lower percentage than in any other region—pointing to the important roles of greater affluence and liberal political views.

Californians seemed a little less willing to make personal financial sacrifices in order to protect the environment. Nonetheless, a majority said that more oil drilling off the California coast should not be allowed, even if this environmental policy resulted in higher gasoline prices for the state's drivers. Four in ten thought that more oil drilling *should* be allowed if it meant lower prices at the gas pump.

Once again, this environmental issue reflected a deep partisan divide. Republicans were not that supportive, while Democrats and independent voters were very supportive of preventing more oil drilling off the coast. Fewer than half of lower-income and non–college educated residents and Latinos supported the proenvironmental position on oil drilling. Whites, upper-income residents, and college graduates were willing to pay higher prices at the gas pump for the sake of blocking additional oil drilling off the California coast. Following their left-leaning politics and upscale demographic trends, San Francisco Bay Area residents were by far the most likely to want to limit offshore oil drilling, even if it resulted in personal financial sacrifice.

In a position consistent with their proenvironmental stands on stricter environmental laws and regulations, most Californians said they would oppose building new housing that threatened endangered species, even if it meant higher home prices. This was a particularly timely issue, since housing prices were rising sharply in most regions of the state during 2000. Yet only about one in three residents said that new housing should be built, even if it threatened endangered species. Interestingly, we do not see the sharp differences across regions, political groups, and demographic groups that were so common in some of the other environmental policy arenas. Perhaps this is a result of broad, popular support for protecting endangered species.

Whatever the real motivation for this proenvironmental stand, a majority across all regions, political parties, and gender, age, income, race and ethnicity, and education categories said that new housing should not be built if it threatened endangered species. Residents of the San Francisco Bay Area—typically more inclined to take the proenvironmental policy position but also living in the most expensive housing market in the state—are indistinguishable from other residents on this particular issue. Republicans were more inclined than other voters to say new housing should be built to make housing more affordable despite the effects on endangered species. Surprisingly, there were no differences between home owners and renters.

Even though Californians seem to want the government more involved in environmental protection, there are limits to their enthusiasm. When asked to choose between two competing values—individuals' property rights and government regulation of land use and development—state residents leaned toward protecting the rights of individuals (see Table 5-7). Four in ten Californians said that the ability of government to regulate residential and commercial development for the com-

TABLE 5.7   ENVIRONMENTAL POLICIES
AND GOVERNMENT DISTRUST

"If you had to choose, which is more important: (a) the ability of individuals to do what they want with the land they own; (b) the ability of government to regulate residential and commercial development for the common good?"

	All Adults	Democrats	Republicans	Other Voters
Individual rights	54%	46%	64%	60%
Government regulations	42	49	31	38
Other, don't know	4	5	5	2

"The state budget surplus may reach $5 billion for the current year and $8 billion for the next year. Most of the surplus funds will go to education and other state programs. Assuming that about $1 billion is left, would you prefer to use the remaining surplus on reducing your taxes or creating a conservation trust fund to purchase lands for parks and open space?"

	All Adults	Democrats	Republicans	Other Voters
Reduce taxes	44%	35%	55%	46%
Conservation trust fund	49	56	37	49
Other, don't know	7	9	8	5

SOURCE: PPIC Statewide Survey (2000c).

mon good was more important, but a majority thought that individuals should be able to do what they wanted with their land. It is worth noting, however, that Californians were much more likely than Americans as a whole to say that the ability of government to regulate the land was more important than individual property rights.[11]

We found deep political, regional, and demographic divisions on this issue. Two in three Republicans and independent voters said the ability of individuals to do what they wanted with their land was more important, compared with fewer than half of Democrats. Public support for government regulation of development increased with income and education and was also higher among whites than Latinos. Homeowners valued the ability of individuals to do what they wanted with their land

11. In a Yankelovich Partners survey in 1999, 25 percent of Americans said land use regulation by government is more important. See PPIC Statewide Survey (2000c).

more than did renters, and men were more likely than women to choose individual property rights as the more important priority. Following these political and demographic trends, Central Valley residents were by far the most sympathetic toward individual property rights, while many San Francisco Bay Area residents felt that the ability of government to regulate land for the public good was more important.[12]

Earlier, we reported that many Californians liked the idea of using existing taxes to purchase open space and also the idea of nonprofit organizations using their funds to preserve land from development. Residents became less supportive of the idea of purchasing open space when the choice was between using surplus funds for land preservation and getting a tax refund. At the time of the survey, the state budget surplus was about $5 billion for the current fiscal year and was estimated to reach $8 billion in the next year. While most of the surplus funds was headed into education and other state programs, there were proposals to set aside about $1 billion to create a conservation trust fund to purchase lands for parks and open space. We confronted residents with two hypothetical options for using the $1 billion in surplus funds—create a conservation trust fund or reduce taxes. Interestingly, voters were almost evenly divided between tax reduction and land preservation.

We found strong partisan differences in reactions to this proposed use of the state surplus. A solid majority of Republicans preferred to have their money returned in a tax refund, while an equally strong majority of Democrats wanted to start a conservation trust fund; independent voters were evenly divided. Along similar political lines, San Francisco Bay Area and Los Angeles residents were the most in favor of setting up a conservation trust fund, while the residents in the Central Valley were the most supportive of a tax refund. Interestingly, this question did not generate much variation across the socioeconomic spectrum: there were no significant differences between Latinos and whites or across education or income groups in the support for using surplus funds to purchase lands for parks and open space. Once again, support for the environment does have its limits, even in times of prosperity.

12. Multiple regressions were analyzed for the "individual property rights" question in June 2000, with age, education, income, gender, region, political party, and race and ethnicity in the equation. The following B values and significance levels (in parentheses) are for the significant variables from the final equations with all variables. Positive correlations indicate a perception that government regulation is more important: Republicans = −.56 (.001), Central Valley = −.42 (.001), Latinos = .53 (.001), Education = .30 (.001), and Women = .44 (.001).

ELECTION 2000: THE POLITICAL SIGNIFICANCE
OF THE ENVIRONMENT

How much do environmental issues really matter to people when it comes to making political decisions and real policy choices? We know from our surveys, for instance, that Californians were fairly attentive to new information on this topic during the course of the 2000 elections. Moreover, many residents told us that the presidential candidates' stands on environmental issues really mattered to them. However, not all Californians could be described as environmental activists, and many other issues trumped the environment during this election year. We now look to evidence on the importance and role of environmental issues in statewide elections and ballot measures.

Eight in ten residents expressed at least some interest in news about growth, land use, and environmental issues, although only about one in three residents claimed to be "very interested" in this kind of news. Strong interest in environmental news was more common in the urban coastal regions—Los Angeles and the San Francisco Bay Area—than elsewhere in the state.

State residents were equally likely to get most of their environmental news from television and newspapers, and few expressed a high degree of satisfaction with the quality and quantity of information they were receiving. In fact, only one in eight said they were satisfied with the amount of news coverage on this topic, and an equally small number placed a great deal of trust in the news they were receiving on these issues.

In all, Californians seem highly attentive to environmental issues, yet their news interests did not translate into active participation in environmental movements. Only one in ten residents actually belonged to an environmental group. Even among those most concerned about environmental issues—Democrats, college graduates, upper-income individuals, and San Francisco Bay Area residents—no more than one in six was a member of an environmental organization.

Californians' appreciation of the environment was evident in their leisure pursuits. However, they had a mixed record when it came to environmentally friendly practices in their daily lives. Three in four residents spent a substantial amount of their leisure time at parks or beaches, two in three frequently took trips to national parks and scenic destinations, and about four in ten residents at least sometimes took day trips or camping trips in wilderness areas. While an overwhelming majority

regularly recycled newspapers, aluminum cans, and glass, and half tried
to purchase recycled papers and plastic goods, only one in five residents
said they routinely carpooled and bought organic or pesticide-free foods.
Personal involvement and household activities focused on the environment tended to increase with income and education. Californians were
somewhat more engaged in environment-friendly practices than the rest
of the nation, but most residents certainly did not fit the profile of hard-
core or even active environmentalists.[13]

Environmental issues did seem to play an important role in the 2000
presidential election, at least in the minds of California voters. In the
June 2000 survey, eight in ten residents said that the presidential candidates' positions on growth, land use, and environmental issues were important to them. Four in ten described environmental issues as "very important." There were partisan differences: nearly half of Democrats, four
in ten independent voters, and three in ten Republicans considered environmental issues highly significant. We found little variation across regions or between demographic groups. Most residents across political
parties, regions of the state, and demographic groups said environmental issues were at least somewhat important.[14]

Whether stands on environmental issues translated into votes at the
ballot box for the presidential candidates is less certain. Clearly, support
for the Green Party candidate, Ralph Nader, ebbed and flowed during
the campaign; however, his support base was never very substantial. Another candidate who was well-known for taking strong proenvironmental positions—Democrat Al Gore—won the state by a 12-point margin of 1.3 million votes over Republican George W. Bush. Throughout
the presidential campaign in California, the Democrats were eager to
point to what they saw as Governor Bush's weak record on the environment in Texas. To what extent the environmental issue contributed
to the lopsided victory by Al Gore is difficult to say.

Other indications of the political significance of environmental issues
are evident in the votes on two bond measures on the March 2000 ballot. Proposition 12 called for a bond issue of $2.1 billion to protect land

13. See PPIC Statewide Survey (2000c) for comparisons with Pew national survey.
14. Multiple regressions were analyzed for the "environmental issues importance"
question in June 2000, with age, education, income, gender, region, political party, and
race and ethnicity in the equation. The following B values and significance levels (in parentheses) are for the significant variables from the final equations with all variables. Positive
correlations indicate that individuals place more importance on environmental issues: Republicans = $-.39$ (.001); Latinos = $.42$ (.001), and Income = $-.01$ (.003).

around lakes, rivers, streams, and the coast; to protect forests and to plant trees to improve air quality; to preserve open space and farmlands threatened by unplanned development; and to repair and improve state and neighborhood parks. It passed by 63 percent to 37 percent, or a margin of almost 2 million votes. Proposition 13 called for a bond issue of $1.9 billion to provide funds for water quality, flood protection, and safe drinking water. It passed by 65 percent to 35 percent, or a margin of almost 2.2 million votes.[15] These two propositions—totaling $4 billion in state bonds—were the largest environmental bond measures in the state's history. They were placed on the ballot by the state legislature and were supported by environmental groups, and they faced little organized opposition, even among the antitax activists in the state. The overwhelming support received for these substantial bond issues perhaps best reflects the public's mood on this issue in the 2000 election. Voters in prosperous times wanted an expanded role for government in the arenas of growth, land use, and the environment. However, bonds are not like new taxes—they are paid over time out of existing revenues. Other findings in our public opinion surveys remind us of the limits of taxpayers' generosity and their deep skepticism with respect to whether government can do the job.

CONCLUSIONS AND IMPLICATIONS

In this chapter, we examined at the rebirth of public concern about growth and environmental issues in California's time of plenty. We would anticipate that the mixture of growth and economic security in the state would provide a surge of interest in policies aimed at limiting local development and protecting the environment. The public's focus on so-called quality of life and its emphasis on lifestyle issues over economic concerns during prosperous times is predicted in the scholarly literature on postmaterialist values and the New Political Culture. For the most part, that is what we found in our analyses of local and state elections and public opinion.

We looked at several ways in which environmentalism expressed itself in the course of the 2000 elections—that is, through residents' perceptions and policy preferences, local growth control initiatives, the pres-

---

15. California Secretary of State (2000b) for votes on Propositions 12 and 13.

idential campaign, and statewide ballot measures. We see, everywhere, signs of the influence of distrust in government.

We found that public interest in addressing both local growth and broader environmental issues has its limits, even during these good economic times. For instance, people in different regions, communities, and socioeconomic groups vary in their level of support for proenvironmental and antigrowth policies. This is largely because of differences in actual experiences with growth and its environmental consequences and because of varying levels of security with current economic circumstances. Moreover, there are sharp partisan differences when it comes to levels of support for government regulation of growth and the environment and to willingness to pay higher taxes for open space and environmental protection. Clearly, this reflects ideological differences toward government involvement and varying levels of public trust. The public is more likely to see government as a major cause of regional problems than as a part of the solution. The public's distrust limits its willingness to pay more for a better environment and pushes it toward local initiatives to control growth.

The public is well aware of local population growth, and they are expecting more in the future. Many residents complain about traffic and growth-related problems in their regions. In response, most people prefer to institute local growth controls through the initiative process. They would also like to see funds devoted to purchasing open space, and they would like to have environmentally sensitive areas protected from development. But we do see important variations in these growth policy preferences across regions, ranging from stronger support in the economically booming San Francisco Bay Area to limited favor in the economically challenged Central Valley. Moreover, residents are reluctant to support efforts to preserve open space if they think it will cost them more of their own money to do so. Those in weaker economic circumstances are even more resistant to tax increases for environmental purposes.

Californians express a number of concerns about the condition of the environment in the Golden State. They worry about air pollution; water pollution from urban runoff; toxics contaminating the land; ocean and beach pollution; and the loss of farmlands, open space, and forests. Overall, Californians are not impressed with their governor's efforts in the environmental arena, and they would like to see the government doing more to protect the environment. There are partisan differences, with

Democrats and independent voters wanting the government to do more for the environment, while Republicans generally believe the government is already doing enough. However, no one is expressing much confidence and trust in state government's performance in this area.

There is strong support for proenvironmental policies, even when the economic costs of such programs are kept in mind. Californians want more environmental restrictions, even if it costs some jobs; they want the government to become more involved in reducing global warming; they prefer the preservation of endangered species, when given that choice or the construction of housing that would threaten wildlife and the environment; and they oppose offshore oil drilling, even if it means higher prices at the gas pump. However, in most cases, we see that economic security and political ideology do limit support for environmental programs, even in good times. Californians who are less affluent, residents of the Central Valley, and Republicans are less in favor of environmental policies. Moreover, many Californians would prefer a tax refund from the state surplus rather than to see the state government use the money to purchase open space.

When Californians went to the polls in 2000, they did express their concerns about growth and environmental issues in a number of ways. Facing a large number of local ballot measures, they passed most slow-growth measures and rejected most progrowth measures. In the March primary, the voters passed two state bond measures for open space and environmental protection by very large margins. Voters told us that environmental issues mattered in their presidential vote, and they strongly supported the candidate with the proenvironment record, Al Gore. Clearly, this was a time when growth and the environment were top priorities for voters. Yet even in this time of prosperity, residents of the Golden State expressed little confidence in their government and little willingness to give government the ability to tackle problems they cared about.

The Latino Century Begins

The 2000 Census confirmed what some demographers were already claiming: California was the first large state to enter the uncharted territory of majority-minority status. This meant that no longer did any racial or ethnic group account for a majority of the population. For the first time in the state's 150-year history, the white population fell below 50 percent. This change was driven by the growth of the Latino population in the state, which was due to a large influx of new immigrants and a high birth rate within this group.

Latinos are not only altering the social character of the state; their growing number raises significant questions about the state's political future. Latino population growth may also have long-term implications for the level of distrust in government in the state. In this chapter, we see that Latinos exceed all groups in California when it comes to trust in government. In a state that has been dominated for more than two decades by white voters who lack confidence in public institutions and elected officials, nothing could have as profound an effect on politics and policymaking as trust among the growing Latino electorate.

There are good reasons to expect Latinos to subscribe to a different point of view about government than most California voters. Latinos do not fit the profile of suburban, affluent, college-educated, issue-focused, and more loosely partisan voters with postmaterialist values and thus are unlikely to join the New Political Culture (Clark and Inglehart,

1998). Their demographics are more like the ethnic voters of the American past—many are immigrants, have children, live in lower-income households, and reside in big cities—qualities that provide a focus on meeting basic needs and a desire for government to offer more public services to help achieve the American Dream.

While many Californians had come to subscribe to a more secular and individualistic worldview that de-emphasizes the role of government and political party in their lives, many Latinos follow the lead of earlier European immigrants to America in valuing the importance of government, political party, church, and family in their decisions. So the growth of the Latino population offers a potentially powerful countervailing force in the state's political climate: they are fiscal liberals and social conservatives at a time when many voters are fiscal conservatives and social liberals.

But the growth of the Latino population also raises some important social and economic issues. Lieutenant Governor Cruz Bustamante best summarized a chief concern raised by racial and ethnic change in an August 1999 speech in which he launched the Commission for One California. He said, "Many significant challenges face California today— water, the environment, the quality of schools, affordable housing. Today, I want to talk about the most important challenge facing us. It is the challenge of living together as one California. Our future demands finding common ground."[1]

The violent and deadly conflicts that surfaced in the spring of 1992 in response to the Rodney King beating trial verdict had placed many of the state's residents on alert about the fragile nature of multiethnic/racial relations.[2] Moreover, a series of controversial ballot initiatives that passed in the mid-1990s seemed to indicate that white voters were uncomfortable with the racial and ethnic changes underway in the state, as they were favorably responding to cuts in programs that benefited the growing ranks of minorities. Latinos, in particular, were taken aback, and they mobilized in response to some politicians' efforts to use their group as the scapegoat for the state's problems.

1. Remarks of Lieutenant Governor Cruz M. Bustamante (1999). Sections of this chapter updated from earlier work I did for Hajnal and Baldassare (2001). I was helped by discussions with Zoltan Hajnal.
2. See Baldassare (1994a, 2000); Dear, Schockman, and Hise (1996); Fulton (1997); Keil (1998); Rieff (1991); Scott and Soja (1998); Sonenshein (1993); and Steinberg, Lyon, and Vaiana (1992) concerning the Los Angeles civil disturbance and racial and ethnic tensions in Los Angeles.

But that was then, and circumstances changed. The negative feelings toward immigration and pessimism about intergroup relations were generated during a deep recession. By the late 1990s, the state had seen its employment levels rise and its budget woes disappear, so the economic and fiscal pressures of immigration were not as relevant. And while racial and ethnic tensions may have flared up from time to time, there had been no repeat of the serious episode of the 1992 civil disturbances in Los Angeles.

Californians were mellowing toward racial and ethnic issues that in earlier times were tearing the state apart. In our focus groups, one respondent remarked simply, "Diversity is always better." Another respondent said, "The positive is that you get to meet a lot of different people from a lot of different backgrounds, and you get to expand your knowledge," while another individual added, "They come here from other parts of the world because they have talent we need." Another respondent said, "I think it's a welcome change. We have the influx of all the new folks coming in, and it's done nothing but make it better." The state's diversity had a broad public appeal in times of prosperity, and once-popular anti-immigrant sentiments were now out of favor. Candidates from both parties were courting Latino voters, who had been previously ignored, and were preaching the politics of inclusion and avoiding racially divisive issues.

In our surveys, Californians were keenly aware of the rapid demographic change occurring in the state, but they were taking it in stride. Seven in ten residents thought the racial and ethnic composition of their region was changing, while four in ten said it was changing "a lot." Yet in all of the surveys we conducted during the 2000 cycle, only a handful of residents named race and ethnic relations as the most important problem facing the state. Eight in ten Californians thought that racial and ethnic groups were getting along very well or somewhat well in their regions (PPIC Statewide Survey, 2000b).

Similarly, Californians were very aware of the trends in immigration but had softened their attitudes about its effects. Nine in ten residents were aware that the state's immigrant population in California has been increasing in recent years. Throughout the 2000 elections, no more than one in twelve residents said that legal and illegal immigration was the most important issue facing the state. The majority of residents held the view that immigrants were a benefit to California because of their hard work and job skills, and those who thought that immigrants were a burden to California were now in the minority. A strong job market and large budget surplus in state government had helped to improve the public mood toward immigrants (PPIC Statewide Survey, 2000b). The contrast with a few years earlier was striking: Californians were very concerned about illegal and legal immigration early in the 1990s. Many cited immigration as the most important issue in the 1994 elections, and many supported an anti–illegal immigration initiative (Baldassare, 2000; Hajnal and Baldassare, 2001).

Clearly, no topic is more important for the state's political and economic future than what happens with the Latino population over the next several decades. The year 2000 was a turning point and could be viewed as the beginning of the "Latino century" for the state. Not only in sheer population size but also in shifts in public attitudes and political significance, there were signs that Latino growth was having statewide effects.[3]

The remainder of this chapter reviews the population growth and socioeconomic conditions of Latinos and their growing presence in the state's political and policymaking arena, including their voting record, voter profiles, and presence in elected office. We look at the 2000 elections for evidence of how the Latino vote was expressed in the presidential and U.S. Senate races and several state initiatives and, in particular, how the Latino vote influenced the process and the outcome of the 2000 state election. Latinos have tilted partisan politics in the state and could have an even more profound influence on the role of government. This potential is evident in how Latinos relate to issues such as government trust, government regulations, and taxes and spending.

LATINO POPULATION GROWTH

Passing the majority-minority milestone in California had been anticipated for some time before it actually happened in 2000. As recently as 1980, two in three of the state's residents were white, and fewer than one in five were Latino. In the five decades between the Great Depres-

---

3. See Ayon (2000); Bustillo (2000); Del Olmo (2000); Lesher (1998); Latino Issues Forum (1998); Rodriguez (1999); Scott (2000); Skelton (1998); and Walters (1998). There are a number of important academic books and articles on Latino politics such as Cain, Kiewiet, et al. (1986); Cain, Kiewiet, and Uhlaner (1991); Chavez (1998); De la Garza (1987); Fernandez and Neiman (1997); Moore and Pachon (1985); Neiman and Fernandez (1998); Pachon (1998); Pachon and DeSipio (1995); Preston, Cain, and Bass (1998); Uhlaner, Cain, and Kiewiet (1989); and Uhlaner and Garcia (1998).

sion and the Vietnam War, the state's population was driven by migration of whites and blacks from the east to the Golden State. This was reflected in the fact that three in four of the state's residents were white or black. The migration from inside the United States slowed markedly by the mid-1970s, and a historic level of migration from other countries, notably Mexico, was in full swing in the 1980s.

As of the 1990 Census, the white population had declined to 57 percent of the state's residents. One in four residents was Latino, and one in ten was Asian. The growth of the Latino and Asian population reflected a sharp increase in the number of immigrants from Latin American and Asian countries during the decade of the 1980s. By the early 1990s, demographers felt that continuing immigration and higher birth rates among the younger immigrant population compared with the aging white population would result in no groups being in the racial or ethnic majority by 2000. They were right.[4]

The state's racial and ethnic transformation was initially fueled by immigration. The state gained almost 3 million legal residents between 1980 and the mid-1990s. Mexico, by far, accounted for most of the legal immigrants to California during this time. Moreover, there are estimates that the number of illegal immigrants from Mexico added anywhere from 1 million to 2 million additional residents to the state's population.[5] However, most of the growth and change in the 1990s can be attributed to natural increase—births over deaths—within the Latino population. Latino births outnumbered Latino deaths by a wide margin for every year in the 1990s, reflecting that this is a young population from a culture that has traditionally had high birth rates. By contrast, the white population was older and had a lower birth rate and a higher death rate, and many whites were actually moving out of the state during the recession of the 1990s.[6]

While this social transformation of California is remarkable—indeed, California is the first major state to be defined as majority-minority—it

4. See Becerra and Alvarez (2001); Booth (2001); Hillburg (2000); Korber (2000); Nelson and O'Reilly (2000); Purdum (2001); Saavedra and Campbell (2000); Schevitz (2000); Verdin (2000); and Woolfolk (2000). See also Maharidge (1996); Schrag (1998); and Walters (1992) on the declining white population.

5. See California Department of Finance (1997); Clark (1998, 2001); Rodriguez (1998); and Johnson (1996). See also McConnell (1999); Portes and Rumbaut (1990); and Vernez (1992) on immigration trends and their consequences.

6. See Baldassare (2000); California Department of Finance (1998); Johnson (1999, 2000); Tafoya and Johnson (2000).

TABLE 6.1   CALIFORNIA'S LATINO POPULATION

	Population (in millions)	% of Total California Population
1990	7.8	26
1995	9.1	28
2000	10.9	32
2005	12.3	33
2010	14.0	35
2015	15.6	37
2020	17.8	39
2025	20.1	42
2030	22.5	44
2035	25.2	46
2040	28.1	48

SOURCE: Baldassare (2000); U.S. Census (2001); population estimates beyond 2000 are from California Department of Finance (1998).

represents an interim step in the state's demographic transition. (See Table 6-1.) In 2000, the state's Latino population reached almost 11 million, making this ethnic group larger in number than the population of Los Angeles County and larger than most states in the nation. Much bigger changes lie ahead for the state in the next several decades, all largely as a result of a growing Latino population. By 2020, when the state's population swells to around 45 million, most of the state's residents will be either Latino or Asian. In fact, Latinos are expected to outnumber whites sometime around 2020, as the Latino population reaches 18 million. Whites are expected to dwindle in number and proportion of the population in the early twenty-first century as a result of the continued aging of the Baby Boomers, low birth rates, and migration to other states.

By 2040, the Latino population is expected to be close to a majority of the state's population and to total about 28 million residents. This is largely a reflection of the continued natural increase of a relatively youthful population and does not take into account any large surges in immigration from other countries. At this point, the state's overall population is predicted to reach 59 million by 2040.

The Latino population in 2040 would be equivalent in size to the overall state population in the mid-1980s. Another way of looking at this long-term prediction of demographic change is that the state will be the opposite of what it was in 2000—from just under half white and one in three Latino, to just under half Latino and one in three white. What will it mean for state politics and policymaking as this demographic transformation is translated into Latino voting for candidates and initiatives in statewide elections? We explore the possibilities when we look at political preferences in this chapter.

THE SOCIOECONOMIC DIVIDE

In every indicator of economic privilege in the state, a socioeconomic divide exists across racial and ethnic sectors of the population. Although no racial or ethnic group is in the majority, whites are still the dominant group when it comes to having all of the advantages of well-to-do residents. Moreover, while Latinos may be a growing population, they are woefully underrepresented in the state's upwardly mobile groups. We examined the measures of socioeconomic success through the cumulative results of nine PPIC Statewide Surveys conducted from September 1999 through January 2001 (see Table 6-2). These surveys included the responses of a large number of residents in each major racial/ethnic group, including more than 3,500 Latinos, over 10,000 whites, and nearly 1,000 each among black and Asian groups. The Asian population is highly diverse and thus includes some nationalities that are doing much better and some that are doing much worse than the averages presented.

The reality is that most Latinos were not living the California Dream in 2000. Most had not attended college, and most did not own their own homes. Most had annual household incomes under $40,000 and had never logged on to the Internet. In all, Latinos and blacks lagged far behind Asians and whites on the key indicators of socioeconomic well-being, including income, education, home ownership, and Internet use. Latinos also fell behind blacks in all of these commonly utilized measures of economic success.

For instance, two in three Latinos and a majority of blacks reported having incomes of less than $40,000 per year, while one in three Asians and whites fell into these lower-income categories. Moreover, one in three Latinos reported having a very low income—under $20,000 per year. Also, only one in six Latinos and one in four blacks reported having an annual income of $60,000 or more, compared with four in ten Asians and whites.

We found a similar racial and ethnic divide in the level of education completed. One in four Latinos reported having no high school diploma;

TABLE 6.2   CALIFORNIA LATINOS AND
THE SOCIOECONOMIC DIVIDE

	Latinos	Whites	Asians	Blacks
Income				
Under $20,000	33%	13%	16%	21%
$20,000 to $39,999	34	23	19	31
$40,000 to $59,999	16	22	22	22
$60,000 or over	17	42	43	26
Education				
No high school diploma	26	5	3	8
High school diploma	32	20	14	25
Some college	25	31	27	34
College graduate	17	44	56	33
Home Ownership				
Own	43	68	55	46
Rent	57	32	45	54
Use Internet				
Yes	47	69	82	62
No	53	31	18	38

SOURCE: PPIC Statewide Surveys from September 1999 to January 2001, all adults.

such a low level of educational attainment was fairly rare among whites, Asians, and blacks. In another stark contrast, nearly half of whites and the majority of Asians had college degrees, compared with one in three blacks and only one in six Latinos.[7]

Home ownership rates also varied dramatically across racial and ethnic groups. Nearly seven in ten whites said they owned their current residence, as did a solid majority of Asians. By contrast, the majority of Latinos and blacks were renting their current residences.

To some degree, the socioeconomic divide that separates Latinos from others is tied to citizenship and time living in the United States. For instance, noncitizens were much worse off than either naturalized citizens

7. Reyes (2001) indicates even lower rates of education among Latinos.

or U.S.-born Latinos in terms of their income levels, high school graduation rates, and home ownership rates. In general, U.S.-born residents were better off than naturalized citizens. Still, even Latinos who were U.S.-born were much less likely than whites to earn $60,000 or more, to have a college degree, and to own their own home. Moreover, a high proportion of Asian residents had also arrived as immigrants from other countries, yet many of them were doing as well as whites and better than Latinos and blacks on levels of income, education, and home ownership. Of course, *Asian* is a diverse category, and some nationalities were doing worse than blacks and Latinos; on average, however, Asians were showing socioeconomic strength. In sum, we cannot assume that the socioeconomic divide will simply disappear over time as Latinos represent a higher proportion of Californians.

To succeed in the state's high-tech economy, computer skills have become almost essential. For this reason, there is a great deal of interest in the "digital divide" in California, defined as a lack of access to computers and the Internet by certain groups that will play a critical role in the state's future. In our analysis of the cumulative data from the PPIC Statewide Surveys, we found a digital divide between young adults and adults over age 64, between those with low incomes and those with high incomes, between those with no college education and college graduates, and between those living in the San Francisco Bay Area and those residents of the Central Valley. A digital divide also existed across racial and ethnic groups. We found that Latinos were much less likely than whites, blacks, and Asians to use the Internet.[8]

Among Latinos, computer and Internet use did vary by citizenship status and other demographic factors. Most U.S.-born Latinos used the Internet; rates of use were much lower among naturalized citizens and noncitizens. Moreover, the digital divide was less noticeable for Latinos with higher incomes and college degrees. Yet even Latinos born in the United States were less likely than non-Latinos to use the Internet. Moreover, Latinos with college degrees and higher incomes were less likely than non-Latinos with college degrees and higher incomes to use the Internet. Once again, we cannot assume that the disadvantages Latinos had in 2000 will simply disappear with time.[9]

8. See PPIC Just the Facts (2001b) and Hajnal and Baldassare (2001).

9. After controlling for age, education, income, citizenship, and gender in regression analysis, Latinos still have significantly lower computer use ($B = -.40$) and lower Internet use ($B = -.58$), with both trends significant at the .001 level. See also Hajnal and Baldassare (2001) on the digital divide.

An even more dramatic digital divide across racial and ethnic groups appears when we compare those who responded that they frequently used computers and the Internet. Whereas about 60 percent of whites and blacks and 80 percent of Asians said they often used computers, only about one in three Latinos reported frequently using a computer. Similarly, fewer than one in three Latinos said they often used the Internet, compared with two in three Asians, a little over half of whites, and four in ten blacks.

Certainly, computer use has been increasing over time, and Internet use has been growing rapidly since the mid-1990s. There has been some speculation that the digital divide will disappear over time as this technology evolves and costs are reduced in the mass consumer market. The evidence is somewhat mixed from our California surveys. Within the time we tracked Internet use—September 1999 through January 2001— we saw use increase from 60 to 69 percent statewide. While the rates of Internet use increased among Latinos during this sixteen-month period (39% to 56%), they also increased among whites (65% to 72%). So there was a shrinking divide, but large differences still existed when comparing Internet use among Latinos to any other racial and ethnic group in the state.

The importance of the digital divide between Latinos and other Californians gains clarity when we look at differences in specific uses of the Internet. In all, Latinos' socioeconomic disadvantages are accentuated by the fact that they do not have as much access to the plentiful and timely knowledge provided by the Internet.

For instance, at least one in three Californians told us that he or she went online to gather information from government, retail, or financial Web sites. However, frequent visits to any of these types of Web sites was very rare among Latinos. In all, Latinos were about half as likely as whites to visit government, retail, or financial Web sites (PPIC Statewide Survey 2000b). This was primarily because Latinos did not have access to the Internet, not because they were choosing to gather other information instead.

About two in three Californians send and receive email messages among friends, relatives, and work colleagues, while four in ten residents overall receive email messages from organizations. Only one in four Latinos reported sending or receiving email on a frequent basis, in contrast to half of whites. Likewise, group email was more of a rarity among Latinos than for the population as a whole (PPIC Statewide Survey, 2000f).

Again, this is largely because Latinos did not have computers at home, and most were thus unable to use the Internet for communications.

In a PPIC Statewide Survey (2000g) in October 2000, about half of all Californians said they used the Internet to gather information for their job and to receive news and information, while four in ten logged on to purchase goods or services. A minority of Latinos uses the Internet for gathering news or work information or for purchasing goods and services, and the gaps in specific uses are especially large in comparison with whites and Asians. If one considers the lost possibilities among those with limited means and options, it places the human toll of the digital divide among Latinos in perspective.

There are other tangible ways in which an economically disadvantaged group falls behind in economic boom times such as California experienced in the late 1990s. Take, for instance, the patterns of ownership of stocks and stock mutual funds in the state. Overall, more than half of Californians owned stocks in some form, but there were large differences across racial and ethnic groups. Two in three whites owned stocks, while only one in three Latinos had any money at all invested in the stock market. Moreover, whites were three times as likely to have large sums of money invested in the market—that is, $50,000 or more. As a result, the bull market of the 1990s had no effect on the finances of most Latinos. In contrast, many whites became wealthier—at least on paper.

Latinos, as a group, lack the funds to buy houses and have not benefited, as have whites and Asians, from the increase in home values over the last several decades. For many Californians, their largest and most profitable investment is the home they own and live in. While the vast majority of whites and Asians own their own homes, most Latinos and blacks do not have this investment. So when housing was appreciating in the late 1990s, it was the whites more often than the Latinos who were in a position to benefit financially. Moreover, a PPIC Statewide Survey (2000f) in the fall of 2000 indicated that the benefits of owning a home were tied closely to race and ethnicity. Nearly half of whites and Asians said their home values had increased a lot in recent years, compared with about one in four Latinos and blacks. These reports suggest that even the minority of Latinos who owned their homes did not benefit as much financially as white home owners, perhaps because their homes were more likely to be found in lower socioeconomic neighborhoods or in less desirable urban areas.

In summarizing the trends, whites tended to be better off economically than Latinos. Whites comprised three in four of the California adults who owned stocks, owned their own homes, and had annual household incomes of $80,000 or more. Two in three state residents who were college graduates or who frequently used the Internet were also white. Latinos were highly underrepresented in all of these categories, numbering only one in six (or fewer) of high-income residents, college graduates, home owners, stock owners, or frequent Internet users. It is clear that it was whites and not Latinos who had benefited the most from the run-up in housing prices and the stock market and the high-tech jobs generated in the New Economy during the late 1990s.

Moreover, Latinos had the unfortunate distinction of outnumbering whites and other groups in some of the more disadvantaged categories. Our surveys revealed that the majority of Californians with annual household incomes under $40,000, with no college education, and with no use of the Internet were Latinos. By contrast, Latinos were an underrepresented minority among all of the moderate-to-upper socioeconomic indicators. These demographic trends raised some nagging questions about the state's economic future, and none of these trends showed signs of measurable change at the time of this writing.

LATINO VOTING PARTICIPATION
AND POLITICAL POTENTIAL

The fact that the Latino population has been growing at a rapid pace could have huge implications for politics and elections in California. Latinos are expected to be an increasing proportion of the electorate in coming decades, making Latino voters and politicians all the more relevant. Moreover, many of the important policy decisions on schools and other government programs made by state and local elected officials and voters at the ballot box will have an impact on the large and growing Latino population. There is perhaps no topic that is receiving more attention from the political parties and pundits than the size and preferences of the Latino vote in California.

Latinos have had relatively poor voting records in the past. (See Table 6-3.) This trend raises some fundamental doubts about the real potential of Latino political participation. Typically, voter registration and voting are related to factors such as age, home ownership, income, and education. As a youthful group with relatively low socioeconomic status, many Latinos do not fit the profile of "high propensity" voters. But we

TABLE 6.3   LATINO VOTING SHARE
IN THE GENERAL ELECTIONS

	Latino	Asian	Black	Other	White
2000	14%	6%	7%	2%	71%
1998	14	4	7	1	74
1996	12	4	6	2	76
1994	9	4	8	2	77
1992	8	4	7	2	79
1990	4	4	8	2	82

SOURCE: Voter News Service (1990, 1992, 1994, 1996, 1998, 2000).

know that other racial and ethnic groups have overcome socioeconomic obstacles when they have become politically mobilized over issues. The 1960s civil rights movement led blacks throughout the nation to register to vote in large numbers, and this pattern of frequent voting has continued. Some have argued that the anti-immigrant initiative on the ballot in 1994 led many Latinos to register to vote and participate in elections and was thus a turning point.

When we conducted focus groups around the state in the spring of 1999, many of the Latino participants were upbeat about their growing role in the political process. "If we are going to be the majority, we will be dominating politics," remarked one Latino. However, other Latinos were aware that the potential for political power existed but that it remained largely unrealized. One respondent noted, "So far, Latinos are not voting. But the next generation will be legal and voting." Some expressed a general optimism about being part of the political decision-making process in the state—for example, the Latino who said, "Latino voting could have positive benefits we can't foresee." Another group member expressed an attitude toward taxes that is rare among California voters: "We Latinos will pay taxes and help pay for the infrastructure." It is interesting that there was little mention of Proposition 187 (the measure that denied public services to illegal immigrants) and the anti-immigrant feelings that were a mobilizing factor after the 1994 elections.

The number of Latinos who are registered to vote and are actually voting has increased over the course of a decade. In the presidential election in 1992, Latinos represented only 8 percent of the electorate. By 1996, the percentage of Latino voters had increased to 12 percent. By the 2000 presidential election, 14 percent of the California electorate was Latino.

While there were numerous signs of a growing potential for Latino political power, there were also some equally discouraging trends in levels of political involvement. For one, only 7 percent of the March primary electorate was Latino, according to the *Los Angeles Times* exit poll (2000a). If accurate, this was actually lower than the March 1998 turnout (see Baldassare, 2000). Moreover, although 14 percent of the November electorate was Latino, this represented no change from the 1998 election, after steady increases in the 1990s. The voting record for Latinos in 2000 reflected an increase in the number of voters. However, because a higher percentage of all voters participate in presidential years, Latinos registered no increase as a proportion of the electorate between 1998 and 2000.

Clearly, there is a long way to go before the voting population reflects the diversity of the adult population. In 2000, the electorate remained largely white. While the population as a whole might be majority-minority, seven in ten voters in California elections were white. While one in three Californians were Latino, only about one in seven voters was Latino. This underrepresentation at the ballot box arises from a variety of reasons. A large proportion of the Latino population was nonadult and thus not of voting age. Many Latinos were noncitizens and thus ineligible to register to vote. Today, perhaps about one in four adults who can vote is Latino (Reyes, 2001). As the U.S.-born population of Latinos grows older and as more Latinos become citizens, we would expect a growing number to participate in the political process.

However, as noted earlier, there are other factors constraining the number of Latino voters at the polls. Most notable is the lower socioeconomic status of Latinos, as measured by their income, education, and home ownership rates. How much and how quickly the Latino vote grows will depend at least partly on the extent to which Latinos are able to improve their social and economic status.

In the PPIC Statewide Surveys, the proportions of Latinos who said they were registered to vote and frequently vote were well below average for the state's residents. Even taking into account the large number of noncitizens, we see that voter registration rates and reports of frequent voting were still lower for Latinos than other groups. Latinos who were U.S.-born were more likely to participate in voting and elections than Latinos who were naturalized citizens. Still, U.S.-born Latinos were less likely than whites or blacks to register to vote or to often show up at the polls. When we take into account demographic differences—such as income, education, and home ownership—the differences between Latinos, whites, and blacks disappear. In other words, Latino political participation rates look very similar to those of other politically under-represented groups.[10]

A related trend involves Latinos' general interest in political issues. Only about one in four Latinos claimed to follow public affairs on a consistent basis. By comparison, almost half of whites expressed this level of interest (PPIC Statewide Survey, 2000b). Throughout the March primary and November election, Latinos lagged behind whites in attention to news stories about the presidential elections. To some degree, this trend is a reflection of different patterns in watching the news: Latinos got most of their news about government and public affairs from television; few were avid newspaper readers. Whites were more likely to say that newspapers were their main source of news. Of course, these differences in attention to the media also relate to age and socioeconomic trends.

There is no doubt, though, that the size of the Latino vote grew dramatically during the 1990s. California added 1.1 million new registered voters to its rolls, and about 1 million of these newly enrolled voters were Latino. During this time, the number of white voters actually declined in the state numerically and as a proportion of the voters. About 16 percent of registered voters were Latino as of 2000, for a total of about 2.4 million voters. In particular, there was a surge of Latino voters after the 1994 elections, presumably motivated by the victory of the Proposition 187 anti–illegal immigrant initiative. New voters tended to be younger and lower-income than Latinos who had registered earlier. The facts that large numbers of Latinos may register to vote in the coming decades and that whites and others groups have less potential for growth are among the reasons that parties and politicians are paying close attention to Latinos (Marinucci, 2000; Willis, 2000). They could tilt the balance of political power and shift policymaking preferences through the election of federal, state, and local representatives as well as through the initiative process.

10. After controlling for age, education, income, citizenship, and gender in regression analysis, Latinos are not less likely to register to vote or to vote frequently in elections. See also Hajnal and Baldassare (2001) on racial and ethnic trends in voting.

LATINO VOTER PROFILES

At its current size, the Latino voting body could significantly affect state races and initiatives. With this in mind, we looked at the demographic and political profile of "likely voters" in all of the PPIC Statewide Surveys between September 1999 and January 2001 (see Table 6-4). We compared the results for Latinos with whites, Asians, and blacks and found that Latino voters are, in particular, quite different from white voters, who have been the dominant group in state elections.

Most notably, we found a strong partisan difference in voting registration. Six in ten Latinos said they were registered as Democrats, while only one in four were registered Republicans. By contrast, whites were more likely to be Republicans, although they were fairly evenly divided along party lines. Asians were less inclined to be Democrats, and blacks more inclined to be Democrats, than were Latinos. In all, the fact that the fastest-growing voter group in the state is heavily Democratic is good news for the Democratic party and bad news for the GOP.

Latino voters who regularly went to the polls were most likely to describe themselves as liberals. Survey responses indicate that four in ten Latinos were liberals, three in ten were moderates, and three in ten were conservative in their politics. With respect to political orientation, Latino voters were similar to Asians and blacks. All three groups were more liberal than white voters. Once again, the growing presence of Latino voters, combined with their similarities to other nonwhite voters, could cause a left-leaning shift in statewide races and initiative outcomes.

As noted previously, Latino voters were strikingly different from white voters with respect to socioeconomic status. The latter were generally older, more affluent, and better educated. Latinos were similar to Asian voters in terms of their youthfulness, reflecting that both groups included large numbers of immigrants, but Asians had income and education levels comparable to whites. By contrast, Latinos were similar to blacks in having lower income and education levels. However, they were dissimilar to blacks in that the latter were older, reflecting that most were U.S.-born and not immigrants. In terms of economic differences, white and Asian voters tended to be home owners, while the likely voters among Latinos and blacks tended to be renters.

We also found important gender differences across racial and ethnic groups. White voters numbered about half men and half women. Men represented Asian voters and women represented black voters by a three-to-two margin in each case. However, while white women were equally likely

TABLE 6.4   LATINO VOTER PROFILES

	Latinos	Whites	Asians	Blacks
Democrat	59%	39%	45%	78%
Republican	24	45	31	8
Independent	17	16	24	14
Liberal	40	31	38	41
Moderate	29	30	32	32
Conservative	31	39	30	27
18 to 34	41	18	38	26
35 to 54	40	42	44	47
55 and older	19	40	18	27
College graduate	32	51	64	42
Some college	33	32	28	34
Less education	35	17	8	24
Under $60,000	69	53	49	67
$60,000 or more	31	47	51	33

SOURCE: PPIC Statewide Surveys, September 1999 to January 2001, likely voters.

to be registered in the two major parties, Latino women registered as Democrat rather than Republican by a three-to-one margin, black women by a six-to-one margin, and Asian women by a two-to-one margin. Among men, whites were more likely to register as Republican, Asians were only slightly more likely to register as Democrat, Latinos by a two to one margin were Democrat, and blacks by a ten-to-one margin were Democrat. In other words, much of the "gender gap" between the parties occurred for women who were Latino, Asian, and black. The gender gap could grow into a larger advantage for Democrats if the number of white voters continues to decline and the number of Latino and Asian voters increases.

There were also some distinct geographic patterns in terms of where the voters from the different racial and ethnic groups resided in the state. Two in three lived in either Los Angeles or the surrounding Southern California suburban region. Four in ten Latinos lived in Los Angeles County proper. By contrast, only about one in four white voters lived in Los Angeles County; nearly half lived in the Southern California suburbs outside of Los Angeles or in the Central Valley. As for Asian and black voters, about three in four lived in Los Angeles and the San Francisco Bay Area, while relatively few lived in either the Central Valley or the Southern California region outside of Los Angeles. Obviously, this means that Latino and other nonwhite voters can have the most pronounced influence on local election outcomes in Los Angeles.

LATINO VOTERS AND STATEWIDE RACES

Latinos have had a measurable effect on statewide races as the number of voters from this group has increased in recent years. Notably, Latinos contributed to a string of successes that the Democratic candidates have enjoyed and to a growing belief among pundits that it is very difficult for Republicans to win a statewide race. Will Latino voters make California a one-party state? Some think it is possible.

Latinos have been strongly supportive of Democratic candidates in statewide elections. (See Table 6-5.) Not coincidentally, Democrats have been on the winning side of big races in recent state elections. In 1992, Latinos supported Bill Clinton over George Bush for president. By two-to-one margins in U.S. Senate races, they supported Barbara Boxer over Bruce Hershensohn in 1992 and Dianne Feinstein over Michael Huffington in 1994. Latinos favored Clinton over Dole in the presidential race in 1996 (Baldassare, 2000). In all of these cases, the Democrats won the statewide races.

In 1998, Latinos supported Gray Davis over Dan Lungren in the governor's race and Barbara Boxer over Matt Fong in the U.S. Senate race by at least two-to-one margins. Democrats went on to big victories in both cases. While Latinos may not be a large enough voting group to determine the outcome of these recent Democratic successes, together with Asians and blacks they have contributed to the margin of victory through their lopsided support of the Democrats. Consider the fact that Davis received a bare majority of the white vote and Boxer did not have a majority at all, yet both won the state handily.[11]

California Latinos received an unprecedented level of attention from the presidential campaigns and initiative supporters during the 2000 elections. There were at least three reasons that the political establishment turned their focus on Latinos. First, given the widespread recognition that the state and the nation were becoming more ethnically and racially diverse and, in particular, more Latino, what better way to establish cre-

---

11. See Voter News Service (1992, 1994, 1996, 1998); Los Angeles Times poll (1994, 1998); Field Institute (1999); Baldassare (2000); and news reports by Covarrubias (1998) and Tobar (1998) on the Latino vote in the 1998 California elections.

TABLE 6.5   LATINO VOTING PREFERENCES
IN STATEWIDE RACES

	Latino	White	Black	Asian
2000 President				
Al Gore (D)	68%	47%	86%	48%
George W. Bush (R)	29	48	11	47
Ralph Nader, others	3	5	3	5
2000 U.S. Senate				
Dianne Feinstein (D)	67	49	87	64
Tom Campbell (R)	24	42	11	33
Others	9	9	2	3
1998 Governor				
Gray Davis (D)	78	50	83	67
Dan Lungren (R)	17	46	11	29
Others	5	4	6	4
1998 U.S. Senate				
Barbara Boxer (D)	72	46	85	54
Matt Fong (R)	23	50	13	44
Others	5	4	2	2

SOURCE: Voter News Service (1998, 2000); PPIC Just the Facts (2000c).

dentials as an "inclusive" candidate or political cause than reaching out to the Latino community? Second, there was the immediate political reality that Latinos had become a sizable enough vote to make it very difficult for the GOP to counter the California trend of overwhelming support for Democratic candidates and that Latino votes were sufficient to tip the balance in favor of ballot initiatives if the contests were close. Third, the political parties and causes were seeking to build rapport with Latinos, given the widely recognized long-term trend of an increasing Latino population and future voting strength in the state.[12]

There were great expectations for the Latino vote in the presidential race in California. The proportion of the electorate that was Latino had

12. See Ayon (2000); Bustillo (2000); Del Olmo (2000); Rodriguez (1999, 2000); and Skelton (2000b).

been steadily increasing, and the strong support of Latinos for Democratic candidates had been helping to provide a comfortable cushion in a recent string of Democratic successes at the ballot box. Republicans in California were among the first seeking to encourage George W. Bush to run for president, in part because he had proven in recent Texas gubernatorial elections that he could appeal to Latino voters. The California GOP had alienated Latino voters since the election in November 1994, and although the Republicans did not expect to win the Latin vote, they also knew that their chances of victory in the state would be slim without at least narrowing the margin of their defeat among Latinos.[13]

In the three surveys that we conducted prior to the open primary in March 2000, the state's voters consistently ranked Gore as their top choice and Bush as a distant second when given the full list of candidates. Among Latinos, a similar pattern was evident, with four in ten voters supporting Gore and one in four favoring Bush. When asked to choose between a hypothetical match-up between Bush and Gore, the state's voters were fairly evenly divided in the surveys leading up to the primary, but Latino voters consistently favored Gore by huge margins averaging over 20 points. In many ways, the underlying attitudes of Latinos reflected a solid core of Democratic support: eight in ten liked Clinton's policies, two in three liked Clinton, three in four said issues and experience mattered most in choosing a presidential candidate, and topics such as schools and health care reform ranked high on their list of concerns.

The *Los Angeles Times* exit poll (2000a) reports that the Latino vote in the March primary was 7 percent of the vote. The Latino vote went 57 percent for Gore, 21 percent for Bush, 10 percent for McCain, and 8 percent for Bradley. Once again, Latinos showed overwhelming support for the Democratic candidate in an open primary.

In the three surveys leading up to the November presidential election, Gore was always ahead of Bush in our statewide surveys. One important component of this lead was a large margin of Latino support. On average, six in ten Latinos supported Gore, while only about one in four favored Bush. Latino voters told us they cared the most about schools, health care, social security, and taxes. On all of these issues, they felt that Gore would do a better job than Bush if he became president. Most Latinos continued to support the policies of Clinton and said they liked the

---

13. The survey results in this section are from the PPIC Statewide Surveys in December 1999 and January and February 2000 (1999c, 2000a, 2000b) and PPIC Statewide Surveys in August, September, and October 2000 (2000e, 2000f, 2000g).

president, while ranking "the issues" and "experience" as their top factors in deciding whom they would vote for.

The Voter News Service exit poll (2000) reported that Latinos comprised 14 percent of all voters in the November 2000 election. The Latino vote went 68 percent to Gore and 29 percent to Bush, with 3 percent supporting Ralph Nader and other candidates. This level of Democratic support was very similar to the presidential elections in 1992 and 1996. The only significant difference was that there were more Latinos voting in 2000, thus helping to provide an even larger margin of victory for the Democratic candidate.

As for the U.S. Senate race, Democratic incumbent Dianne Feinstein coasted through the open primary against four Republicans seeking to challenge her in November. In the three surveys leading up to the March primary, Feinstein received about 50 percent of the vote, while U.S. Representative Tom Campbell led the Republican pack with support from only one in seven voters. Among Latinos, about two in three supported Feinstein and fewer than one in ten favored Campbell. According to the *Los Angeles Times* exit poll (2000a) the Latino vote in the March primary went 66 percent to Feinstein and 8 percent to Campbell, with 24 percent to all others.

In the three surveys before the November election, Feinstein was receiving support from six in ten voters, while only one in three favored Campbell. Among Latinos, six in ten said they would vote for Feinstein, while two in ten would vote for Campbell, and most of the rest were undecided. According to the Voter News Service exit poll (2000), 67 percent of Latinos voted for Feinstein and 24 percent voted for Campbell, while 9 percent chose other candidates. The Latino support for Feinstein was similar in her previous U.S. Senate election wins in 1992 and 1994 and comparable to the support for U.S. Senator Barbara Boxer in 1998.

In the 2000 elections, neither Al Gore nor Dianne Feinstein was able to win a majority of the white vote, but they both walked to easy victories in the statewide totals. Once again, the difference was that there were now more Latinos in the electorate, voting in concert with other non-whites, and thus more votes for the Democrats. At this point, Latinos do not yet have the political strength on their own to tilt partisan outcomes.

As of this writing, one of the most significant facts about the Latino vote is that it is one of the few large and growing voting groups that is still *somewhat* up for grabs. Upper-income and older white voters are solidly Republican, blacks are strongly Democratic, and the Asian vote is not that large. The two major parties are still making a strong play for the Latino vote, seeing in this group a power and influence that goes beyond its current size and hoping that they can attract a sizable number of new voters.

LATINOS IN ELECTED OFFICE

Latino candidates have achieved some notable successes in recent California elections. The highest elected position held by a Latino is the lieutenant governor's office, which was won by Cruz Bustamante in 1998. Two of the past three speakers of the state assembly have also been Latinos—Cruz Bustamante and Antonio Villaraigosa.

The number of Latinos holding federal, state, and local elected office in California increased dramatically in the past two decades. There were 460 Latinos holding elected office in 1984, and that number increased to 789 in 1998. This includes federal, state, and local elected representatives. At the same time, there has been a large increase in Asian office holders—from about 100 to 500—while blacks have held steady in a range between 200 to 300 elected office holders. Latino office holders now actually outnumber the Asian and black office holders combined (see Reyes, 2001).

Why the upsurge in Latino representation? There are more districts than in the past represented by a majority-minority makeup or a majority of Latino voters (Gay, 2001), and moreover, in 1990 the voters enacted term limits for their state legislators. One possibility is that the turnover in the state senate and state assembly has benefited Latino candidates, who might have otherwise had to wait to run for office until incumbents to retired or legislative district boundaries had been redrawn after the 2000 census.

Indeed, twenty of the eighty seats in the state assembly, and seven in forty of the seats in the state senate were held by Latinos after the 2000 elections. The fact that Latinos held one in four seats in the state assembly is particularly impressive. Latinos also held six of the U.S. House seats in California after the 2000 election. (See Table 6-6).

The partisanship of Latino state and federal representatives only reinforces the problems that Republicans are having with demographic change in the state. In looking at the racial and ethnic composition of the legislative offices, we find a serious shortage of Latinos. While Democrats have become increasingly diverse along racial and ethnic lines, Republicans have not.

TABLE 6.6   LATINO ELECTED OFFICIALS
AFTER THE 2000 ELECTIONS

	Seats	Latinos	Whites	Blacks	Asians
U.S. Congress	52	6	40	4	2
Democrats	32	6	20	4	2
Republicans	20	0	20	0	0
State senate	40	7	31	2	0
Democrats	26	7	17	2	0
Republicans	14	0	14	0	0
State assembly	80	20	53	4	3
Democrats	50	16	27	4	3
Republicans	30	4	26	0	0

SOURCE: California Secretary of State (2000c); PPIC Just the Facts (2000b).

Among the fifty-two members of the California congressional delegation after the 2000 election, twelve were either Latino, Asian, or black. All of the nonwhite members of the delegation were Democrats. Looking at it another way, twelve of the thirty Democrats in the House seats were nonwhites, while all twenty Republicans were white. As for the state senate, nine of the forty members were Latino or black. All of the nonwhite members were Democrats. While nine of the twenty-six Democrats were Latino or Asian, all of the Republicans were white. In the state assembly, twenty-seven of the eighty members were Latino, Asian, or black, making this the most diverse legislative body in the state. Twenty-three of the twenty-seven nonwhite members of the state assembly were Democrats. In all, the Democratic membership was split between whites and nonwhites (27 to 23), while twenty-six of the thirty Republican members of the state assembly were white.

The racial and ethnic trends for legislative officials point to the difficulties that the GOP is having in their efforts to reach out to the Latino voters in the state. With no nonwhite members in Congress or the state senate and only a few Latinos in the state assembly the GOP is presenting the image of a party that is seemingly not inclusive. Latino voters who are looking for GOP representatives from their own ethnic group to support in elections will find few to choose from in legislative elections in California.

Latinos also garnered important gains in local representation at the turn of the century. The elected mayors of two of California's largest cities were Latino—Miguel Pulido in Santa Ana and Ron Gonzales in San Jose. Gloria Molina was elected county supervisor in Los Angeles, and Rocky Delgadillo was elected Los Angeles city attorney. Notably, there was also a Democratic setback in the city of Los Angeles in 2001. Antonio Villaraigosa received the most votes in the primary and many expected him to win. However, he lost the runoff to a city official, James Hahn. Villaraigosa lost the election despite the fact than nearly half of the city is Latino. The reasons point to why Latinos are lagging in political power. While Latino voting has increased, only one-quarter of the electorate in the 2001 runoff was Latino. Non-Latinos supported Hahn, pointing to the Latinos' continued reliance on multiracial coalitions.

Latinos still account for only about one in ten of all office holders, and that is well below the percentage of Latinos in the population, Latino adults in the population, and Latino adults eligible to vote. In fact, Latinos, Asians, and blacks are all underrepresented in the ranks of federal, state, and local elected representatives, even though they have gained much success at the ballot box in recent years (see Reyes, 2001).

LATINOS AND THE INITIATIVE PROCESS

The initiative process is an electoral area in which Latino voters have had a more mixed record in recent years. Overall, Hajnal and Louch (2001) point to a pattern over time of Latinos not being on the winning side of initiatives as often as whites. This outcome has been most likely for initiatives with racial and ethnic dimensions. Three initiatives that passed despite Latino opposition exemplify this pattern:

- Proposition 187, which denied public services to illegal immigrants and their children, passed overwhelmingly by 59 percent to 41 percent. Two in three whites and the majority of Asians and blacks supported this initiative, while only one-third of Latinos voted in favor of it (see Clark, 1998).
- Proposition 209, the initiative that banned affirmative action programs in government, passed by 55 percent to 45 percent. Two in three whites supported it. As a result, it passed despite the fact that the overwhelming majority of Latinos, Asians, and blacks voted against it (Chavez, 1998).
- Proposition 227, the initiative that ended bilingual education programs in the public schools, passed by 61 percent to 39 percent. Two in three whites supported it, as did a majority of

Asians, while blacks were evenly divided and only one-third of
Latinos voted for the initiative (*Los Angeles Times*/CNN exit
poll, 1998).

The fate of two statewide initiatives on the March 2000 primary ballot demonstrates both the distinct voter preferences of Latinos and their
potential effects on policymaking through the state's initiative process.
Latinos are socially conservative in a state where most white voters are
socially liberal, and Latinos are also fiscally liberal in a state where most
white voters are fiscally conservative. These predilections put Latinos
even more at odds with the majority of voters in California, who are
white. Yet the outcomes of these initiatives indicate that these positions
sometimes place Latinos on the winning side of initiatives that most
Democrats oppose and other times places them on the losing side of initiatives that most other voters support.

Proposition 22, the "limit on marriage" initiative, required that only
a marriage between a man and a woman would be recognized in California. The PPIC Statewide Surveys (1999c, 2000a, 2000b) showed this
measure consistently winning by large margins, with Latinos supporting
it by a two-to-one margin, even while fellow Democrats opposed it.
Proposition 26, the local majority vote for school bonds, sought to
reduce the vote needed to pass school bonds from a two-thirds to a
simple-majority vote. The last two PPIC Statewide Surveys (2000a,
2000b) before the March primary showed Proposition 26 losing by a
slim margin, while a strong majority of Latinos supported it.

The elections confirmed these outcomes and voting trends (*Los Angeles
Times* exit poll, 2000a). Proposition 22, the ban on gay marriages, passed,
overwhelmingly supported by "all voters" and Latinos but not by Democrats. Proposition 26, the local majority vote for school bonds vote, failed
by a slim margin, even while six in ten Latinos voted in favor of the measure. If there had been a larger turnout among Latinos, Proposition 26
would probably have had enough support to pass in the March primary.

The November 2000 ballot included two education reform measures.
Supporters of the "school vouchers' initiative" (Proposition 38) and the
"55 percent local vote for school bonds" initiative (Proposition 39) targeted the Latino vote because they were expecting a large turnout from
this group. The initial enthusiasm for school vouchers that we found in
early surveys diminished rapidly over time, and the same pattern held
for Latino voters (PPIC Statewide Surveys, 2000e, 2000f, 2000g). Seven
in ten Latinos voted against school vouchers on election day, similar to

the trends among all voters (*Los Angeles Times* exit poll, 2000b). In the two surveys prior to the election, we found close to a majority supporting the 55 percent vote on local school bonds, helped in large part by strong support among Latinos and other nonwhite voters. On election day, Proposition 39 passed by 53 percent to 47 percent, primarily because six in ten Latinos, Asians, and blacks supported it; only 50 percent of whites voted for the measure (*Los Angeles Times* exit poll, 2000b). A fiscally liberal measure that was twice defeated by a more predominantly white electorate had narrowly passed, demonstrating the potential for nonwhites to influence outcomes when they have similar voting preferences in statewide initiatives.

MORE TRUST IN GOVERNMENT

Latinos' fiscal liberality is consistent with their greater trust in government at all levels. Californians overall distrust the federal government's ability to perform its functions. (See Table 6-7.) Fewer than one in three said the federal government can be trusted always or most of the time, while most thought that Washington can only sometimes be trusted to do what is right. In contrast, nearly half of Latinos said that they trust the federal government either always or most of the time. Whites, blacks, and Asians all expressed a lower degree of trust in the federal government than Latinos. U.S.-born Latinos were less trusting than those who are naturalized citizens, but even they trusted government more than Californians as a whole.

The vast majority of California residents believed that people in government waste the money paid in taxes, and six in ten thought they wasted a lot of it. Latinos were less likely than whites to hold this point of view. Slightly more than half of Latinos thought the government wastes a lot of money. Latinos were more confident than others in the fiscal performance of government even after we controlled for other factors.

Two in three residents believed that the federal government is pretty much run by a few big interests looking out for themselves. While seven in ten whites held this negative view of Washington, only about half of Latinos were of the opinion that their government is run by and for special interests. Latinos also had a little more faith than others that the federal government pays at least some attention to what the people think when it decides what to do, and they were much more likely than whites to have at least some confidence that when the federal government de-

TABLE 6.7   LATINOS AND
GOVERNMENT TRUST

	All Adults	Latinos	Whites
"Federal Government can be trusted always or most of the time"	32%	49%	27%
"Government wastes a lot of money we pay in taxes"	58	51	61
"Government run by a few big interests looking out for themselves"	64	53	68

SOURCE: PPIC Statewide Survey (2000a, 2000e, 2000g), all adults.

cides to solve a problem that the problem will actually be solved (PPIC Statewide Survey, 2000g).

Latinos also tended to hold their state government in higher regard than other Californians did. The trend was consistent when we repeated the questions we asked about overall trust, fiscal performance, special interests, and problem solving at the federal level (PPIC Statewide Survey, 2001a). About half of Latinos said that they trust the state government to do what is right always or most of the time, compared with four in ten whites. Only four in ten Latinos believed the state government wastes a lot of the taxpayers' money, in contrast to half of the white respondents. About half of Latinos believed that the state government is run by big interests looking out for themselves, compared with six in ten whites. Latinos were a little more likely than whites to have confidence that when the state government decides to solve a problem, the problem will be solved.

Latinos were less cynical about the way in which the election process affects policymaking in California, both for statewide candidates and initiatives. For example, two in three whites said that the fact that there were virtually no limits on campaign contributions in state and legislative elections was a "bad thing" in making state laws and policies. By contrast, only one in three Latinos saw the lack of stringent campaign finance laws in a negative light. Similarly, nearly six in ten whites perceived the initiative process in California to be controlled by special interests. Only four in ten Latinos held this pessimistic view of citizens' initiatives (PPIC Statewide Surveys, 2000e, 2001a).[14]

14. A series of multiple regressions controlling for age, education, income, gender, party, and citizenship, indicate Latinos are more likely to trust the government to do what

MORE PRAISE FOR ELECTED OFFICIALS

Latinos were more likely than other Californians to praise state and federal officials. This is consistent with their greater feelings of trust and confidence in government. Californians gave President Bill Clinton high marks through the final years of the presidency, even during the ordeals of a sex scandal, House impeachment, and a Senate trial. In six surveys we conducted between October 1998 and October 2000, about six in ten residents consistently said the president was doing an excellent or good job in office. Latinos were constant in their greater approval than whites of the president. In the last survey before the end of the Clinton presidency, seven in ten Latinos thought the president was doing an excellent or good job compared with half of our white respondents. One possibility is that the higher ratings among Latinos were a result of their higher registration rates as Democrats. However, since these surveys interviewed all adults, they included many Latinos who were not registered to vote and thus who may not have necessarily had Democratic leanings. Nonetheless, we found that Latinos were more positive than others toward the president, even after controlling for political party.

Further confirmation of the possibility that Latinos' ratings of federal elected officials derive from their more positive attitudes toward government and not from partisan leanings is seen in the legislative ratings. In six surveys we conducted between October 1998 and October 2000, fewer than four in ten Californians rated the performance of the U.S. Congress as excellent or good. During this time, the Republicans led the House of Representatives and U.S. Senate. The last survey in this series was indicative of the trend we saw throughout this two-year period: About half of Latinos rated the Congress as excellent or good, compared with one in three whites. Again, this trend persisted even after we controlled for party, socioeconomic status, and citizenship.

We saw confirming evidence of Latinos' positive attitudes toward federal elected officials in other survey responses. For instance, residents were asked to rate U.S. Senator Dianne Feinstein's job performance in the course of her reelection campaign. In all, a little over half of Californians approved of the job the senator was doing, but six in ten Lati-

---

is right ($B = .73$) at the .001 significance level, less likely to believe that the government does not waste much money ($B = .26$) at the .07 significance level, and less likely to think that the lack of campaign contribution limits is a bad thing ($B = .58$) at the .001 significance level. The same trend was evident for the role of special interests but was not statistically significant. See also Hajnal and Baldassare (2001).

nos gave her positive marks compared with half of our white respondents. When it came to rating their own representative to the U.S. House of Representatives, a little under half said their legislator was doing an excellent or good job. Once again, Latinos were more generous than whites were in their evaluations (PPIC Statewide Surveys, 2000b, 2000f).

If these patterns persist, we would also expect that the state's elected officials be viewed more favorably by Latinos. In surveys conducted in September and October 2000 and in January 2001, about six in ten Californians said they approved of the job Governor Gray Davis was doing. In each of these three instances, Latinos gave the governor much higher marks than whites did. A good example of this trend was reflected in our September 2000 survey—when two in three Latinos approved of the governor's performance in office, compared with about half of the white respondents. Moreover, the governor's ratings on the handling of specific issues—crime and punishment, the state budget and taxes, education, transportation, the electricity problem, and health care reform—were consistently higher among Latinos than whites (PPIC Statewide Survey, 2001a). Again, Davis enjoyed higher ratings among Latinos than others, even when controlling for party registration, socioeconomic status, and citizenship.

Ratings of the state legislature showed a generally positive trend, with similar variations across groups. In two surveys that we conducted in the fall of 2000 and early in 2001, just under six in ten residents approved of the job the California legislature was doing. Latinos were much more glowing in their reviews than were the white respondents. For instance, in September 2000, three in four Latinos approved of the job being done by the state legislature, compared with less than two in three whites (PPIC Statewide Surveys, 2000f, 2001a). Again, the trend is significant, even after taking political party and other personal characteristics into account.[15]

POSITIVE ATTITUDES TOWARD GOVERNMENT REGULATIONS

The fact that Latinos hold a more trusting view toward government and have a more favorable attitude about their elected officials would seem

15. Latinos are significantly more positive than others toward the president, Congress, governor, and state legislature after controlling for age, education, income, gender, political party, and citizenship in multiple regression analysis. See also Hajnal and Baldassare (2001).

to have very important implications for the kinds of public policies they would prefer. This, in itself, could have major implications for public policy directions. Most Californians distrust government involvement and thus assume that less government is better. Most also view government officials as less than competent and, furthermore, do not want government intrusion in their personal lives. Latinos feel differently and have less of a problem with the notion of government playing a more active role in regulating economic, social, and even personal-choice interests. These differences were borne out in Latino attitudes toward government regulations during the 2000 elections.[16]

Californians as a whole were generally ambivalent about government involvement in the private sector. They were about equally likely to say that "government regulation of business is necessary to protect the public interest" as to agree that "government regulation of business often does more harm than good" (see Table 6-8). In fact, Americans in general were about evenly divided in their attitudes toward business regulations. This is not the case among Latinos in California, most of whom believed that government regulation of business is needed to protect the public interest. In this respect, Latinos were distinct from whites, most of whom felt that government regulation of business often does more harm than good.

The favorable attitudes Latinos had toward regulation of business extended to land use and development decisions. When asked to choose between two values—individual property rights and government regulation of development—Californians favored individual property rights by a large margin. Americans as a whole leaned even more heavily toward the idea that individuals should be able to do what they want with their own land. Latinos, however, were evenly divided on this issue, with nearly half saying it is more important for the government to regulate development for the common good. By contrast, whites in California leaned heavily toward the idea that individual rights have the top priority.

16. For business regulations, see PPIC Statewide Survey (2000b) and 1999 national survey by the Pew Research Center; for land use, see PPIC Statewide Survey (2000c) and 1999 national survey by the Yankelovich Partners; for both abortion regulations and gun controls, see PPIC Statewide Survey (2000a) and 1999 national survey by the *Wall Street Journal* and NBC News; for more gun control laws, see PPIC Statewide Survey (2000f) and 2000 national survey by Fox News/Opinion Dynamics; for HMO reforms, see PPIC Statewide Survey (2000b) and 1999 national survey by the Pew Research Center; for health care for the uninsured, see PPIC Statewide Survey (2000b) and 2000 national survey by the Kaiser Family Foundation.

TABLE 6.8   LATINOS AND GOVERNMENT
REGULATIONS

	All Adults	Latinos	Whites
"Government regulation of business is necessary to protect the public interest"	46%	57%	41%
"Government should pass more laws that restrict the availability of abortion"	27	41	23
"Federal government should create standards for HMO patients rights"	63	75	57
"Government does not do enough to regulate guns"	62	70	59

SOURCE: PPIC Statewide Survey (2000a, 2000b), all adults.

On another controversial issue, in this case involving government regulation of private activities, the overwhelming majority of state residents have long held pro-choice positions on abortion. In a January 2000 survey, only three in ten residents wanted the government to pass more laws restricting abortion, while seven in ten thought the government should not interfere with a woman's right to abortion. Latinos differed sharply from fellow Democrats on this issue of abortion regulations, with more of them than even Republicans holding antiabortion positions. Four in ten Latinos thought the government should pass more restrictive laws with regard to abortion, while fewer than one in four whites felt this way. One might argue that it was their socially conservative or religious and cultural background that influenced Latinos in their opinions about abortion. Nonetheless, their policy preferences on this issue reflect a certain willingness to allow the government to intervene in private decisions.

Most Californians have reached the point of fearing gun violence so much that they have for some time favored greater government restrictions on gun ownership. Their pro–gun control attitudes were in line with those expressed by Americans as a whole. Two in three Californians believed that "the government does not do enough to regulate access to guns," while just one in three residents felt that "the government goes too far in regulating access to guns." On this issue, Latinos were even more overwhelmingly in favor than whites of increasing government regulation of guns.

We also asked residents what they thought was more likely to reduce gun violence—better enforcement of existing laws or more laws and re-

strictions on obtaining guns. This provided another opportunity to identify preferences for more government regulations. A solid majority of
Californians chose better enforcement, while only one in three preferred
more laws. In fact, state residents were more likely than the nation as a
whole to think that the answer lies in better enforcement of existing laws.
Latinos were more divided on this issue and thus much more supportive than whites of having more laws and restrictions on guns.

Latino support for more government involvement is also evident in
their responses to the issue of health care reform. By a two-to-one margin, Californians agreed that the federal government ought to create standards to protect the rights of patients in HMOs and managed health care
plans. Only one in three believed that such efforts would get the federal
government too involved in health care. Californians were similar to
most Americans in their desire for more government involvement in
HMOs and managed care. While a solid majority of whites were in favor
of more government regulations, Latinos were overwhelmingly supportive of this proposal for health care reform.

When asked their preference for providing guaranteed health insurance coverage for all Americans, half of Californians felt it would be better to build on the existing health care system, in which working people
get health care coverage from their employers and the government is involved in providing care for the poor and unemployed. Fewer were interested in switching to a private system in which all individuals buy their
own health insurance and those who could not afford to buy a plan
would receive a tax credit or subsidy. The policy choice was between
having the government or a private system provide the health care for
the uninsured. Californians were even more inclined than Americans as
a whole to want the current level of government involvement continued.
Moreover, we see the consistent pattern of greater support among Latinos than whites for having the government involved in the health care
decisions for the uninsured.

In areas in which one might expect limited Latino support for increased
government involvement, because there could be personally adverse economic consequences, Latinos' strong tendency to support government
regulations still took precedence. One such issue is environmental regulations. Since Latinos had lower socioeconomic status and more limited
job opportunities, one might expect a greater reluctance to support regulations that would limit jobs and economic growth. In fact, such was
not the case. Two in three Californians said that "stricter environmental
laws and regulations are worth the cost," and only one in three believed

that "stricter environmental laws and regulations cost too many jobs and hurt the economy." Latinos were as likely as whites to say that environmental laws and regulations are worth the cost, with only one in three worrying about the impact that government regulations in the environmental arena might have on their jobs.

We might expect that Latinos more than others would favor school vouchers, because taxpayer vouchers could be used to pay for private and religious schools, presumably benefiting many Roman Catholic and lower-income Latinos whose children might be attending underperforming public schools. Californians were equally divided when asked if "government funding should be limited to children who attend public school." Interestingly, Latinos and whites were equally likely to think that government funding should be limited to public schools. The voucher issue speaks to the high regard that Latinos have for public institutions such as the public schools, even when weighed against the possibility of making private school options more likely for themselves.[17]

One final piece of evidence regarding Latinos and their preference for government involvement comes from a series of questions on income inequality. In a survey after the 1998 election, we established the fact that most Californians saw the state divided into two economic groups—the haves and the have nots—and there was no difference in this perception between Latinos and other groups (PPIC Statewide Survey, 1999a). When asked whether the government should do more to make sure that all Californians have an equal opportunity to succeed, fewer than half of the state's residents agreed that this was the right approach, while slightly more than half felt that the government need not do anything because people already have an equal opportunity to succeed. Interestingly, the majority of Latinos felt that the government should do more to assure equal opportunity, while only four in ten whites agreed. Once again, Latinos expressed a more accepting attitude than others toward government involvement in both social and economic issues. This could result in a major shift in the political status quo if Latino voting increases and Latino preferences for a more active government role are expressed at the ballot box.[18]

17. For environmental regulations, see PPIC Statewide Survey (2000a) and the 2000 national survey by the Pew Research Center; for school vouchers, see PPIC Statewide Survey (2000a) and the 1999 national survey by the *Wall Street Journal* and NBC News.

18. In a series of multiple regression controlling for party, age, education, income, gender, and citizenship, Latinos were significantly more likely to want the government to restrict abortion ($B = .32$), do more to regulate guns ($B = .32$), and create federal standards

MORE GOVERNMENT SPENDING

There are several reasons why we would expect Latinos to favor more government spending when it comes to programs. Their positive impressions of government and its elected officials would make them more inclined to feel confident that government funds would be used efficiently and effectively for specific purposes. The fact that Latinos were heavily registering as Democrats rather than Republicans placed them in the company of voters who were ideologically in favor of more government funding for schools, health care, and social services. The inclination of Latinos to have a more active and involved government would also lead them in the direction of supporting more public spending. Lastly, the fact that many Latinos were lower-income workers or recent immigrants, and thus represent some of the key constituencies for a variety of social programs, would make them among the prime beneficiaries of increased government funding.

In fact, throughout the election cycle, Latinos were consistently among the groups most in favor of increased government spending. While many Californians were encouraged by talk of tax cuts and a smaller government with fewer services, most Latinos were in favor of using surplus funds to expand the role of government. In this respect, Latinos are having an impact on the state's political landscape, which has been dominated by fiscally conservative attitudes favoring lower spending and reduced taxes.

In early 2000, Californians were divided on the issue of the appropriate use of the federal budget surplus. Half said that the surplus should be used to cut taxes, and half said the surplus should be used to pay for social programs. Americans were similarly split on what to do with the surplus. A solid majority of Latinos wanted the federal government to use the surplus to pay for social programs, while an equally solid majority of whites preferred to see the extra money spent on tax cuts.

At another point, Congress and President Clinton were debating the amount of money in the federal surplus that should be dedicated to a tax cut. The Republican legislative leaders wanted a very large tax cut and smaller increases in federal spending, while the Democratic president proposed a more modest tax cut and larger increases in popular services such as Medicare and educational and environmental programs. Again,

---

for HMO patients (B = .31)—all significant at the .05 level or less. Attitudes toward environmental and business regulations were not significant.

Latinos were much more in favor of increased spending than were Californians as a whole. They favored the prospending plan by a four-to-one margin, while whites supported spending over a larger tax cut by a two-to-one margin (PPIC Statewide Survey, 1999b).

It was also apparent that Latinos placed a higher priority on government spending than shrinking the national debt. In further questioning about how the federal government should use the federal budget surplus over the next several years, we asked residents whether the surplus should be used for an across-the-board tax cut, for reducing the national debt, or for improving funding for needed government programs. Californians were most likely to choose a tax cut first, followed by reducing the debt and, in last place on their wish list, improving government funding. Latinos were much more likely than whites to call for increased spending on government programs and much less likely to favor debt reduction.

With regard to achieving tax cuts, Al Gore and the Democrats made a point of distinguishing their plans from those of George W. Bush and the Republicans. Gore emphasized that his plan targeted the lower- and middle-income families, while Bush stressed that his plan involved tax cuts for all. When asked to choose between these two options, Californians were divided. Latinos showed a solid preference for targeted tax cuts that excluded higher-income households, while whites were divided on this issue.

The desire among Latinos to have the government increase funding and assistance for lower-income families is evident in other survey responses as well. A little more than half of Californians believed that poor people have difficult lives because government benefits do not go far enough to help them live decently, while about four in ten thought that the poor have easy lives because they can get government benefits without doing anything in return. Latinos were much more likely than whites to think that government benefits do not go far enough: six in ten Latinos were of the opinion that government funding for poor people is inadequate, while fewer than half of whites held the view.

Latinos also expressed strong support for government spending on entitlement programs such as Social Security and Medicare. Two in three Californians thought that strengthening the Social Security system should be a higher priority for the next president than cutting taxes. Latinos were only slightly more likely than whites to express a desire to have the president focus on Social Security, since most groups had a strong preference for this policy direction. Another issue on which there was strong agreement among residents statewide was coverage of prescription drugs by Medicare. Three in four Californians wanted prescription drugs covered, even if it meant an increase in premiums for Medicare patients and an increase in costs for the Medicaid program. In this case, Latinos were even more strongly supportive than whites.[19]

PREFERENCE FOR A LARGER GOVERNMENT, MORE SERVICES

The unique orientation of Latinos toward spending by the federal government came into focus most sharply in a question we asked in the weeks before the November 2000 presidential election (see Table 6-9). When asked if they would prefer a smaller government with fewer services or a larger government with many services, the majority of Californians preferred the former to the latter. Although whites preferred a smaller government providing fewer services by a two-to-one margin, six in ten Latinos wanted a larger government with many services.[20]

The inclination of Latinos to support increases for government spending at the federal level extends to state-level funding. After the 1998 gubernatorial elections, we asked Californians to rate four areas of the state budget—K–12 public schools, public colleges and universities, public health and welfare, and prisons and corrections—as high, medium, or low priorities for state spending. Residents overwhelmingly identified public schools as a high priority, and a majority said that higher education and health and welfare were very important; only one in four said that prisons and corrections should receive high priority in state spending. In all instances, Latinos were more likely than whites to rate state programs as high priorities for public spending. There were especially large differences with respect to higher education, health and welfare,

19. For tax cuts, see PPIC Statewide Survey (2000a) and the 1999 national survey by CBS News; for the national debt, see PPIC Statewide Survey (2000f) and the 2000 national survey by the *Wall Street Journal* and NBC News; for targeted tax cuts, see PPIC Statewide Survey (2000g) and the 2000 national survey by the Pew Research Center; for government benefits for the poor, see PPIC Statewide Survey (2000b) and the 1999 national survey by the Pew Research Center; for Social Security and Medicare, see PPIC Statewide Surveys (2000e, 2000f) and the 2000 national surveys by CBS News; for larger government with more services, see PPIC Statewide Survey (2000g) and a 2000 national survey by the ABC News/*Washington Post*.

20. In multiple regressions controlling for age, education, income, party, gender, and citizenship, Latinos were more likely than others to say they preferred a larger government with more services ($B = .29$) at the .03 significance level.

TABLE 6.9   LATINOS AND
GOVERNMENT SPENDING

	All Adults	Latinos	Whites
"Prefer smaller tax cut and larger increases in federal spending"	69%	78%	65%
"Federal budget surplus should be used to pay for social programs"	47	55	44
"Favor Medicare system paying for the cost of prescription drugs"	74	81	73
"Prefer larger government with many services"	39	58	31

SOURCE: PPIC Statewide Survey (1999b, 2000a, 2000f, 2000g), all adults.

and corrections and prisons, since very few Californians ranked K–12 schools as less than a high priority.

The greater desire for state government spending was also evident in future-oriented questions in the same postelection survey. We asked people how important it was for the state government to be spending public funds on various infrastructure needs now in preparation for future population growth. The programs mentioned included building schools, building roads and freeways, and building and expanding water storage facilities. Seven in ten residents said it was very important to build schools, and half believed it was very important to build water systems and roads. In all three cases, Latinos were much more likely than whites to say that it was very important for the state to invest money in the infrastructure (PPIC Statewide Survey, 1999a).

Latinos also expressed a greater interest in state spending on environmental programs than in receiving a tax cut. We asked Californians how they would like to see the state budget surplus allocated after most of the funds are set aside for education and other state programs. A near majority of Californians said they would prefer a conservation trust fund to purchase lands for parks and open space, while almost as many said they wanted to use the remaining surplus to reduce their taxes. A slight majority of Latinos preferred that the state retain the funds for conservation programs, while just shy of a majority of whites supported this position.[21]

21. See PPIC Statewide Survey (2000c) on the state conservation trust fund.

There is also considerable evidence from our statewide surveys that Latinos held a generous attitude toward local government spending. Most of our local questions pertained to the public schools. For instance, seven in ten Californians thought there should be more resources going to low-performing schools—eight in ten Latinos favored this option, compared with six in ten whites. Seven in ten residents said they would support a local school bond to pay for school construction projects; once again, eight in ten Latinos said they would vote for the bond, compared with two in three whites. Latinos were also less favorable than whites toward local tax limitations. While most Californians felt that it was a "good thing" to require a two-thirds vote to raise local property taxes, Latinos were more likely than whites to say the supermajority vote has been a "bad thing."[22]

In sum, Latinos are distinct in their strong and consistent preferences for government spending at the local, state, and federal levels. Their liberal positions on fiscal issues stand in contrast to the state's white voters, who have been inclined to take a hard line against spending and tax increases since Proposition 13 passed in the late 1970s. As Latinos vote in larger numbers, they could tip the balance in local and statewide initiatives concerned with spending for government programs. Moreover, fiscally conservative candidates for statewide office will have to moderate some of their positions, since such attitudes do not reflect the spending preferences of Latino voters.

UPBEAT ECONOMIC OUTLOOK

Although lagging behind whites, blacks, and Asians in socioeconomic achievement, Latinos exceed all groups in California when it comes to positive feelings about their own economic circumstances. These are among the most consistent trends we have noted in our surveys, offering a seemingly contradictory view of the Latino experience in California. On the one hand, socioeconomic statistics offer a discouraging picture of lagging Latino economic outcomes. On the other hand, Latinos are exuding a level of confidence we cannot find in other groups.

Californians were consistently upbeat about the overall condition of the state and their own financial circumstances throughout the late 1990s

22. See PPIC Statewide Surveys (2000a, 2000b) in January and February 2000 on local government spending.

and the 2000 election cycle. Once again, Latinos led the way in terms of expressing the most positive sentiments.

By a two-to-one margin, Californians were more likely to say that the state was headed in the right direction rather than the wrong direction. This was consistent across all of the PPIC Statewide Surveys conducted between April 1998 and January 2001. The trend was the same in every survey wave: Latinos were always significantly more positive about the state of the state than whites were. Over time, about seven in ten Latinos said the state was headed in the right direction, in contrast to six in ten whites.

The differences between Latinos and other Californians were even more striking when we asked people about the trends in their personal financial situation. In surveys conducted in September 1999 and September 2000, we asked residents how their financial situation compared with their situation a year earlier and whether they thought they would be better off financially a year from now. Four in ten residents reported that they were better off financially than they were a year earlier. About half of Latinos felt they were better off, compared with one in three white respondents. Similarly, almost half of Californians believed they would be better off a year from now. Almost six in ten Latinos expected to see financial improvements in the year ahead, compared with only four in ten whites. The variation between groups is accounted for by more Latinos reporting that they had experienced or would experience improvements, while more whites felt that their financial condition had not or would not change.[23]

OPTIMISM ABOUT THE STATE'S FUTURE

The long-term perspective of Latinos on the state of the state is remarkably more optimistic than the views expressed by others. In looking out to the year 2020, half of whites believed the state will be a worse place to live compared with only one in three Latinos. Latinos were considerably more likely than whites to foresee the state as a better place to live. Latinos were also much more likely than whites to believe that the pub-

23. Latinos are more positive than others about their current finances ($B = .35$), future finances ($B = .36$), and the direction of the state ($B = .36$) at the .001 significance level, taking into account age, gender, education, income, and citizenship in multiple regression analysis. See also Hajnal and Baldassare (2001).

lic education system will improve, that the quality of the natural environment will get better, and that the gap between the rich and the poor will get smaller in their region. The two groups had similarly optimistic outlooks on the likelihood that race and ethnic relations will improve, that jobs and economic conditions will improve, and that the crime rate will decrease by the year 2020 (PPIC Statewide Survey, 1999d).

In sum, Latinos offered an upbeat assessment of the economic conditions as well as the political conditions in the state. The Latino trends were similar when it came to evaluations of their own financial circumstances. Their optimism was far and away greater than the views expressed by the rest of the public. Latinos have raised the level of confidence and optimism overall in the state. In fact, the continued growth of the Latino population gives rise to the prospects of an improving public mood in California. More optimistic feelings about the economy and the state are generally related to a greater willingness to increase government spending and taxes. Once again, the greater prominence of Latino attitudes could have implications for the role of government.

A mysterious element in the high levels of trust and optimism among Latinos is that the views were being expressed by a group that was underachieving in both political and economic terms. Why Latinos had more positive sentiments is unknown, but one possibility is their relative improvement in circumstances over time. Many of the Mexican immigrants have left a country where politics have historically been dominated by one-party rule and corruption scandals and where poverty and joblessness are common outcomes. So the American political and economic system certainly must look good by comparison. Moreover, many Latinos have seen improvements in their economic circumstances and political involvement in recent years, and this has generated positive feelings and hope.

CONCLUSIONS AND IMPLICATIONS

In so many ways, knowledge of the Latino population is crucial to understanding the social and political changes under way in California today. The state's population growth, racial and ethnic change, and shifts in the political landscape are largely a result of an increasing Latino presence. There are major advantages of the state undergoing a demographic transition in combination with economic prosperity. The public remains well aware of the fact that racial and ethnic change is occurring in their midst and that immigration has fundamentally changed the population composition of their regions. Yet most Californians are comfortable with these racial and ethnic changes, and they have grown much more positive toward the overall effects of immigration and racial and ethnic diversity in the state, after a very rocky start during the last economic downturn.

Latinos are beginning to change the look of politics in the Golden State. As their numbers grow, so does their presence as voters at the ballot box and as elected representatives in local, state, and federal offices. Statewide candidates, legislators, and initiative campaigners are paying an increasing amount of attention to Latino voters. We find that Latinos do not fit the typical profile of California voters who are liberal on social issues and conservative on fiscal issues. In emphasizing a broad role for government, they present a different trend from that of postmaterialist values and the New Political Culture. In recent California elections, Democratic candidates and spending initiatives appeared to be the main beneficiaries of the growing Latino political clout.

In the 2000 elections, most Latino voters described themselves as registered Democrats who were moderate to liberal in their politics. The Democratic party once again benefited from the overwhelming support their candidates received from Latinos in the presidential, U.S. Senate, and legislative races. Latinos joined other voters in the state in passing an initiative to ban gay marriages and in rejecting an initiative offering a school voucher system. Latino voters, along with blacks and Asians, were the groups whose support made it possible to pass an initiative that made it easier to approve local school bonds. This victory came after two earlier defeats by an electorate dominated by whites, demonstrating the possibilities of new multiracial/ethnic coalitions in the state.

Yet the possibilities of coalitions must be examined in light of the fact that Latinos differ from other Californians in critical attitudes toward government and do not toe a partisan line. Latinos are distinct from other Californians in their more trusting attitude toward all levels of government in terms of both overall performance and fiscal responsibility. Latinos are more likely than others to approve of the jobs that elected officials are doing and to look favorably on government involvement in aspects of their personal lives and in the regulation of businesses. Latinos are more willing to see their government spend money and raise taxes to address a variety of social problems. However, Latinos also support some socially conservative proposals, such as restricting abortions or banning same-sex marriages. This makes it difficult to apply the normal political categorizations of left or right: Latinos appear to be distinct from other Californians in their liberal fiscal preferences and their conservative social attitudes.

Latinos are also more likely than others to think that the state is in good shape, that their own financial circumstances will show improvement, and that California's future will be a bright one. It is likely that this attitude reflects the immigrant experience. To some extent, their optimism is derived from improving economic conditions. Whatever the reasons, Latinos have injected a more positive tone at a time when public attitudes have become decidedly pessimistic and cynical toward government.

Despite these positive attitudes, the effects that Latinos will have on social, economic, and political trends is not at all certain. We are at a critical juncture, because the reasons to be optimistic or pessimistic about the state's future depend on what happens next with Latinos. Many of the challenges the state faces affect Latinos more than other groups. When the topic turns to the state's public school system, whatever problems exist fall disproportionately on Latino children, who represent a large and growing proportion of all students. When it comes to the issues of lack of job training for a high-tech economy, of bridging the digital divide, or of the income gap between rich and poor, it is Latinos who are most affected. When we are referring to the needs for health care for the uninsured or to public assistance programs for poor families, once again, Latinos are the crucial group to which these apply.

In recent years, many political observers have been keen on describing Latinos as a "sleeping giant that has awakened." It is true that voter registration and exit polls point to increasing political participation among Latinos, as do also the number of elected Latinos in federal, state, and local offices. However, compared with whites, Latinos are still vastly underrepresented in every aspect of the political process.

They are also vastly underrepresented among the state's economically privileged. Latinos did not fully participate in the economic boom of the late 1990s—lacking the college education and skills that bring access to high-paying jobs, home ownership, the stock market, and the Internet economy. Thus, growing income inequality poses a real threat as the state moves into the Latino century. If current patterns of social and economic inequalities persist, placing Latinos on the bottom rungs of the income and education ladders, then the state's economic future could be a bleak one. Latinos' prospects are in doubt today. The ability to achieve any real, significant changes probably rests on the success of current efforts to improve the state's public educational system and on the hope of future periods of prosperity.

Many questions are raised by the current political trends involving Latinos. Will their trusting and progovernment attitudes change with assimilation? Maybe not, given that their attitudes toward government trust, regulations, and spending did not change when we controlled for socioeconomic status, age, and citizenship. But those who have studied postmaterialist values and the New Political Culture would think otherwise. Will Latino voting increase without a big jump in income and educational attainment? Certainly it could, since many Latinos were mobilized to vote in response to Proposition 187.

However, Latinos' moving into the middle class in large numbers— and, with it, gaining high-paying jobs, buying a home, reading newspapers more frequently, and logging on to the Internet—offers the most likely scenario for increased voting on a regular basis. Moreover, if their positive predisposition toward government persists in light of increased voting, then Latinos may offer the best chance of changing the politics of government distrust that have dominated California politics for twenty years.

There are other large issues at stake besides the future of the political climate of government distrust, however. At this point, the grim prospect exists that, lacking substantial socioeconomic gains, Latinos could fall still further behind in voting in elections and representation in political offices. They could be further underrepresented in the all-important initiative process. All of this means that policy decisions that affect the large Latino population would be handled by others. But if Latinos are able to achieve a more prominent role in politics in the next two decades, they will have a strong voice not only in their own destiny but also in the future of the Golden State.

The Un-Party State

Should he or should he not? This was the big question on the minds of GOP political consultants as they pondered the possibility of George W. Bush's spending his time battling in the presidential race in California. Bush did spend millions of dollars on television commercials, but he gained little traction from these efforts.

Will he or will he not? Al Gore's supporters wondered if they would ever see their candidate set foot in the Golden State. During the closing moments of the fall campaign, Bill Clinton was sent out to California to do one last victory lap, while Gore focused his efforts on Florida and the "battleground" states. While the nation was riveted by the closest presidential race in memory, California's election night was dull and predictable. Once again, the Democrats romped to victory, thus raising the specter of California becoming a one-party state.[1]

It was not always this way. The Democrats used to be the party of perpetual loss. After Proposition 13 passed, the Reagan Revolution ruled in California. The GOP had a winning streak of three victories in presidential elections and four victories in gubernatorial elections. Political observers wrote off the Democratic party, both in terms of its national

---

1. I was informed by many news stories and reports on the major parties in California's elections, including Barabak (2000); Benson (2000); Broder (2000a, 2000b); Chance (2000); Chance and Balzar (2000); Coile (2000); Decker (2000); Jeffe (1999, 2000b, 2000c); Mendel (2000); Schneider (2001); Schwieren (1999); Shields (2000); Skelton (2000a, 2000c, 2000d); Unz (2000); and Walters (2000a, 2000b).

platform and its most visible leaders—too liberal for the state. The voters were fiscally conservative, law-and-order, and hawkish on military issues. They lined up solidly with the Republicans in fighting communism, crime, and big government. California was thought to be safely in the hands of the GOP—until the state's voters became disillusioned with the first Bush administration during a deep recession.

The pendulum swung toward the Democrats in the mid-1990s. The state's economy was in the midst of prolonged prosperity, and budget deficits were giving way to surpluses. The Cold War was over, and there were no significant military threats on the horizon. Crime was declining, and city streets were safer to walk at night. The earlier fears of tax increases had given way to the possibility of increased spending on neglected items such as schools, freeways, and health care. Suddenly, the Democratic party was back in favor.

To explain this shift, many people pointed to the fact that changing demography had fundamentally altered political life and elections in the Golden State. The white population had been the dominant group at the voting booth ever since Americans had begun venturing out west in search of the California Dream, and this group had a substantial following in the GOP and conservative camps. However, in the 1990s, other racial and ethnic groups, offended by the GOP's recent stance on race and immigration policies, began to exert their influence in elections. New Latino and Asian voters joined blacks in finding the Democratic party a more welcoming home. Thus the argument went.

However, this argument is too simplistic. As we have noted before, even though the state had reached majority-minority status, voters in the state remained overwhelmingly white. Clearly, racial and ethnic trends were a factor in the growing strength of the Democratic party, but they could not explain, in and of themselves, the sizable GOP losses.

If California were a safely Democratic state, for whatever reasons, it would have major implications for national politics. California is the state with the largest population, biggest economy, most voters, largest congressional delegation, and most electors in the electoral college. George W. Bush proved that you could win a national election without taking California and without winning the popular vote. But he demonstrated how difficult it is to gather enough electors to do so.

Still, both parties' establishments fretted over the national media stereotype that California was not in play in 2000. The state's elected officials had just moved up the presidential primary so that California could be a part of the presidential selection process. The state's Democrats boasted about the national party convention being held in Los Angeles. The state's Republicans had pleaded with then–Texas Governor Bush to run for president in the hope that he could heal the wounds inflicted by former Governor Pete Wilson's anti–illegal immigrant stances and attract Latino voters to the GOP. In the end, the California presidential election was as dramatic as statewide races are in Hawaii for Democrats or Utah for Republicans. It fueled the perception that California had transitioned from conservative-Republican to liberal-Democrat.

This chapter examines the convincing evidence against the popular notion that California has become politically irrelevant and has entered a new era as a one-party state in the "Democrat" column. The more important trend—and the one accounting for the recent history of support swinging from the GOP to the Democrats—is the emergence of the "un-party" state in these times of distrustful voters. By this we mean that the growing political clout has come to rest outside of the major parties—in the dual form of independent voters and an enthusiastic use of the initiative process. The compelling reasons for this political trend are, once again, found in the power forces at work in postmaterialist values and the New Political Culture (Clark, 1998; Inglehart, 1998) that were discussed in earlier chapters. In California, the state's mostly affluent voters have gravitated in prosperous times toward a political philosophy that includes a weak party loyalty and an issue-oriented focus in voters' ballot choices. The growth of voter registration outside of the major parties and the fluid formation of loose political coalitions through the initiative process provide validation of a new and politically unpredictable trend toward an un-party state, and they counter the conventional wisdom that there has been a consolidation of political power by one party.

THE DEMOCRATS: WINNING WAYS IN THE 1990S

How low can you go? The Republican party thought it had hit bottom after the 1998 statewide election. All of the state constitutional offices were up for election, as they are every four years, and one U.S. Senate seat had entered the contest. Beyond that, there were the congressional elections, all of the state assembly seats, and half of the state senate seats. President Bill Clinton was seemingly on the ropes, caught in the middle of an embarrassing episode of sex and lies under oath and on the verge of House impeachment and a Senate trial. But the president's troubles did not matter. Californians liked Clinton and showed overwhelming support for Democrats in 1998.

By the time the 2000 election rolled around, Democrats were firmly in control of the state. The Republicans had lost every statewide race but two in 1998—insurance commissioner and secretary of state. Many of the Democratic victories, such as the governor's race, were won by large margins (Baldassare, 2000). As if there were not enough problems for the Grand Old Party, Insurance Commissioner Chuck Quackenbush had been embroiled in a financial scandal leading to his resignation in 2000, leaving Secretary of State Bill Jones as the lone GOP survivor. The Democrats were in control of the governor's office, both U.S. Senate seats, the lieutenant governor's office, and the offices of the attorney general, the controller, the insurance commissioner (appointed), the treasurer, and the superintendent of schools. The political scene had deteriorated badly since Republican Governor Pete Wilson was reelected in 1994 and the attorney general, secretary of state, insurance commissioner, and treasurer were all won by the GOP.

The statewide races went from bad to worse for the GOP in 2000. Al Gore ended up winning in California by 12 points and 1.3 million votes. The "compassionate conservative" Governor Bush from Texas ended up with a lopsided loss in the presidential race, despite the fact that his campaign had not folded its tent after Labor Day, as some had complained about President George Bush in 1992 and Bob Dole in 1996. The Republicans fought hard and spent considerable money in California yet had little to show for it, and that made the defeat all the more stinging. The news was even more depressing in the U.S. Senate race. Tom Campbell was a moderate, pro-choice Republican congressman from the Silicon Valley who had run in statewide GOP primaries before and lost to more conservative Republican candidates. This time, the Republicans thought they had a chance to make a decent showing, especially since their candidate matched the philosophical profile of California voters, and the incumbent Democratic U.S. Senator Dianne Feinstein had won by only a narrow margin in her last run against a conservative Republican in 1994. Campbell lost by nearly 20 points and over 2 million votes. This was an even more uneven match than in 1998, when Democratic U.S. Senator Barbara Boxer won her reelection bid against Matt Fong.

The bad news for the GOP in the 2000 elections did not end with the top-of-the ticket statewide races. The Democrats extended their already overwhelming control among the state's members of the U.S. House of Representatives and in the two branches of the state legislature. When the election was over, the Democrats had won thirty-two of the fifty-two house seats, twenty-six of the forty state senate seats, and fifty of the eighty state assembly seats. The Democrats had picked up four seats in the U.S. House, one seat in the state senate, and two seats in the state assembly. Particularly impressive was the fact that the Democrats were able to succeed in several of the hotly contested House races, which attracted national attention. In the end, Republican U.S. House members Tom Campbell, Brian Bilbray, James Rogan, and Steve Kuykendall had all been replaced by Democrats.

If we look at the trends over time in California's legislative arena, we can see a fairly steady deterioration in the fortunes of the GOP in local districts in California. We begin with 1994, the last time that a Republican won a major statewide race—the governorship. In that year, there were almost as many Democrats as Republicans in the House seats representing the state, a narrow margin for the Democrats in the state senate, and more Republicans than Democrats in the state assembly. In the 1996 presidential year, the Democrats gained back a few seats in each of the three legislative arenas. In 1998, the Republicans picked up one House seat while the Democrats continued to pick up a few seats in the state senate and state assembly. When we look at the results after four statewide elections, we see that the Democrats had gained five seats in the U.S. House, five in the state senate, and a whopping eleven seats in the state assembly.

The Republicans are now facing the 2002 election with trepidation. How will they field candidates in the governor's race and other state offices when so few GOP hopefuls have any experience winning statewide races? Also, the Democratic governor and state legislature are in control of the legislative redistricting process. Moreover, the trends in these legislative elections suggest further losses unless the Republicans hold onto slim hopes that the remaining districts are "theirs." The talk of the nation was about California moving sharply to the left of the rest of the nation and at the same time becoming a Democratic state for good. But is this the case?

CALIFORNIA'S ENDURING POLITICAL RELEVANCE

Pundits argued insistently during the 2000 presidential election that California had become irrelevant on the national scene.[2] A combination of

2. Those who have written about California's political irrelevance and liberal leanings include Barnes (2000); Block (2000); Meyerson (2001); and Schrag (2000b, 2001).

factors had pushed the state so deeply into the Democratic column that
there was no point in the Republicans spending their time and money
trying to win a statewide race in California. The liberal ideology of the
state's residents was simply too much at odds with the Republican party's
political platforms. Moreover, the political demography of the nation
had shifted to the extent that the Republicans *could* win the White House
without California, and the Democrats could *not* win it without the
Golden State. So how politically essential is the state to the hopes of presidential aspirants, and how different are Californians' political views
from the positions of other Americans?

California and the nation walked in lockstep for most of the twentieth century when it came to selecting a president. If we look at the
twenty-five presidential elections that occurred between 1900 and 1996,
in twenty-two instances the winner in California went on to take up oc-
cupancy in the White House in January. The three exceptions in which
the Democrats lost in California and yet went on to win in the national
election were Woodrow Wilson (1912), John Kennedy (1960), and
Jimmy Carter (1976). In the latter two cases, the Republicans won in
California by razor-thin margins. So the pattern is straightforward: becoming president has almost always required a victory in California. The
historical data present a solid case for the state's relevance in national
elections.[3]

The 2000 presidential election did little to weaken the case for California's importance. If for no other reason, it demonstrated how relent-
lessly the need to win without California can drive campaign strategy,
including the use of campaign funds. Of course, the 2000 presidential
election was an anomaly in many respects. It was determined by a close
win in Florida by Bush, and only after the U.S. Supreme Court stepped
in and decided to halt the recount efforts. Certainly, if Republicans are
looking for ways to win the presidency without taking California, the
2000 election does not provide much of an answer. It took a hard-fought
political campaign and even an eventual court battle to win enough electoral college votes in other states to overcome the loss in California.
Moreover, Bush entered office with questions about the legitimacy of his
presidency, given that he had lost the popular vote.

With the state's long historical track record of contributing to the winning side of the national presidential vote, it is hard to accept the claim

3. I wish to thank Jon Cohen for providing the historical data on the California vote
in presidential elections in this section.

that California has become irrelevant. The most notable political change is that California has gone from being predictably Republican in the post–World War II era to solidly Democrat in recent elections. This must be a troubling trend for the GOP, because they now have to compensate for the deficit of a very large loss. The last election showed how difficult this is and will be.

CALIFORNIA'S MAINSTREAM POLITICAL CULTURE

Given that pundits had diagnosed California as an ultraliberal state out of step with the nation, we took pains to use questions from national surveys in our PPIC Statewide Survey to provide an objective basis for comparison of state and national political orientation. Beginning in early 2000 and continuing into the weeks just before the November election, we asked a series of questions on trust in government and public policy preferences in all of our statewide surveys. The questions were taken from national surveys by organizations such as Gallup, Pew, Yankelovich Partners, the Kaiser Family Foundation, CBS, NBC, ABC, the *Washington Post,* and the *Wall Street Journal.*

The results showed that the state's political orientation was not much different from the nation's. About three in ten California adults consistently described themselves as liberals, just a little over one in three said they were political moderates, and a little more than one-third of residents described themselves as conservatives. Compared with the rest of Americans, Californians were a little more likely to say they were liberal and a little less likely to describe themselves as conservative (Baldassare, 2000). Nevertheless, six in ten residents in California called themselves middle-of-the-road to somewhat conservative. This moderately conservative tendency held true for Democrats, Republicans, and independent voters. This California voter profile has not shown a shift to the left since we began conducting statewide surveys in 1998.

We found that Californians were slightly more likely than Americans as a whole to express confidence in the federal government and to trust the government in Washington to do what is right. They were less likely to think that the government wastes a lot of the taxpayers' money, and they were considerably less likely to say that the government is run by a few big interests looking out for themselves.

On other measures, Californians were also somewhat more trusting than their fellow citizens. Half of the residents believed the federal government pays at least some attention "to what the people think when it decides what to do," in contrast to about four in ten Americans generally. Almost six in ten Californians had at least some confidence that, "when the government in Washington decides to solve a problem, the problem will actually be solved." Only half of all Americans shared that confidence. Still, it is important to note that these are relative differences: Californians were quite "American" in their cynicism about government.

There is little evidence that California is far to the left of the nation on policy issues. There are no major disagreements between residents of the state and the nation with respect to what they want from their government. In our survey in early 2000, most Americans told us that "the government should not interfere with a woman's access to abortion," that "stricter environmental laws and regulations are worth the cost," and that "the government does not do enough to regulate access to guns." Californians agreed with all of these policy perspectives, although they were more likely than Americans as a whole to favor gun control and a woman's right to an abortion without interference. Californians were as evenly divided as other Americans over the issue of whether government should give parents taxpayer-funded vouchers to pay for private or religious schools or if government funding should be limited to public schools.

Most Californians, just like most Americans, overwhelmingly supported both national standards to protect the rights of HMO patients and a Medicare system that would cover the costs of prescription drugs. The only difference is that Californians were even more strongly in favor of Medicare coverage of prescription drugs. Finally, the majority of Americans said they prefer a "smaller government with fewer services" to a "larger government with many services." Most Californians agreed that a smaller government would be preferable; however, slightly fewer held this perspective than other Americans.

Overall, Californians were highly skeptical about government and reluctant to see it expand. They were pretty much in agreement with Americans on what they thought of their government and what they expected the government's role to be in the policy arena.

MAJOR PARTY REGISTRATION: TRENDS OVER TIME

One would expect that the recent string of Democratic successes in statewide elections would be accompanied by either a surge in voter registration for the Democrats or a decline in the voting rolls of Republicans. (See Table 7-1.) The Republicans won three consecutive presidential elections in 1980, 1984, and 1988. They also won four consecutive

TABLE 7.1   PARTY REGISTRATION:
TRENDS OVER TIME

	Democrats	Republicans	Others	Total
1988	50.4%	38.6%	11.0%	100%
	7,052,368	5,406,127	1,546,378	14,004,873
1992	49.1%	37.0%	13.9%	100%
	7,410,914	5,593,555	2,097,004	15,101,473
1996	47.2%	36.4%	16.4%	100%
	7,387,504	5,704,536	2,570,035	15,662,075
2000	45.4%	34.9%	19.7%	100%
	7,134,601	5,485,492	3,087,214	15,707,307

SOURCE: California Secretary of State (2000c).

gubernatorial elections in 1982, 1986, 1990, and 1994. This was followed by Democratic victories in the presidential elections in 1992, 1996, and 2000, and a Democratic victory in the 1998 gubernatorial election. These election outcomes are not explained by voter registration trends (i.e., the parties that voters list as their affiliation when they register to vote). In fact, there has been little change in the number of registered voters in major parties or in the Democratic party's margin over the Republican party in California.

The last time the Republicans won a presidential race (1988), the Democrats had an 11-point margin among the 14 million registered voters in the state: 50 percent were Democrats, 39 percent were Republicans, and 11 percent were registered to other parties (e.g., Libertarian, American Independent) or as "decline to state" (i.e., independent). The Republicans won the presidential race that year by a 4-point margin. In fact, the Republicans won every top-of-the ticket race for governor and president between 1980 and 1990, despite the fact that Democrats had at least a 10-point edge over the Republicans in the voter rolls. Thus, the voter registration margin was not a crucial factor.

When Californians went to the polls to vote for president in 1992 and 1996, the Democrats maintained an 11-point and 12-point edge, respectively, over the Republicans. In these two elections, the Democratic candidate, Bill Clinton, defeated the Republican candidates by 13 points. It is important to point out, however, that the Democrats were defeated by the GOP by a 15-point margin in the gubernatorial race in 1994, which occurred between the two presidential victories. It is thus hard to make the case that Democratic registration rates explain the Democratic victories in these two presidential elections.

There were 15.7 million registered voters in California preceding to the 2000 presidential election. The Democrats maintained the same 11-point margin over the Republicans that they had just before the 1988 election. The Democratic candidate, Al Gore, won by a 12-point margin. In the dozen years preceding the 2000 election, the ranks of the Democratic voters had increased by only 82,233, or 1.1 percent, while the ranks of the Republican voters had increased by a similar 79,365, or 1.5 percent. In other words, there had been no mass exodus from the Republican party to the Democratic party over the course of time that the Republicans consistently lost and the Democrats won.[4]

The greatest change in voter registration since 1988 involved voters outside the two major parties, the vast majority of whom registered as "decline to state" (independent voters who did not register as belonging to either a major or a minor party). There were 1.5 million "other" voters registered at the time of the 1988 presidential election. The "other" group—consisting of independent voters and those registered as members of minor parties—consistently grew by a half-million voters after each of the three presidential elections leading up to the 2000 elections. By November 2000, there were nearly 3.1 million independent and minor party voters in California—2.3 million of whom were "decline to state" or independent voters. The numbers of "other" voters had doubled between 1988 and 2000, making this the fastest growing group in the electorate. These "other" voters had climbed from one in eleven of the state's voters to one in five within a dozen years. In the meantime, the percent of registered Democrats actually declined by 5 points, while the percent of registered Republicans fell by almost 4 points. Looking at these voter registration statistics in another way, the voting rolls had grown by about 1.7 million from 14 million to 15.7 million voters between 1988 and 2000. Ninety percent of this growth occurred outside of the two major parties.

A number of factors contributed to the growth in the number of voters who registered as independents. Certainly, a preference to remove oneself from the ideological limits of the major parties was one. Among other reasons may have been the fact that California voters had passed

4. California Secretary of State Bill Jones made a major effort to clear deadwood from the voter rolls after he was elected in 1994, and many voters who had moved, died, or were otherwise ineligible were removed from the rolls (see Baldassare, 2000).

an open, blanket primary initiative in 1996. This allowed voters to choose the candidate they wished to vote for in every office, regardless of the voter's party or the candidate's party. In many ways, this initiative and its support reflected, as well as affected, the movement toward the independent ranks. The blanket primary rules applied to the June 1998 and March 2000 California primaries, including the presidential selection. The U.S. Supreme Court invalidated this version of the blanket primary later on in 2000. Nevertheless, the open primary offered an additional reason for voters to register outside of the major parties between 1996 and 2000: They could voice their preferences for whichever party or candidates they preferred in the primaries.[5]

Of course, not all Californians cast ballots in an election. The November 2000 election was history-making in two ways: a record number of Californians cast ballots (11.14 million), and yet it was the lowest turnout of eligible adults in a presidential election (52%). These statistics reflect that voter participation in California is not keeping pace with population growth. Large numbers of eligible adults are not registering to vote, and large numbers of registered voters are not voting. In the November 2000 election, about seven in ten registered voters cast their ballots, amounting to about half of Californians who were eligible to vote. The performance was much weaker in the California primary: less than four in ten eligible adults participated. In other words, while the prospects of an open primary may have motivated additional people to register to vote outside of the major parties, the reality was still that on primary election day, most adults who were eligible to vote did not.

It is possible that voters who go to the polls are different from registered voters generally. In particular, there may be a higher proportion of Democrats and a lower proportion of Republicans voting than in the past. If so, this could explain the changing fortunes of the major parties. However, exit polls of voters on election day indicate that this was not the case: the 11-point gap between registered Democrats and registered Republicans is not found in exit polls from 1992 to 2000. Democrats consistently outnumbered Republicans at the polls, but by a smaller margin than the registration gap (11%). The average margin between Democrats and Republicans was 5.4 percent between 1992 and 2000, based on the exit polls from these elections. In the 2000 elections, 43 percent of voters were Democrats, 35 percent were Republicans, and 22 percent identified themselves as outside the major political parties.

5. See Baldassare (2000) and Cain and Gerber (2002).

This amounted to an 8-point margin in favor of the Democrats. So despite the fact that the Democrats had a smaller edge over the Republicans than in the voter registration rolls, the Democratic party won the presidential race by a 12-point margin.[6]

In looking at the PPIC Statewide Surveys during the entire 2000 election cycle, we reach similar conclusions about the political party profile of active voters. This includes the responses of over 14,000 registered voters and almost 9,000 likely voters in our surveys. The Democrats outnumbered the Republicans by 10 points (i.e., 45% to 35%) among all registered voters; however, the Democrats led the Republicans by only 5 points (44% to 39%) among those who were most likely to vote in the state's elections. Clearly, there is no indication that Democrats were more likely to flock to the polls than were Republicans. If anything, the opposite appears to be the case, yet Democratic candidates were winning by margins larger than the Democratic registration edge (PPIC Just the Facts, 2001b).

There is some evidence that trends over time in who actually votes have not been working in the favor of Republicans. Between 1994 and 2000, the number of self-identified Republicans declined by 1 point (36% to 35%). However, the exit polls do not show any surge in Democratic support: this party's voters increased by 1 point (41% to 42%) during the same time frame. Between 1994 and 2000, the voters outside the major parties also increased by 2 points (20% to 22%). These all represent relatively small changes; however, they do not reflect a particular surge in voting by Democrats.

Obviously, the growth of voters outside of the major political parties coincided with the state's progression toward single-party domination in the late 1990s. To argue that the Democratic party became bigger and more powerful or that the Republican party lost more of its voters is untenable. Nor is there any evidence that voter turnout was crucial. The Democratic party's candidates benefited from independent voters.

THE POLITICAL ROLE OF INDEPENDENT VOTERS
IN THE UN-PARTY STATE

The facts that both Democrats and Republicans fall short of the majority needed to win and that there is no strong third party that consistently

6. See Baldassare (2000); Schwieren (1999); and Voter News Service (2000).

votes for its candidates means that the statewide races of the major parties hinge on the decisions of over 2 million "decline to state" voters. Indeed, recent successes of the Democrats are a result of winning the majority of the unaffiliated vote.[7]

Independent Voters in Recent Elections

The basic arithmetic dictates that Republicans need a large share of the independent vote to win California. Simply put, Republicans are dependent on achieving more votes from independents than are Democrats, because the GOP trails in registration by about a 10-point margin. Assuming that GOP voters remain overwhelmingly loyal and that a small contingent of Democrats defect, it is still not likely that Republicans can win without the solid support of independent voters. The GOP had enjoyed the support of many independent voters in presidential, U.S. Senate, and gubernatorial elections from 1980 though the mid-1990s. However, their favor seems to have dwindled, with independent voters leaning more toward Democrats lately.

The 1998 election provides a good example. (See Table 7-2). Exit polls indicate that one in five voters were neither Democrat nor Republican. In the governor's race, voters outside of the major parties favored Gray Davis over Dan Lungren by an 18-point margin (53% to 35%), leading to a 20-point victory for the Democrat. In the U.S. Senate race, independents went for Barbara Boxer over Matt Fong by an 8-point margin (50% to 42%), helping to provide the Democrat with a 10-point win.

In the 2000 presidential election, both Al Gore and George W. Bush had the support of nine in ten voters in their respective parties. Right away, this would force Bush into the position of needing a very strong showing among independents in order to win the state because of a Democratic edge in the numbers. Instead, Al Gore was supported by independents and other-party voters by a 6-point margin (46% to 40%), while one in seven independents supported Ralph Nader and other third-party candidates. Even though neither candidate received a majority of the vote, Gore was able to build an insurmountable lead because he was the favorite among independent voters.

7. See Baldassare (2000); Clark and Inglehart (1998); Greenberg (1995); Keith et al. (1992); and Lipset and Schneider (1983) on independent voters and related trends.

TABLE 7.2 PARTY PREFERENCES IN STATEWIDE RACES

	Democrats	Republicans	Independent/ Other Voters
2000 President			
Al Gore (D)	90%	11%	46%
George W. Bush (R)	7	88	40
Others	3	1	14
2000 U.S. Senate			
Dianne Feinstein (D)	89	21	43
Tom Campbell (R)	6	75	38
Others	5	4	19
1998 Governor			
Gray Davis (D)	90	20	53
Dan Lungren (R)	7	79	35
Others	3	1	12
1998 U.S. Senate			
Barbara Boxer (D)	87	15	50
Matt Fong (R)	11	82	42
Others	2	3	8

SOURCE: Voter News Service (1998, 2000); PPIC Just the Facts (2000c).

In the U.S. Senate race, the Republican challenger Tom Campbell tried to reach out to independent voters by emphasizing his moderate positions. Nine in ten Democrats supported Dianne Feinstein, while three in four Republicans favored Campbell. Among voters outside of the major parties, Feinstein had a 5-point advantage over Campbell (43% to 38%), while about one in five of these voters favored other candidates. Feinstein's big margin of victory was assured by support from independents.

The Democrats also had the advantage with independent voters in the 2000 elections for House seats. In our preelection surveys, Democrats and Republicans were equally strong in their desire to vote for congressional candidates inside of their party of registration. However, independent and other-party voters favored Democratic over Republican candidates by 14 points (44% to 30%). The Democrats' ability to attract independent voters was part of their success story in the House races, especially in the "swing" districts, where there was a close competition between parties.

Independent Voters and the Gender Gap

One of the longest-running sequels in California's elections has been the Year of the Woman. It began in 1992, resurfaced in 1996 and 1998, and was on the scene in the 2000 election. For the third straight presidential election, women's strong support of a Democratic candidate sent the Republican candidate another crushing defeat. In fact, much of the credit for the Democrats' success has focused on the gender gap. Truly understanding how the gender gap works in California calls for an accounting of the un-party trends: men have moved toward independent status, while women have not.

How was Gray Davis able to capture the governorship by such a landslide margin, after the Republicans had won in four straight elections? He managed to carry the women's vote by a 25-point margin (60% to 35%), while carrying the men's vote by half of that margin. Similar trends were evident in the U.S. Senate races won by the Democrats in the 1990s. In 1998, Boxer won the women's vote by an 18-point margin (57% to 39%), while Fong and Boxer divided the men's vote (48% each).

In the 2000 elections, the Democrats had two solid statewide wins because of the large numbers of women supporters. The exit polls indicate that Bush won over Gore by the slimmest of margins among men, while Gore beat Bush by a 21-point margin among women. In the U.S. Senate race, men supported Feinstein over Campbell by a slim margin, while women favored Feinstein over Campbell by a two-to-one margin.

The GOP's problems in the Golden State begin with simple arithmetic: more women voters than men voters showed up at the polls in statewide elections, about 52 percent to 48 percent, respectively. Among women voters who went to the polls, Democrats led the Republicans by a 14-point margin (50% to 36%). In other words, Republicans started each election with a large deficit in voter registration among women.

Given the Democrats' overwhelming support among women voters, why does the GOP not simply try to build a big lead among men voters to counter this trend? Simply put, the numbers are not there in terms of voter registration advantages. Among male voters, Republicans outnumbered Democrats by only a four-point margin (42% to 38%). While many new voters in the state have been registering as independents, it turns out that these independent voters are much more likely to be men than women. During the 2000 elections, about 20 percent of men were independent voters. Starting from only a small advantage among men voters, the GOP is left with the daunting task of attracting most independent voters and some crossover Democrats if they are to win a big enough victory among men to counter the Democrats' margin of support among women.[8]

Clearly, the Democrats are the favorite among women voters for a variety of reasons. Partly, their support comes from being the party more likely to elect women candidates. Most of the women holding high elected offices in the state are Democrats. California's two U.S. senators are women, and both are Democrats. As for the 52-member congressional delegation, there are sixteen women in House seats, and all but one is a Democrat. In the forty-member state senate, there are ten women in office, and all ten women are Democrats. In the eighty-member state assembly, there are twenty-five women, and all but five are Democrats. In practical terms, women voters have few GOP-elected officials they can identify with. Moreover, the GOP has lost its edge with women voters because of issues: Democrats have stressed abortion choice and a range of social and fiscal issues that appeal to moderate and independent women.

There was a time when Republicans in the state could work the gender gap to their advantage. That is, the GOP could overcome the voter registration disadvantages and absorb substantial losses among women by winning by large margins among men. In fact, Republicans enjoyed great successes over an extended period of time, even though Democrats enjoyed a major advantage in voter registration. In those earlier days, Republicans had the issues on their side. For instance, they could convince independent male voters that they had the better answers to the Cold War, rising crime rates, a soft economy, budget deficits, and higher taxes. In the 2000 elections, GOP candidates struggled to find issues that resonated with independent male voters during times of peace and prosperity.

Independent Voters: The Distrustful Centrists

California's independent voters have shown themselves to be a truly independent lot. Although they were more likely to support the Democrats

8. See PPIC Just the Facts (2000b, 2001c).

in 2000, many of their attitudes indicate that the Democrats should not assume they have a lock on independents' votes. Who are these independent voters, and what do they seem to want from the candidates? Compared with the voters of the two major parties, they tend to be younger, more likely to be employed, less likely to own a home, and much more likely to be men than women. In other respects, their demographic characteristics are not much different from the major parties' voters. Independent voters generally show only a passing interest in politics, are not that focused on elections, and tend to get most of their political news from television rather than newspapers. They are likely to tell us that issues rather than political party drive their decisions to vote and whom to vote for (Baldassare, 2000).

When independent voters were asked which party they felt closest to, Democrats edged out Republicans by a 12-point margin (43% to 31%), although a sizable one in four said neither was their favorite. When asked about their politics, four in ten called themselves middle-of-the-road, three in ten said they were liberal, and another three in ten said they were conservative. Here, the key for Democrats have been their ability to stress their political moderation, while Republicans have been inclined to focus on socially conservative themes.

As a voter group, independents fell somewhere between liberal Democrats and conservative Republicans in their lack of confidence in government. (See Table 7-3). For instance, only three in ten independent voters thought they could always or mostly trust the government to do what is right. By comparison, one in four Republicans and four in ten Democrats believed the government can be trusted on a fairly consistent basis. Independent voters were a little less likely than Democrats to believe that the government is run for the benefit of all the people and were similar to Republicans in their thinking that the government wastes a lot of taxpayer money (PPIC Statewide Surveys, 2000a, 2000g). On the issue of government responsiveness, independent voters had even more doubts than major party voters: Nearly two in three believed that elected officials do not care what people like them think.

Independent voters shared with Republicans a strong desire to reduce the size of government. (See Table 7-4.) In stark contrast to the state's core of Democratic voters, they overwhelmingly preferred government to be smaller in size with fewer services. During the 2000 elections, nearly half said they would like to see the federal surplus spent on a tax cut, while Democrats strongly preferred that the surplus be directed toward

TABLE 7.3   GOVERNMENT DISTRUST BY
PARTY STATUS

	Democrats	Republicans	Other Voters
Overall Government Trust			
Always/Mostly trust the federal government	41%	25%	31%
Sometimes/Never trust the federal government	59	75	69
Government Responsiveness			
Elected officials care what people like me think	49	43	36
Elected officials do not care what people think	49	56	62
Don't know	2	1	2

SOURCE: PPIC Statewide Survey (2000a).

spending on social programs. On many different fiscal issues, independents side more with Republicans than with Democrats (Baldassare, 2000). Nonetheless, the majority has favored Democratic candidates, and this support has assured that party's success in recent elections.

In recent times, Democratic statewide campaigns have wooed independent voters by drawing sharp contrasts between the records of Democratic and Republican candidates on three issues—abortion, gun control, and the environment (see Table 7-5). Independents have been overwhelmingly pro-choice on abortion, have strongly favored stricter gun controls, and have been major supporters of stricter environmental regulations. On all of these issues, independent voters were more closely aligned with Democrats than with Republicans. This strategy seemed to work once again in the 2000 election.

Other issues have also attracted independent voters to the Democrats, if only for the time being. In 2000, with peace and prosperity in place, independent voters were not fretting about the Cold War, crime rates, unemployment, inflation, budget deficits, or the prospects of higher taxes. They were worried enough about the future, even in these good times, to be ambivalent about the government's role in solving the problems that Californians were likely to encounter.

TABLE 7.4   GOVERNMENT SPENDING BY
PARTY STATUS

	Democrats	Republicans	Other Voters
What Size Government?			
Smaller with fewer services	37%	78%	63%
Larger with many services	54	17	34
Don't know	9	5	3
What to Do with Federal Surplus?			
Cut taxes	35	68	49
Pay for social programs	59	28	46
Other, don't know	6	4	5

SOURCE: PPIC Statewide Survey (2000a, 2000g).

While independents have not been proponents of big government, their lack of attachment to party and ideology has allowed them some pragmatic flexibility. For instance, they could admit that local governments need more money for roads (because their commute has become unbearable); that their local public schools need more funds to provide a better quality education; or that the president and Congress need to focus on how to save Social Security, to protect HMO patients' rights, and to counteract against the threat of global warming. They could, in effect, exercise their postmaterialist values, acknowledging that there are specific roles for government in their lives, even if public institutions are not entirely trusted.

At the same time, it is important to remember that these independent voters were divided when put to the ultimate test—choosing between a tax cut and more spending on government programs—while Democratic and Republican voters fell more solidly into one camp or the other. They were probably not only divided in numbers but were truly ambivalent about whether to set aside their doubts about government to get things accomplished, since the government had the money to do so.

Independent Voters and Issue-Oriented Politics

One of the most striking features of both the 1998 gubernatorial and the 2000 presidential elections was the Republican refusal to believe voters

TABLE 7.5   DEFINING ISSUES:
ABORTION RIGHTS, ENVIRONMENTAL
PROTECTION, GUN CONTROL

	Democrats	Republicans	Other Voters
Abortion Rights			
Government should restrict abortions	18%	34%	26%
Government should not interfere	81	63	71
Don't know	1	3	3
Environmental Protection			
Stricter regulations hurt economy	25	40	31
Stricter regulations worth the cost	70	57	66
Don't know	5	3	3
Gun Control			
Government goes too far	23	48	41
Government does not do enough	73	49	55
Don't know	4	3	4

SOURCE: PPIC Statewide Survey (2000a).

when they said that, in assessing candidates' qualifications, issues mattered much more to them than character. Ever since President Bill Clinton was caught in the middle of a sex scandal, the Republicans, without much subtlety, had been telling the voters that a person's character should count the most in choosing a leader. That was a subtext of the 1998 elections, and it did not work well in the Golden State. Voters told us in our surveys that there were more important considerations than a candidate's character, but the GOP pressed on (Baldassare, 2000). In the end, independent voters gave their support to Democratic candidates in 1998, perceiving the Democrats to be more focused on the issues they themselves embraced.

Early in the 2000 primary season, we asked voters once again what the most important factor was in selecting a presidential candidate; once again, six in ten voters said "the candidate's stands on the issues." Fewer than one in four mentioned character, and only one in eight mentioned experience in office. Stands on the issues was the top qualification among every voter group. Among independent voters, the response was similar to that of other voters: six in ten chose the candidate's position on the issues as the most important factor. Latino voters offered an interesting contrast with whites, one that fit their higher level of trust in elected officials: they were more likely than white voters to value experience in office (27% to 10%).

A further indication that issues matter most was evident in a survey question we asked between the major party conventions in the summer of 2000. What do people want the conventions to tell them about a presidential candidate? A solid majority of voters said they were most interested in learning about the candidates' positions on issues that mattered to them, while one in five mentioned character, one in six said experience in office, and fewer than one in ten wanted to hear about party platforms. Once again, issues were the number one choice across all of the political groups. Character was of most interest to Republicans and of least interest to Democrats, while independent voters were in line with all voters in preferring to learn more about issues.

Many voters indicated that they thought the presidential debates would be critical when it came to making a decision at the ballot box. Many did watch at least one of the debates, and about half told us that the debates helped at least somewhat in deciding who to vote for in the presidential election. What did voters learn the most about the candidates from the debates? They were more likely to say they learned the most about the candidates' stands on the issues than about character, intelligence, or experience in office. Once again, independent voters were more impressed with learning about the candidates' stands on the issues than were voters in the two major parties.[9]

While the presidential candidates had their favorite issues, what did California voters most want to hear them talk about? A month before the California primary, the answer was schools, followed distantly by other topics such as tax cuts, health care, and Social Security and Medicare. Our surveys had consistently shown that schools were the one issue on people's minds for state action, and this was exactly what captured their interest in the early stages of the presidential race. Independent voters also chose schools as their number one issue. Few chose crime, defense and the military, the economy, rising taxes, or immigration—all of the issues that the GOP had success with when competing against the Democrats in the 1980s and early 1990s. These preferences

9. See PPIC Statewide Survey (1999d, 2000e, 2000g) for "stands on issues" questions at the beginning of the election, during the party conventions, and after the debates.

persisted in our surveys throughout the summer months and the conventions and right up to the November 2000 election.[10]

We asked voters whether they thought Gore or Bush would do a better job in handling the five issues they were most likely to identify as their top concerns. The importance that independent voters placed on the candidates' ability to handle the issues was abundantly clear, providing a crucial signal in the campaign. They were more confident that the Democrat could handle the job.

Gore was favored over Bush by large margins on three issues that four in ten voters ranked as their first priorities (i.e., schools, health care, Social Security). A majority of independent voters felt more comfortable with having the Democrat handling schools, health care, and Social Security. Eight in ten Democrats had more confidence in the way that Gore would handle all three of the latter issues. By way of contrast, about two in three Republicans felt that their party's candidate was better suited to take on these three issues, while one in five Republicans admitted that the Democrat would do a better job.

Bush did lead Gore as the candidate considered as most capable of handling tax cuts and the military—two issues that the Bush team emphasized heavily in the closing weeks of the campaign. Republicans were convinced that their candidate would have the best strategy for cutting taxes and strengthening the military defense, and even three in ten Democrats thought that Bush would do a better job. Independent voters also favored Bush over Gore on tax cuts and the military, but by narrower margins than they favored Gore over Bush on schools, health care, and Social Security. However, in our September and October surveys, the bottom line is that only one in six voters listed either of these issues among their top concerns.[11]

In sum, the Democrats' edge over Republicans was largely a function of the list of issues that independent voters cared about at the time of the 2000 elections. Voters were emphatic that issues mattered more than anything else in their voting decisions. They were very specific about the issues they had in mind—domestic programs that offered a brighter outlook for the state and the nation, such as schools, Social Security, and health care. The list of issues that rose to the top were ones in which the

10. See PPIC Statewide Surveys (2000b, 2000e, 2000f, 2000g) for questions on the "most important issue" for presidential candidates, asked before the March primary, party conventions, presidential debates, and November elections.
11. See PPIC Statewide Surveys (2000f, 2000g) for questions on which presidential candidate would do a better job of handling these five issues.

Democrats were able to make a convincing case for their expertise, while the Republicans' strengths were further down on the voters' lists of concerns during the entire year. Politicians who claimed moral superiority for either themselves or their party did not sway the independents a bit. But then, it is little wonder that a focus on character would not work, given the generally low regard that independent voters have toward anyone holding public office.

THE INITIATIVE PROCESS IN 2000: GROWING DISTRUST, CALLS FOR REFORMS

Besides the growing importance of independent voters, the increasing use of the initiative process befittingly characterizes the un-party state of California. In a state where distrust makes a "divided government" seem like a better idea than one-party control of the legislative and executive branches, the voters have turned to the initiative process to accomplish their issue-focused orientation and to directly affect the policymaking process. For independent voters who are not in the habit of voting for one party or a philosophy, the initiative process has great appeal. Democrat and Republican voters have also liked the initiative process, because they, too, have shown distrust toward representative democracy. (See Table 7-6.)

Nevertheless, as part of the fallout from their 2000 election experience, Californians seem to be reassessing their state's trend toward allowing voters to play a major role in the policymaking process. The voters' role in the direct democracy process was supposed to increase public participation and government responsiveness. However, as it is currently being practiced, the initiative process is developing its own problems of voter distrust. Having faced another bewildering array of state propositions on the 2000 ballot and a barrage of television commercials on everything from school vouchers to drug treatment programs, Californians were ripe for reconsidering their attitudes toward citizens' initiatives in the state.[12]

State Assembly Speaker Robert Hertzberg had this to say in launching the Speaker's Commission on the California Initiative Process, which was exploring reforms: "Those who gave California voters this power-

---

12. See Schrag (2000c), who discusses the "fourth branch of government."

TABLE 7.6   THE INITIATIVE PROCESS:
PRAISE FOR THE CONCEPT

"In general, do you think it is a good thing or a bad thing that a majority of voters can make laws and change public policies by passing initiatives?"

	All Adults	Democrats	Republicans	Other Voters
Good thing	69%	66%	69%	73%
Bad thing	23	25	23	21
Don't know	8	9	8	6

"Do you think public policy decisions made through the initiative process are probably better or probably worse than decisions made by the governor and legislature?"

	All Adults	Democrats	Republicans	Other Voters
Probably better	56%	50%	56%	60%
Probably worse	24	27	22	22
Don't know	20	23	22	18

SOURCE: PPIC Statewide Survey (2000g).

ful tool to reform would have a hard time recognizing the initiative process we know today, where powerful interests clutter the ballot with contradictory proposals incapable of passing constitutional muster."[13] Certainly, many voters today would share this point of view about ballot initiatives.

The citizens' initiative process began in California's progressive era. The state's voters passed a series of reforms in 1911 aimed at reducing political corruption and the power of railroads and big business over the state government. These reforms included the referenda and the recall and, perhaps most important, the initiative process, which allows voters to pass new laws and amend the constitution with a majority vote in a statewide election. For an initiative to appear on the ballot, the state

13. The quote from press release issued by State Assemblyman Hertzberg in October 2000 (Hertzberg 2000). See Weintraub (2001) on the Speaker's Commission on the California Initiative Process.

attorney general must first review the measure, then a minimum number of valid signatures from voters must be collected. If all goes well, the initiative is qualified for an election.[14]

Indeed, the initiative process has evolved from a rarely used to a frequently used procedure for fashioning public policies in a variety of domains. Many credit the Proposition 13 tax revolt with the increasing use of initiatives. Since 1980, there have been 626 statewide initiatives circulated for signatures, 123 qualified for elections, and 52 passed into law. This is far more activity than in the period from 1912 to 1979. By far, the most popular topics for initiatives have been taxation, government regulations, and fiscal and governance issues. However, initiative proponents have often delved into more domestic policy issues such as education, health care, the environment, and crime. It is also common for initiatives to tackle specific issues that serve an organized interest or cause, such as gambling, labor, social issues, and tobacco, drugs, and alcohol (Silva, 2000). Statewide initiatives today often involve slick, expensive media blitzes by professionally staffed campaigns paid for by the causes for and against the initiative—far removed from the populist tool envisioned in the progressive era.

The 2000 elections were fairly typical of the current initiative process. Voters were confronted with twenty state propositions on the ballot in March and eight in November. Seventeen of the measures passed. About half of the measures were placed on the ballot by the legislature, including state bonds, as required by constitutional law, but there were also some public policy decisions that the legislature preferred to hand over to the voters. In March, voters passed several of the more controversial measures, including one that dictated tougher treatment of juvenile criminals and another that banned gay marriages in California. In November, they passed measures that revised the campaign contribution laws, that required law enforcement to offer treatment programs to drug offenders, and that made it possible to pass local school bonds with only a 55 percent local vote. The voters turned down efforts to repeal the tobacco tax passed by voters, to start a school voucher system, to amend the insurance lawsuit laws, and to create a strict campaign finance system. Once again, many millions of dollars were spent on the initiative

14. See Schrag (1998) and Broder (2000c) and also academic assessments of the initiative process, including Bowler and Donovan (1998); Bowler, Donovan, and Tolbert (1998); Cain and Noll (1995); Cain, Ferejohn, et al. (1995); DeBow and Syer (1997); Ferejohn (1995); Gerber (1995, 1998, 1999); and Lupia (1998).

campaigns, but there was a new twist this time—exorbitant funding for certain initiatives by Silicon Valley's wealthy entrepreneurs.[15]

How did Californians feel about the initiative process as they sorted through the latest round of decisionmaking in the 2000 elections? At times, they felt confused and frustrated, but they were always protective of their ability to overrule their elected officials, whom they did not typically hold in the highest esteem. When asked who has the most influence over public policy in California today, most felt that it was either the governor or legislature who called the shots, while only one in five thought the citizens' initiative process was the shaping force. But when asked whom they preferred to be the most influential, nearly half picked the citizens' initiative process, three in ten named the legislature, and two in ten wanted the governor to have the greatest power to shape public policy.[16] This feeling of empowerment through initiatives was best summed up by a focus group participant who said, "I'd like it if we could vote on everything, so they don't make decisions for us."

As a general concept, the initiative process always seems to receive rave reviews from the public. Seven in ten residents told us that it was a "good thing" that a majority of voters can make laws and change public policies, while almost six in ten liked the idea that voters could make permanent changes in the state's constitution with a majority vote. Most voters also believed that they could do a better job of making laws and public policies through the initiative process than their governor and state legislature could do through the legislative process. Why do voters heap praise on their own lawmaking abilities? In part because of their uneasiness about elected officials: two in three said that campaign contributions have a bad influence on policy decisions made by the state's elected officials, and six in ten believed that their state government is pretty much run for the benefit of a few big interests.[17] Further, many believed that their elected officials avoided making difficult and unpopular choices. Another focus group participant summed it up this way, "If legislators did their job, they would make the laws as needed. We only need the initiative process when they table everything."

15. See Silva (2000) for historical information on initiatives, California Secretary of State (2000b, 2000c) for state propositions on the 2000 ballots, the California Voter Foundation (2001) on initiative campaign spending, and Kerr (2001) on Silicon Valley individuals financially backing the school initiatives.

16. See PPIC Statewide Survey (1999d) in December 1999.

17. See PPIC Statewide Surveys (1999b, 2000g, 2001a) in September 1999, October 2000, and January 2001 for questions on the initiative process and voter distrust.

While Californians showed a lot of respect for the initiative process in concept, most were also aware that, in practice, it was far from perfect. A month before the November election, only one in ten residents said they were "very satisfied" with the way the initiative process was working today. Six in ten residents said that they were only "somewhat satisfied," and one in four were not satisfied. Three in four residents said that changes were needed in the initiative process, while only one in five judged the current system as fine the way it was. One in three residents wanted major changes, while four in ten believed that minor changes would be sufficient. Among the many problems that citizens saw in the initiative process were court challenges that invalidated measures voters had passed, confusing language, and the role of special interests.

Disappointments with courts overturning initiatives was best summed up by a focus group member who said, "Initiatives should pass a legal test. It's too frustrating to everyone that the court throws them out later." For example, after the March 2000 primary, the U.S. Supreme Court ruled against the "open primary" initiative voters had passed in 1996. Two in three Californians said they had an unfavorable opinion of the court's decision, and this view was shared across political groups. Similarly, the major political parties had joined forces in a court challenge aimed at blocking a campaign finance initiative that the voters passed in 1996. The majority of the voters—across the political spectrum—had a negative opinion of this effort.[18]

The sheer volume of initiatives on the ballot alone has become overwhelming for the state's voters. What is worse is that many of the measures involve confusing language, such as double negatives. In our focus groups, individuals complained that "initiatives should be worded more simply" and that "initiatives should be in plain English, with no loopholes." Another individual noted with frustration, "On the ballot, no means yes and yes means no." During the fall, our surveys indicated that voters were feeling uneasy about the decisions they were being asked to make regarding numerous and complicated initiatives. Most said they were not getting enough information to allow them to decide how to vote on the measures. Moreover, most believed that the information sources that exerted the greatest influence on the initiative vote—news stories and paid political commercials—were the least useful in helping them decide how to vote. Many Californians strongly felt the need for

18. See PPIC Statewide Survey (2000e) in August 2000.

more objective and unbiased information, such as Web sites and voters' guides.[19]

While Californians may have liked the initiative process because it circumvents the power of special interests in the legislative process, they were not naive about the role of special interests in promoting and supporting citizens' initiatives. Nine in ten residents believed that the initiative process is controlled to some degree by special interests, and half believed those interests wield a lot of control. This cynical view of citizens' initiatives was pervasive across political parties, independent voters, and all regions of the state.

The desire to improve upon an initiative system that is both cherished and frustrating has led to a widespread support for reform (see Table 7-7). In our surveys after the November 2000 election, eight in ten residents favored increasing public disclosure of the financial backers of signature-gathering for initiatives and initiative campaigns—an effort aimed at reeling in the effects of special interests. Six in ten Californians said they would favor a law that requires volunteers to gather signatures to qualify initiatives, thus banning the use of paid signature gatherers—an obvious effort to return the initiative process to its citizen-activist roots. Californians also overwhelmingly approved of reforms to improve the quality of the initiatives that are placed on the ballot: eight in ten residents support a system of review and revision of proposed initiatives to avoid drafting errors and problems with ballot language, while nine in ten favored having a review of proposed initiatives so that voters know if there are legal problems before they vote. Clearly, the support for these two reform proposals stems from voter frustration with confusing ballot language and with initiatives passed by the voters but later overturned after challenges in the courts.[20]

Perhaps the greatest threat of all to the citizens' initiative process is the prospect of low voter turnout in the state's elections. A system of direct democracy would seem to be designed for a time when large numbers of voters are participating in public policymaking. Moreover, the profile of voters should reflect the profile of the public at large. In California's 2000 elections, neither of these conditions was met: Half of eligible adults voted in November, and only four in ten in March. The mostly white voter profile in both elections was in no way representative of the state's diverse adult population.

19. See PPIC Statewide Survey (2000f) in September 2000.
20. See PPIC Statewide Survey (2001a) in January 2001.

TABLE 7.7   INITIATIVES: THE NEED
FOR REFORMS

"Do you think that the initiative process in California is in need of major changes or minor changes or that it is basically fine the way it is at this time?"

	All Adults	Democrats	Republicans	Other Voters
Major changes	32%	31%	27%	33%
Minor changes	43	43	48	41
Fine the way it is	19	19	19	20
Don't know	6	7	6	6

"Overall, how much is the initiative process today controlled by special interests?"

	All Adults	Democrats	Republicans	Other Voters
A lot	52%	55%	57%	52%
Some	40	40	36	40
Not at all	3	2	2	3
Don't know	5	3	5	5

SOURCE: PPIC Statewide Survey (2000g, 2001a).

The initiative process was created in an era when eligible adults voted in large numbers and there were few measures on the ballot to ponder. Today, initiatives crowd the ballots more than ever before, and fewer people are going to the polls and deciding which measures should pass. If current trends persist, Californians may end up with an initiative system that, like the legislative system they distrust, lacks credibility because the laws it creates do not reflect the will of the general public.

AFTERMATH OF THE 2000 ELECTION: MORE DISTRUST, CALLS FOR REFORMS

Many political observers were predicting that the national presidential election would be close, but no one had a clue about how close it would really be. The Election Day ending was surreal, with the major networks calling the crucial state of Florida first for Gore, then for Bush, and then too close to call. Gore telephoned Bush to concede, then called back to say that he changed his mind, and then Bush reportedly became "snippy" about the retraction. The presidential election became even stranger as the vote recount proceeded in Florida and then was stopped by the state government, only to be restarted by the state courts, then halted again by the U.S. Supreme Court. A month after the election, we finally knew who would become the new president.

In California, the state's elected officials told the public, "It could never happen here," but could it? In a survey a month after the election, we looked at how Californians reacted to this entire post–presidential election trauma on the national scene (see Table 7-8). We were interested in how this contentious and confusing process affected their attitudes toward the president-elect and the new presidency. We also asked them if they thought the national presidential selection process needed to be changed and how they thought California might avoid the kind of political fiasco seen in Florida on election night.

A month later, Californians had distinct recollection of the 2000 U.S. presidential election. Some of their memories were embarrassing from the standpoint of how this democratic nation goes about selecting its leader. There were the poll workers in Florida holding up paper ballots to the light in an effort to determine if a hole was punched in one of the columns for a presidential candidate. There were the infamous "butterfly ballots" that caused some Gore voters to mistakenly vote for Pat Buchanan. There were the interventions of courts and state officials and a suggestion that the legislative branch might intervene as well. Of course, partisan politics played a role in what was determined as fair and accurate. In a rare ending to a presidential election, the candidate with the lower popular vote count won a trip to the White House because the electoral college is what really counts. How would an already cynical and distrustful public interpret this experience?

Some complaints about the 2000 presidential election revolved around the fear that Americans had unwittingly ended the election in an inconclusive manner, thereby disabling the new president's ability to gain the legitimacy needed to govern effectively. After the wrenching process had finally ended, just over half of Californians felt that George W. Bush would be able to be a strong and capable president. Most Republicans were optimistic about his chances of leading effectively, but only three in ten Democrats and fewer than half of independent voters felt that he would be able to do so. This uneasy feeling reflected, in part, personal and partisan impressions of the president-elect, but it was also tied to an awareness of the recent bumpy road to the White House, as indicated

TABLE 7.8   PUBLIC SUPPORT FOR
ELECTION REFORMS

*"For future presidential elections, would you support or oppose
changing to a system in which the president is elected by direct
popular vote instead of by the Electoral College?"*

	All Adults	Democrats	Republicans	Other Voters
Support	64%	75%	41%	70%
Oppose	30	19	53	25
Don't know	6	6	6	5

*"In California, would you prefer to use state funding for new
voting technology at local polling places—such as touch-screen
voting systems—or would you prefer that local polling places
continue to use paper ballots?"*

	All Adults	Democrats	Republicans	Other Voters
Voting technology	51%	55%	43%	53%
Paper ballots	42	39	48	43
Don't know	7	6	9	4

SOURCE: PPIC Statewide Survey (2001a) all adults.

by the response to another question. The majority of Californians felt
that the country would be divided and that it would be hard for Bush to
accomplish much in the next four years. Even as many as one in four Republicans held slim hopes for the country uniting behind Bush, while
solid majorities of Democrats and independent voters held little hope for
an effective presidential term.

When the presidential election was over and done with, Californians
were not very happy about the contentious and complicated process the
nation had gone through in selecting its leader. By more than a two-to-
one margin, the state's residents supported the idea of changing to a system in which the president is elected by a direct popular vote rather than
by the electoral college. Americans as a whole had offered similar responses in earlier national surveys, most recently in a *Washington Post*
and ABC News survey in December 2000. In California, there was little
doubt among Democrats and independent voters that a direct popular
vote would be a superior system: more than seven in ten voters wanted

change. Republicans were divided on the issue, perhaps because some saw election reform as an attempt to delegitimize the presidency of George W. Bush. Still, over four in ten Republicans also wanted to change the selection process. Clearly, Californians would get themselves strongly behind any national efforts to eliminate the electoral college. But no such proposal would surface once the traumatic election experience was finally over.

Details of the recount process in Florida prompted claims that punchcard voting systems should be replaced. In California, there were no major problems reported with the election count, except that completion of the massive voting effort was painfully slow. Some had proposed that the state government, in collaboration with county governments (which run the election process), use state funds to upgrade the technology used to vote at local polling places. This idea was floated when the state had a large surplus and before it was determined that these funds would be needed to pay skyrocketing electricity bills. A majority of Californians liked the idea of using state funds for new voting technology at local polling places. Fewer than half of the voters across parties wanted to continue to use paper ballots. One issue at hand was that this election reform faced a digital divide: it was highly popular among Californians who were frequent Internet users and strongly opposed by those who did not use computers.

Californians were more skeptical of plans for Internet voting. About one in four voters in state elections are casting absentee ballots, which involves sending paper ballots through the mail (California Secretary of State, 2000c). It takes considerable time to count these ballots, and the counting of overseas absentee ballots was a topic of great controversy in Florida. Nonetheless, only about one in three residents wanted the state to allow absentee voting over the Internet, while six in ten preferred the current paper ballot system. On this issue, there was consensus across party lines and all demographic groups. Even among Internet users, fewer than half wanted to allow absentee voting over the Internet. Apparently, fears about privacy and fraud severely limited the public's support for this technological change. For the time being, an election reform that might increase voting and accuracy is hampered by a lack of trust in the Internet and an awareness of its possible abuses.

THE FUTURE: A GENERATION GAP IN VOTING

One demographic group that might help us peer into the likely future of California's un-party state is California's young adults. They differ from older adults in voting behavior—but will that change, or will their propensities persist as they age?

Older adults constitute a disproportionate share of today's electorate. In the November 2000 elections, three out of ten voters were age 60 and older, while almost six in ten voters were over 45 years of age. By contrast, only one in seven voters was under the age of 30 (Voter News Service, 2000). The age profile of voters in elections is heavily skewed toward older residents: they comprise a much larger percentage of those who frequently vote than of the population at large. Younger voters tend to be underrepresented in the California political process: they represent a much larger share of the adult population than is reflected in the age-related statistics of who was voting at the polls. Those in their middle years, that is, between the ages of 35 and 54, comprise a roughly equal share of adults and likely voters.

Voter registration rates in California increase sharply with age. In the cumulative results of the PPIC Statewide Surveys, we found a 31-point difference in voter registration rates between adults under age 25 and adults age 65 and older. Today, it is difficult to find adults age 55 and older who are not registered to vote. Even stronger age differences were evident among those who described themselves as most likely to vote in elections. Fewer than three in ten adults in the 18-to-24 age category said they frequently vote, while seven in ten in the 65 and older group told us that they often vote. A solid majority of adults under the age of 45 do not routinely vote, while a large proportion of adults over the age of 45 do. Together, registration and voting trends tell us that many younger adults are either not registered or, if they are registered, do not vote with much regularity. If today's younger adults continue to vote in low numbers, already low voting rates will plummet. While many young adults may join the voting ranks as they grow older, many others may not, especially if they are unable to improve upon the low incomes and educational status they have today.

Looking at only those residents who were registered to vote, older adults were much more likely to align themselves with one of the major parties than were younger voters. This indicates that many new voters coming into the political system were deciding to register as "decline to state." It is thus likely that today's un-party state trends will remain alive and well in the future. Indeed, the influence outside of the major parties should grow substantially. Interestingly, the proportion of voters who were Democrats was similar across all age groups. It is the Republican registration that declined sharply in the younger age groups. As a result,

Democrats outnumbered Republicans by a 12-point margin among those under age 35 and by a 10-point margin among those between the ages of 35 and 54, but only by a 4-point margin in the 55 and older age group. This means that Republicans today are near parity with the Democrats only among the oldest residents. Certainly, this is a disturbing trend for those who are looking for a return to competitive state elections.

So what was the political orientation of the state's younger adults? It was decidedly more liberal. We found a 10-point increase in the proportion of adult residents describing themselves as liberals when comparing those who were in the age group of under 35 with the age group of 55 and older (36% to 26%). In the meantime, there was a 6-point decline in the self-described conservatives when we contrasted the younger and the older age groups (40% to 32%). Looking at this trend in another way, liberals outnumbered conservatives by a 4-point margin among those under age 35, while conservatives outnumbered liberals and by a 14-point margin among those who were 55 and older. However, no one can predict whether those more liberal leanings of younger adults will be voiced in elections.

The state's changing demographics are closely related to the low voting participation rates among younger Californians. Whites make up less than half of the adult population under the age of 35, while older Californians are overwhelmingly white. Younger adults are much less likely to own homes, have college degrees, use the Internet, and have high household incomes. Of course, all of these socioeconomic trends are typically tied to low voting participation. The wealthiest segment of the population is in the prime earning years, 35 to 54 years old. Those most likely to own a home are in the 55 and older age group. The low socioeconomic status of younger adults is strongly affected by the number of Latinos and immigrants.

There were also significant differences in political attentiveness across age groups. Nearly half of adults under age 35 said they have little or no interest in politics. By contrast, only about one in four adults over the age of 55 had little or no interest in politics. Similarly, the majority of older adults followed news about public affairs most of the time, and less than one in ten in this age group said they hardly ever or never pay attention to public affairs. By contrast, fewer than one in four of the under the age of 35 followed public affairs most of the time, while a similar one in four hardly ever or never does.

In sum, our analysis of the age profile in California politics provides some important findings for the future of both representative and direct democracy in California. Younger voters represent a small share of the voting public. They are unlikely to declare allegiance to either of the major parties. As for the future of the state's elections, a lack of voting participation and political interest among young Californians could have two dramatic impacts—a much smaller electorate and an electorate that is even more disproportionately older, white, and affluent than today. Young adults may turn to voting as they get older; but, again, they may not, because of the low socioeconomic status of the many Latinos counted among today's young adults. In sum, the state faces the possibility of a dwindling voting population and a further reduction in a low voter turnout that is already raising serious concerns about the state's elections representing the will of all of the people.

CONCLUSIONS AND IMPLICATIONS

California's statewide elections seem to have become one-sided affairs at a juncture in U.S. history when other large states in the nation seem to be politically competitive in terms of the Democratic and Republican parties. At no time has this trend been more apparent than during the 2000 elections. While the nation waited a month for the outcomes of vote counts in Florida to determine who would become the next president, the race in California was a foregone conclusion. California, it seems, has joined the ranks of the states where partisan elections are predictable. This has led observers to speculate that California has become so predictably Democratic and liberal in voting that it has become an irrelevant player in the national political arena.

We find the current, popular view that California has become a one-party state off base. In reality, the more significant political trend is the growth and flourishing of the un-party state, which is a result of the public's distrust in its political and governance system. Specifically, it is the voters outside of the major parties who are exerting a major influence on elections, while, at the same time, voters are playing a larger role in public policymaking through the initiative process. We see in these political trends further evidence of the powerful workings of postmaterialist values and a New Political Culture emerging in California. Predictably, affluent Californians in prosperous times have become less tied to party loyalties and more enamored with an issue-oriented politics that allows them to choose the policies they want to pursue at the ballot box.

No one can argue with the fact that California voters have moved decisively from the Republicans they supported from the 1980s through the early 1990s. Since the mid-1990s, the state has been a virtual lock for the Democratic top-of-the-ticket. But the notion that California is now a nonplayer in national politics is simply erroneous. Since 1990, the winner in the state's presidential sweepstakes has been highly predictive of the most popular candidate in the nation. This was also true in 2000. The GOP leaders can attest to what it takes for them to overcome the loss of fifty-four electoral college votes in California—finding enough votes elsewhere by arguing about the counting of hanging chads before the Florida and U.S. supreme courts. Moreover, the notion that California voters are now out of step with the nation is highly overstated. Californians for the most part share the views expressed by Americans on a range of policy issues. This is not an ultraliberal state; its political base is dominated by fiscal conservatism and distrust.

The Democrats have not made big gains in voter registration; in fact, in the dominant political trend, both major parties are losing share to the unaffiliated voters. The GOP has lost ground because of issues, which is what drives independent voters at the polls. The Republican party has not responded as quickly as the Democrats to the changing political and economic conditions of peace and prosperity. The GOP's themes in 2000—lowering taxes, fighting crime, defending against the nation's enemies—were dated and out of step. Their emphasis on social conservatism, in particular their stress on further restricting abortions, ran against the current of the many independent voters who mistrust government interference in individuals' private lives. Now, the GOP must come to grips with the voters' image of being both out of touch and out of power in California.

The Democrats, however, should not feel that confident about their newly found status as the dominant force in state politics. Their success has depended on their ability to corral the large and growing number of independent voters in the electorate. These are fickle voters who do not hold allegiance to any political party. They leaned toward the Democrats recently on the basis of the issues that drove them to the polls, because Democrats were perceived as the best problem solvers for those particular issues. But independents' distrust of government and their fiscal conservatism make them similar to GOP voters. Independent voters could shift back to the Republicans without much provocation, thus ending the talk about a one-party state. For instance, events such as the September 11, 2001, attacks—which refocused Americans on the threat of terrorism at home, military efforts abroad, and the economy—could be a stimulus to move the free-floating independent voters from one party to another party in upcoming elections.

The growing use of the initiative process is a major component of the public's lack of confidence in its government and its elected officials' ability to create good policy. However, the initiative process has reached the point where it, too, is suffering from distrust and disenchantment. The public is concerned about the prominent role that special interests are playing in what was supposed to be a populist tool for governance. It is frustrated by the confusion of what it considers to be too many poorly worded ballot measures. It is unhappy about the fact that the courts often reject measures the public has approved. Many Californians are calling for reforms of the institution they cherish.

The state's political future is most uncertain because of Californians' substantial disenchantment with politics and elections. In recent presidential elections, new records have been set for the lowest turnout of eligible adults. The voting groups that are likely to grow the fastest—Latinos and Asians—have been shown to have many impediments to increasing their political involvement. Moreover, independent voters are inclined to pass on elections, unless the issues impassion them. Many young adults are not registered to vote, and few are found among frequent voters. Will California become a state in which even fewer make decisions for the many? Will the economically privileged be the ones who go to the ballot box to vote and implement public policies for all residents in the state—rich and poor, young and old, white and nonwhite? In a direct democracy like California's—where citizens' initiatives on statewide ballots strongly influence policy directions—who participates is more crucial than which party rules.

CHAPTER 8

Lights Out for California?

Immediately after the 2000 election, the long period of public confidence in the economy was suddenly interrupted by an electric power crisis. This complex technical and market failure came out of nowhere, with little warning, and yet its consequences were potentially devastating. It was one of Californians' worst governmental nightmares—fatal flaws had surfaced in the little-known state legislation passed in the mid-1990s to deregulate the private electric companies. It was about to turn off the lights—and much more—on the state's residents and businesses. With this crisis, the state surplus and the good economic times were gone. As the state budget deficit grew in later months, the promise of massive efforts to improve the schools and to build the badly needed infrastructure for future population growth again went on hold. The crisis highlighted yet again the public's reasons for distrusting elected officials and for fearing the worst when it came to the government developing even the most basic plans for the future.

Needless to say, California doomsayers in the national press and late-show comedians had a field day with the state's electricity problem. "California Unplugged," screamed the cover page in *Time*, complete with a map of the state shaped as an electric plug disconnected from an electric cord. California would also have to test its relationship with the newly elected GOP president and ask for help from the person whom it had soundly rejected at the polls a few months earlier. The state would have its first taste of what political life could be like in an increasingly one-party state that finds itself irrelevant to—or at least politically on the outside of—the Washington administration.

This episode provides a compelling story for a book addressing the politics of distrust in times of prosperity. It is most instructive to view Californians and their government as the glow of prosperity began to dim, to see how the crisis came to be and what the already distrustful public's mood was like upon learning of the far-reaching consequences of its government's flawed deregulation plan.

CALIFORNIA'S ELECTRICITY PROBLEM

The electricity problem that surfaced in California in 2000 had its roots in a utility deregulation law that passed with little fanfare and public discussion five years earlier.[1] In 1996, GOP Governor Pete Wilson signed into law a piece of legislation that had passed unanimously in the Democratic-controlled state legislature. Essentially, what it did was to separate the regulation of generating power from the selling of electricity to residential and business customers. The private electric companies were to buy electricity on the wholesale market at whatever cost was available and then sell the electricity to their retail customers at a rate set by state regulators. Accordingly, the private electric companies sold off their power plants and for several years went about buying electricity from wholesalers inside and outside of the state. At the time of the deregulation law, a large surplus of electricity was being generated inside the state, although no new power plants had been built for some years. Everyone was supposed to benefit from deregulation—power producers, sellers, and customers alike.

The first signs of trouble arose during the summer of 2000 in San Diego. The price of electric power had skyrocketed due to an unexpected shortage of supply, and many of the 1.2 million residents in the region were faced with electric utility bills that were more than double what they were used to paying. This was the first region in the nation in which customers would be paying market prices for electric power, as the costs for buying power were passed on by the region's private electric company. Faced with an ugly political situation in just a few months before an election, the governor and state legislature were determined to find a

1. I gained detailed information on the state's electricity problem through many news articles and reports on the state's electricity problem, including Associated Press (2001); Bay Area Economic Forum (2001); Benson (2001); Brownstein (2001a); Geissinger (2001); Kasindorf (2001); Marelius (2001); Rogers (2001); Rose (2000); Schneider (2001); Stanton (2001); Sterngold (2001); and Walters (2001).

short-term solution, and they did. They passed a new law that allowed the private electric company to set up "balance accounts"—which were essentially IOUs or deferments on the higher-than-expected payments. The customers would continue to pay what they were accustomed to for electricity; and then, in a couple of years, they would be charged for the balance of the additional costs. California's elected representatives hoped that the wholesale costs would be lower in the future and that utility bills would decline. In the meantime, the electric companies would borrow money to make up the balance of unpaid bills.

The impression among legislators was that this was an isolated incident that had cropped up in one region and that had been solved by the legislation. It turned out that the problem in San Diego was actually a harbinger of bigger and much worse problems to come. The state's two giant private electric companies, covering most of the residents living in the north and south regions—Pacific Gas and Electric and Southern California Edison—were having to pay much higher wholesale prices than they expected. They had both amassed several billion dollars in debts to power producers, and they were forbidden by law to pass on the costs of buying electricity to their business and residential customers. By the end of the fall, wholesale producers were unwilling to sell electricity to the private electric companies, because they had no promise that these huge debts would be repaid. In the end, Pacific Gas and Electric declared bankruptcy. In the meantime, electricity was in short supply in the western states, and it was becoming increasingly difficult to buy enough to keep the lights on in California. Rolling blackouts and alerts of the threat of rolling blackouts were now a common occurrence.

In this situation, the state government had to step in and buy electricity directly from the wholesalers and give it to the private utility companies to distribute to consumers. The state was able to do this because it had the money and the creditworthiness to act as the buyer, while Pacific Gas and Electric and Southern California Edison had neither. The state government was now using the billions of dollars it had amassed in surplus funds to buy electricity.

While the governor was reluctant to raise electricity rates, the state's regulatory arm eventually did. The purpose of the higher electricity rates was to generate new money to fund the state bonds that would pay for the billions of dollars of surplus funds that were being used to buy electricity. The governor and Democratic-controlled legislature had rejected the idea of simply using the surplus funds to pay for electricity, since they were hoping to regain the surplus funds for use on state programs. In the meantime, the state government had opened up several lines of investigation into the actions of power generators and was looking for illegal actions such as price-fixing.

The state government took some additional actions at this point to try to increase the electricity supply in the summer months. This included expediting the permit process for building new power plants and easing air pollution restrictions so that more power plants in the state could operate for longer hours. In his speeches, the governor urged Californians to conserve electricity and cut household use by at least 10 percent. At the time, there was a shortage of electricity on the spot market. The state had six rolling blackouts and threats of many more in early 2001.

The governor also asked the Bush administration for a very specific kind of help. He did not want money from the federal government. When the state utilities sold their generating capacity, making out-of-state power producers major players in the wholesale electricity market in California, regulatory power shifted to the Federal Regulatory Commission (FERC). Thus, Davis wanted the federal government (in this case, represented by FERC) to place price caps on the cost of electricity sold to California by out-of-state power producers. The Bush administration repeatedly said "no," often with references to the state's "flawed" deregulation laws that did not pass on the charges to customers. The ground for denial was that price caps would discourage wholesale producers from selling electricity to California and that this would reduce the supply available to the state, thus exacerbating the problem. There was a tense encounter between President Bush and Governor Davis in California in late May. Was California irrelevant in the new GOP-dominated federal government? Yes. Then, the U.S. Senate switched to a Democratic majority, as a Vermont Republican left the Republican ranks and became an independent. Senate Democrats invited Governor Davis to present testimony on behalf of the state's problems. A few weeks later, the federal regulatory agency placed a cap on wholesale electric prices.

In the summer of 2001, the electricity crisis appeared to be easing. There was plenty of supply, new power plants were coming online, wholesale prices appeared to be dropping, and the state had secured long-term contracts for electricity. The governor pressed on with efforts to secure billions of dollars in refunds for what he termed exorbitant charges by wholesale electricity producers. The state's attorney general continued to investigate the possibility of criminal wrongdoing. In the meantime, the spike in electricity prices and routine blackouts did not materialize. The state's plan was in place to issue bonds to return the surplus funds that paid to keep the lights on.

As of this writing, the conventional wisdom was that the crisis had passed but that the state government would be paying dearly for the electricity problem for years to come. For one thing, the state government had signed billions of dollars worth of long-term electricity contracts at above-market rates. For another, the state government was going to have to float a record-setting $12.5 billion bond issue to repay the state treasury for the money borrowed to pay the electric bills for the ailing electric utility companies. In the end, the state spent more than its $8.5 billion surplus to keep the power on. The energy crisis had drained the state's precious surplus funds from active use in the closing days of economic prosperity. The electricity crisis had weakened Californians' already wavering confidence in the economy, which would deteriorate even further with the terrorist attacks on the East Coast on September 11, 2001. The state government's focus would return to cutting the state budget in order to avoid massive deficit spending. Meanwhile, in the wake of the Enron collapse, there were investigations into electricity market manipulation leading to California's energy shortage. Still, the electricity crisis had exacted a tremendous toll on Californians' already shaky trust in government.[2]

THE PUBLIC'S EARLY REACTIONS IN 2001: SHOCK AND CONFUSION

How did the public react to these events? The message was loud and clear in our focus groups in early 2001: Californians were worried, bordering on panicky, about the electricity problem. "It seems like it came out of nowhere," and "I don't know what to expect next," commented two Los Angeles residents. "The energy crisis is going to destroy the economy, no one will want to build businesses here, and the economy will go into a recession," said a Sacramento resident. Many were laying the problem on the state government's doorstep. "It seems like they were blindsided by this whole thing," commented a Santa Clara resident. The political problems of the energy crisis for Governor Davis were evident in a remark by a Sacramento resident, "I've lost all confidence in that man [Davis] and his ability to perform, just based on this. Where is the

2. For reviews of the fiscal and political state of the electricity problem in fall 2001, see Borenstein (2001); Howard (2001); Tamaki and Bustillo (2001); and Taub (2001).

control?" One focus group respondent summarized the effects: "This whole episode with the energy crisis has totally shaken my belief in the government having a grip on what's going on."

In our early January 2001 survey, energy captured the attention of residents and surged to the top of the list of residents' concerns. (See Table 8-1.) From this point on through the early summer, we saw public opinion about government and the economy degenerate even further, as Californians faced many uncertainties. Although residents were convinced about the cause of the problem—their government—they were divided about what actions the state's elected officials should take to resolve the electricity crisis. On one issue, there was almost universal agreement: that the electricity problem was a threat to the state's future.

For the first time in the Davis administration, public schools were no longer the dominant topic on people's minds. When asked to name the number one issue that the governor and legislature should work on, Californians were equally likely to name public schools and the electricity problem. One in four mentioned both issues. The public registered little interest in anything else. Problems such as population growth, the environment, jobs and the economy, traffic and transportation, and housing were named by fewer than 5 percent of Californians.

Residents in all of the major regions of the state rated electricity and public schools as the two most pressing issues facing the state. However, electricity prices edged ahead of schools in regions outside of Los Angeles and the San Francisco Bay Area. Los Angeles was the only area of the state where schools were mentioned much more often than electricity, reflecting that Los Angeles residents receive their electricity from a municipal power authority rather than one of the financially troubled private electric companies. Residents in all ethnic and racial groups and demographic categories listed schools and electricity as their top concerns. Whites tended to focus on electricity more than schools, and Latinos to focus on schools, crime, and other issues more than electricity, indicative of the large numbers of Latinos living in Los Angeles.

Whether or not the state's leaders and media were willing to call it a "crisis" at that point, Californians overwhelmingly viewed the issue of the cost, supply, and demand for electricity as a major problem in their state. Three in four residents said it was a "big problem," and more than nine in ten thought that the electricity situation was at least somewhat of a problem. There were regional variations, again, with two in three Los Angeles residents saying that this was a big problem, compared with three in four residents elsewhere. There was a high level of concern about

TABLE 8.1 MOST IMPORTANT
PROBLEM: TRENDS OVER TIME

"Which one issue facing California today do you think is most important for the governor and legislature to work on?"

	1999	2000	2001
Public schools	36%	28%	26%
Electricity	0	0	25
Budget and taxes	6	6	4
Jobs and the economy	5	5	4
Environment	3	5	4
Immigration	5	8	4
Health care	3	5	4
Crime	7	7	3
Transportation	2	3	2
Poverty	5	4	2
Other issues	10	12	10
Don't know	18	17	12

SOURCE: PPIC Statewide Survey (2001a), all adults.

this new issue across all regions and political, racial and ethnic, and socioeconomic groups.

Eight in ten Californians were convinced that the cost, supply, and demand for electricity would have adverse consequences for the state's economy over the next few years. More than half thought the harm to the state's economy would be very significant, while one in four expected at least some damage. While most residents in every region were anticipating that the electricity situation would do a great deal of harm to the economy, once again, the most concern arose among those living outside of Los Angeles. However, even in Los Angeles, half of the residents expected the state's economy to take a major hit as a result of the electricity problem. There was little difference across political, social, and economic groups in these perceptions.

Where did Californians place the blame for the electricity problem? Nearly half said it was their state legislature's deregulation of the industry five years earlier that was most responsible. About one in four blamed the private electric companies, which were close to bankruptcy at the time. Only one in ten said the current governor and legislature were responsible for the problem, while a similar number said the fault lay with

California consumers. Across every region of the state, about half of the public saw their former governor and legislature as the cause of the current crisis. In all political groups and socioeconomic categories, this issue was viewed as a government-made problem. The one exception was a distinction that surfaced between whites and Latinos: whites were more likely to blame government, while Latinos focused on the electric companies and consumers. This, of course, fits with Latinos' tendencies to see government in the most positive light, although it may also be partly explained by differing information sources.

When residents were asked to choose their most-favored solution for the electricity situation, there seemed to be no strong consensus. They were a little more likely to say reregulation of the state's electricity industry, which is explained by their belief that the problem was caused by deregulation. However, nearly as many said that the state needs to build more power plants, a point of view that takes into account that the strong demand for electricity causes both higher prices and the threat of rolling blackouts. There was also considerable discussion at the time about the state's failure to build new power plants for many years, and it is likely that this was considered as contributing to the severe shortage of electricity. About one in five residents felt that the problem could be solved if Californians did a better job of conserving energy. Only 1 percent favored the solution of raising electricity prices, which would have ultimately reduced demand for electricity and paid for the sky-rocketing costs of wholesale prices. At first, the California public seemed highly unwilling to pay for a problem that they viewed as caused by government. This attitude would contribute to reluctance on the part of the governor early in the crisis to raise taxes or increase utility bills as part of the solution to the crisis.

The governor's approach to the electricity problem did not seem to affect the public's confidence in his overall performance. He continued to enjoy high approval ratings, despite emerging concerns with electricity problems. Two in three residents said they liked the way the governor was handling his job, while one in four disapproved, and one in eight were undecided. The governor's approval ratings were the same as they were during the previous fall, when over six in ten residents said they felt he was doing a good job in office. As is typical, there was a partisan split on the approval ratings for the Democratic governor: three in four Democrats, six in ten independent voters, and just under half of Republicans approved of the overall job Davis was doing in office. Solid majorities in all regions of the state and in all racial and ethnic groups were approving of their governor's job performance. However, reflecting partisan differences, those in Los Angeles and the San Francisco Bay Area were more sympathetic toward Davis than others, and Latinos gave him more favorable ratings than whites did.[3]

The frustration that Californians felt toward the electricity problem surfaced in their evaluations of the governor's handling of the issue. We noted earlier that few residents blamed the current state office holders for the situation, yet most were not happy with the way their governor had responded to date. Almost two in three residents disapproved of his handling of the electricity problem, while only one in four approved; one in seven had no opinion. It should be noted that most of the people who disapproved of Davis's handling of the energy problem still blamed the situation on other factors—specifically, deregulation and the utilities—rather than on their current governor. Moreover, many residents who were saying they approved overall of the job he was doing in office, as well as in specific areas such as schools, crime, and the budget, were still not pleased with the way he was handling the electricity problem.

What was unique about this problem in its early stages was that residents experienced its threat more through media reports than through personal inconvenience. Few people were directly affected in any way, either through electricity disruptions or higher bills, but many had seen, heard, or read news stories about the possibility of future problems. It was a story that captivated the public's interest like none other having to do with government and business decisions in recent memory. Perhaps it was because of the potential threat to businesses and the economy, as well as to the lifestyle of individuals, but at any rate, Californians were galvanized by this issue. An astonishing eight in ten residents said they were "closely" following the news about the electricity problem, while nearly half said they were "very closely" following the story.

To say that public interest in the news about the electricity problem was unprecedented would not be an overstatement. By comparison, as many people followed the state's electricity story as mentioned that they had been closely following the around-the-clock news about the outcome of the close presidential election, and far fewer had been watching the news about the transition planning of President-elect Bush. There had

3. The California legislature was also viewed in a positive light by most residents: 58 percent approved, and 27 percent disapproved of the job they were doing; 15 percent remained undecided. Both Davis and the legislature appeared to benefit from the fact that most Californians still thought the state was going in the right direction (PPIC Statewide Survey, 2001a).

also been high profile political events involving the governor and state legislature in Sacramento, since we interviewed people several days before the governor's highly anticipated "State of the State" address in early January, yet we found far less interest in the state government news than in the electricity problem.

There had been a sharp increase in interest in news about the state's electricity problem since the fall. When the problem of utility deregulation and higher electricity bills was seen as confined to San Diego, fewer than half of Californians said they were closely following this story in September 2000.[4]

Yet even if the electricity problem was still one of potential threat rather than real consequences, its appearance on the scene had dimmed Californians' already low expectations for the immediate economic future of their state. The optimism consistently displayed by residents during the latter half of the 1990s suffered a major setback amid increasing worries about the electricity situation. Only half of the state's residents said they expected good economic times for the state in the coming year. Four in ten anticipated bad economic times lying before them in 2001. This presents a very different picture from the previous year and a half, when Californians were overwhelmingly optimistic about the state's economy. Economic optimism in the state had dropped by a stunning 27 points in less than a year.

The decline in economic confidence over time was found across all regions of the state, among all income groups, and in all racial and ethnic groups. In every region of the state, only about half of the residents were now expecting good economic times. Californians with higher incomes were more likely than those with lower incomes to predict good times, yet many in each group had grown pessimistic.

Clearly, there were many other issues that may have been contributing to the economic anxieties. Early in 2001, there were warnings of a slowing national economy, along with a steep drop in value among high-technology stocks. It was increasingly evident that the bubble had burst in the dot.com industry. Still, many of these real economic issues had not yet surfaced in residents' lives. For instance, in our January 2001 survey, we saw only a slight decline in consumer confidence, and few Californians said they were financially worse off than they were a year ago. What

---

4. In September 2000, the governor's handling of the electricity problem in San Diego were not highly noticed in the state: 28 percent approved, 36 percent disapproved, and 36 percent had no opinion (PPIC Statewide Survey, 2000f).

had happened, instead, was that people were more worried about their financial future (PPIC Statewide Survey, 2001a). The threat of blackouts and rising electricity prices contributed to concerns about what lay ahead.

In the early stages, the electricity problem had people worried but not panicking. Despite the dramatic drop in optimism about the state's economic future, six in ten Californians still thought that things in the state were generally going in the right direction, while half that number thought that things were on the wrong track. The public's perception that things in the state were still basically on the right track was consistent with what we had seen since the spring of 1998. The sense that the state was basically in good shape was present in all regions and across all income and racial and ethnic groups. In other words, the present was just fine, but the future was looking doubtful to the public. Of course, this also represents an element of public denial that the electricity problem would ever reach the stage where it would require pain and sacrifices.

THE PUBLIC'S LATER REACTIONS IN 2001: FRUSTRATION AND DISTRUST

As the electricity crisis moved into its more advanced stages, the public mood deteriorated significantly (see Table 8-2). In a statewide survey in May 2001, residents were far more negative than before in their assessment of the state and its handling of the problem. Californians remained riveted on the news about the electricity crisis, which they now perceived as such, with a remarkable eight in ten residents closely following media reports. There was much less interest in other political and economic news. While most residents did not specifically lay blame at the doorsteps of the president and the governor for creating the problem, six in ten residents were nonetheless unhappy with the performance of both Bush and Davis in handling the problem.

By late spring, Californians had also become progressively more pessimistic about the state and the direction of the economy. The majority of Californians now expected bad economic times to lie ahead, and more people thought the state was headed in the wrong direction rather than the right direction. The electricity problem led to a full-blown crisis of confidence, even before there were any signs of widespread discomfort. Many Californians had arrived at the conclusion that it would be "lights out" for California.

TABLE 8.2   CHANGE IN
OVERALL MOOD

"Turning to economic conditions, during the next 12 months do you think we will have good times financially or bad times?"

	August 2000	January 2001	May 2001
Good times	72%	51%	38%
Bad times	21	38	56
Don't know	7	11	6

"Do you think things in California are generally going in the right direction or the wrong direction?"

	October 2000	January 2001	May 2001
Right direction	59%	62%	44%
Wrong direction	32	29	48
Don't know	9	9	8

SOURCE: PPIC Statewide Survey (2000e, 2000g, 2001a, 2001b), all adults.

Californians faced the prospects of a summer of rolling blackouts and higher utility rates with great trepidation. Nearly half now said that electricity was the most critical issue facing the state; fewer than one in ten mentioned the public schools. Eight in ten thought the problem of the cost, supply, and demand of electricity in California was a big problem. Two in three were convinced that this issue would cause a great deal of harm to the state's economy over the next few years.

Residents continued to direct blame toward the former state officials and private electric utility companies that were instrumental in developing and implementing the deregulation laws, rather than toward the current office holders in Sacramento and Washington. With one of the two major utilities having declared bankruptcy, the focus on solutions had shifted from government—in the form of reregulation of the electricity industry—to building more power plants.

Governor Davis saw his overall approval ratings drop by about 15 points (see Table 8-3). Almost as many disapproved as approved of his overall performance, after a long period when most residents consistently approved of the governor's job performance. These ratings were gathered after the state had approved electricity rate hikes to pay for bonds covering the state's electricity costs. More and more, the governor's job

TABLE 8.3   GOVERNOR'S REPORT CARD:
TRENDS OVER TIME

"Do you approve or disapprove of the way that Gray Davis is handling his job as governor?"

	October 2000	January 2001	May 2001
Approve	60%	63%	46%
Disapprove	28	24	41
Don't know	12	13	13

"Do you approve or disapprove of the way that Governor Davis is handling the issue of the cost, supply, and demand for electricity?"

	September 2000	January 2001	May 2001
Approve	28%	24%	29%
Disapprove	36	62	60
Don't know	36	14	11

SOURCE: PPIC Statewide Survey (2000f, 2000g, 2001a, 2001b), all adults.
NOTE: For September 2000, ratings were for handling the electricity problem in San Diego.

performance was being judged on the basis of his ability to resolve the electricity crisis, and he was facing an increasing risk of angering voters as a result of higher utility bills. Once again, approval ratings seemed to rise and fall with the times, since Californians did not have a foundation of overall trust in their government and elected officials.

The effects of the electricity crisis on trust in government was evident in our May 2001 survey: Two in three Californians said the problem made them less confident in the state government's ability to plan for the future. We found this negative reaction across all regions, party lines, and demographic groups. The electricity problem had clearly damaged the already vulnerable relationship between Californians and their government.[5]

In the early summer, worries about the electricity problem persisted, as did the problem's effects on consumer confidence and political trust. In a July 2001 survey, eight in ten Californians continued to closely watch this story. More than half now described the energy crisis as the top issue in the state. More than three in four rated electricity as a big

5. PPIC Statewide Survey (2001b), May 2001.

problem. More than half predicted serious, negative consequences for the state's economy, and half blamed former and current state office holders in Sacramento and Washington. Few saw government involvement as an answer to the problem—only one in four residents called for reregulation. Most thought that marketplace issues were most crucial— six in ten residents thought that increasing supply (i.e., building power plants) and decreasing demand (i.e., conservation) were the way out of the problem.

Even though blackouts had thus far been avoided, far fewer than half approved of the job the governor (39%) and state legislature (45%) were doing to solve this problem. Nearly half of Californians (45%) said they had very little or no confidence in the governor and state legislature when it came to passing new laws to resolve the issue. Even though the voters recognized that the root cause of the electricity problem lay with previous state office holders, they were reluctant to give credit to their current elected officials for averting a more serious crisis. As a true signal that persistent distrust in representative democracy surfaces in times of both normalcy and crisis, two in three residents said the best way to solve California's electricity problem was to let the voters decide through the initiative process.

By the late fall of 2001, the electricity blackouts that people feared had not materialized. Moreover, there were investigations into the manipulation of electricity markets. Still, the damage had been done. The large budget surplus had vanished, huge borrowing costs for electricity were looming before the state, and fiscally austere times had returned to the government's annual budget process. Californians had stopped believing in prosperous economic times, and many still worried that the state's electricity problem could do harm to an already weak economy. Few gave the governor a lot of credit for averting rolling blackouts, and many were displeased with his policies, while fewer than half supported Davis's reelection. The electricity problem had provided further confirmation to a cynical public that they could not trust their state government.[6]

CONCLUSIONS AND IMPLICATIONS

For years, we have been hearing from Californians that their state government is ill-prepared for the future. Californians were reminded

6. PPIC Statewide Survey in July, November, and December (2001c, 2001d, 2001e).

through the electricity crisis—with a real and vivid example—that state elected officials are not good at visualizing what future conditions will be like or at designing the kinds of legislation that will be best suited to providing for tomorrow's public services. The governor and state legislature had passed a utility deregulation law that was firmly grounded in the supply-and-demand circumstances of the mid-1990s, but ill-suited to the rapid population growth occurring in California. This episode left Californians worrying and wondering: What state government errors and miscalculations would be next? How would the governor and state legislature handle the growing scarcity of water, the need for rebuilding the state's infrastructure, diminishing quality of schools, or other unforeseen crises?

Since Californians are generally distrustful toward government, the fact that their government was directly responsible for the electricity problem through passing flawed legislation led to more than simple disappointment. We tracked a range of emotions among the public as this crisis evolved from its early days to the time of this writing: denial that the problem could spread from San Diego to other regions, followed by shock and confusion as it became a statewide issue, and then anger, frustration, and further distrust of the current state office holders. California thus far has averted a serious crisis, but people will likely remember this as an example of their state government's failure for years to come. It will be viewed with some bitterness as the beginning-of-the-end of a remarkable time of surplus and prosperity.

The electricity problem in this state, like the natural disasters before it and the calls for help from the East Coast after the terrorist attacks in September 2001, did show that Californians were more than willing to make sacrifices when they were called upon to do so. It suggested once again to people that they were more capable of solving problems than were the politicians they had elected to office.

In January 2001, the governor pointed out that the solution to the electricity shortage lay partly in the hands of the state's 34 million residents: if they could conserve energy, then the state might be able to avert blackouts. The governor asked every household to reduce its electricity use by 10 percent. Some doubted that Californians would meet such lofty goals, but they actually exceeded them.

Without the public spirit of cooperation, the lights may very well have gone out in California. Amidst this looming problem, one hopeful sign in particular emerged: Californians can be counted on when it comes to playing a helpful role in a state of crisis. But, as we indicated earlier, Californians soon remarked that they wanted to take the lead role in solving the problem away from elected officials. By mid-year, only a handful of residents had a great deal of confidence that their elected officials could rectify the problem, and most felt it was a better idea to have voters resolve the issue at the ballot box. In the end, many residents saw the electricity crisis as a problem created by the politicians and solved by the public.

CHAPTER 9

Insights after a
Golden Moment

As California approached the threshold of the twenty-first century, it seemed to be entering a golden era. Confidence in the economy was at an all-time high, and there were even economists who spoke of a different economy, one for which new rules would have to be written. Yet for the public, there was a dark shadow in that golden glow, something that made Californians less sanguine about the more distant future. That something was largely a distrust of government and a lack of confidence that the government could cope with some of the more formidable challenges taking shape for the state. Then came the electricity crisis early in 2001, and with it corroboration of some of the public's deepest apprehensions about the abilities of state government. Then, in September 2001, the nation was shaken by terrorist attacks on New York and Washington. The state's budget deficit ballooned as the economy weakened. The remaining hopes for extending this all-too-brief period of peace, security, and prosperity now seemed gone for good. The golden "era" in California proved to be more of a golden "moment," but it provided sharp insights into how distrust has played out on the state's social, economic, and, most important, political stage and what it portends for the future of the state and perhaps even the nation.

THE BLIGHTING EFFECTS OF DISTRUST
IN CALIFORNIA POLITICS

At the turn of the century, Californians' lack of confidence in government and elected officials, evident in so many dimensions, had led to major uncertainties about the future. While it is too early to tell at this writing, it does not seem that the terrorist attacks will lead to a public reassessment of government at all levels, as it appears to have for the federal level at the early stage of the terrorist threat. At any rate, the intent of this volume is to focus on Californians and their government: our detailed analysis of the state in its most recent, and seemingly fleet, moment of prosperity has led us to the following conclusions.

1. *Californians were in good spirits due to prosperous times but worried about the future because of a lack of faith in their government's abilities.* Most Californians were feeling comfortable about the way life was going in the state for several years up to and through the 2000 elections, yet they were uneasy about what lay ahead for California's future. Their upbeat mood was reinforced by some powerful economic trends in the late 1990s: among the many positive signs were ample job opportunities, strong income growth, housing appreciation, and a booming stock market. Yet it took little probing to recognize that there was only a superficial sense of happiness about the state of the state.

What were residents worried about? They were keenly aware that California is unprepared for the rapid and continuous changes occurring in the state. There were signs of decades of growth without careful planning, such as worsening traffic, lack of affordable housing, creeping urban sprawl, and vanishing open space. There were even more troubling indications of inequality: Latinos, the fastest growing racial and ethnic group in the state, were the least well off. Californians knew that their current prosperity, in and of itself, could not address future issues. Only the government could do that, but it was not addressing these issues, and there were serious doubts that it was up to the challenge.

The electricity problem was the state's wake-up call for how much work remained to be done—at least that is how average residents saw it. In the spring of 2001, three in four residents said that population growth in recent years had contributed to the state's electricity shortage, and two in three felt this new problem made them less confident in the state's ability to plan for the future (PPIC Statewide Survey, 2001b).

Many experts who were closely observing the growth and change in California had been uneasy about the state's lack of forethought and planning for the decades yet to come. They had issued warnings that public officials were not keeping a close eye on the roads, water systems, and basic infrastructure needed to keep the state functioning at a higher population level (Baldassare, 2000). While much of the focus to date had been on the lack of adequate infrastructure spending, the electricity problem pointed to the fundamental issues of mismanagement.

2. Prosperity and budget surpluses did little to change the public's feelings of distrust; voters were unwilling to increase spending and taxes, and public officials were hesitant to ask for more funds.

In the late 1990s, following years in which they scrambled to make ends meet and postponed spending on important items, the state and federal governments were in the unusual position of having to decide what to do with all of the excess cash they had on hand. In California, the public responded with some ambivalence. They heaped praise on the immediate performances of their state and federal elected officials, but they gave them little credit for the prosperous times they were enjoying and barely budged from their long-held perspective that their elected officials were incompetent when it came to managing money and solving problems. While many were eager to see the surplus spent on needed programs rather than returned through tax cuts, there was hesitancy about expanding the role of government.

The state government had been able to avert a more serious electricity crisis, largely because there were billions of dollars in surplus funds that could be spent on electricity. It is interesting to speculate about what would have happened if there had been no surplus to bail out the state. Would the government have borrowed money, or would it have asked the public to share the pain and pay higher taxes and utility bills? Probably not the latter, judging from the response of state politicians at every stage.

Elected officials remained very anxious about asking the public for more money, to such an extent that their reluctance compromised their ability to make sound policy judgments. For example, their reluctance to mandate assistance from the public led to a critical flaw in the deregulation plan: residents' utility bills could be increased even when wholesale prices spiked. In San Diego, where residential electricity rates skyrocketed, the legislature sought to quiet residents' fears with long-term IOUs, thus postponing a serious discussion about what went wrong with deregulation until it became a full-fledged statewide problem. As the crisis spread, the governor announced that he would not raise electricity rates, and he stubbornly followed this self-imposed restriction until the state ran low on surplus funds. In the end, six in ten Californians said they preferred paying higher electricity rates to pay off the debts rather than using the surplus funds that would otherwise go to state programs (PPIC Statewide Survey, 2001a). There was no public outcry against the plan of the legislature and governor to increase utility bills to pay for state bonds, but there was plenty of evidence of nervous politicians. We expect politicians will continue to avoid asking the public to pay for problems, fearing that such requests will be remembered come election time.

3. *Schools may be the main focus in plentiful times, but distrust limits the public's willingness to spend money on their priority issue, and public support for improving schools is fleeting in the face of other troubles.* California had allowed its public schools to drift from excellent to mediocre, just at the time when the schools were needed the most to teach and train the state's new majority-minority. Residents were dedicated to improving their schools at the turn of the century, even when their lights began to flicker in early 2001. They recognized that the schools' fall from grace was partly financial—a lack of local funding created by Proposition 13, which was put in place by voters like themselves. Still, they were reluctant to support efforts making it easier to raise local taxes for schools, even in the height of prosperity. Ironically, a measure easing the requirements to pass local school bonds may have succeeded only because some voters thought they were *tightening* the restrictions. If California has any chance of overcoming a future filled with income inequality, the reforms that have already been implemented have to be working, and the state must remain steadfastly committed over the long haul to the difficult and expensive task of improving the quality of public schools. However, the electricity crisis demonstrated the difficulty of staying focused on schools when prosperity ends and other troubles are brewing.

Schools had no competition as the number one problem in California, as long as people were rating the economy as strong and the state as heading in the right direction. By early 2001, schools were tied with the electricity situation as the number one problem in the state. Later in the year, schools barely registered in responses to our survey questions about the most important issue facing the state. Electricity had become the single, dominant issue du jour.

Many observers of California's times of plenty expressed skepticism about the state's fixation on schools. They thought that it was an oddity that could be explained by the conditions of a strong economy, a budget surplus, and no serious competing problems. Interest would fade, they said, as it had in the 1980s and 1990s, leaving schools with little public support to carry through on the long-term investments and reforms that would be needed to turn the situation around. Certainly, voter reactions to the initiatives in 2000 that sought to lower the threshold for passing local school bonds had raised serious doubts about the public's commitment to education spending. Then, the importance of schools faded with the first signs of deteriorating economic conditions. Obviously, the public's commitment to following through on their state government's plans to improve the public schools rested on shaky grounds. Unfortunately, without better public schools, any long-term hopes of addressing the socioeconomic inequalities clouding the state's future are dim.

4. The environment was a heightened concern in prosperous times, and residents approached local growth issues by taking matters into their own hands.
The state's residents were truly worried about how the environment was affecting their quality of life, and they had many reasons to be concerned. Close to home, they saw their cities growing rapidly and their regions beset with traffic and other growth-related problems. The state had (and has) a host of environmental problems ranging from air pollution to toxic waste to loss of farmland and open space to pollution at its beaches. Certain regions are more vulnerable than others—with notable differences in environmental and growth-related concerns between the more affluent urban coastal areas and the economically challenged and fast-growing Central Valley.

Californians want more environmental help from the state government, but there is little awareness of or confidence in the state's handling of complex issues involving growth, land use, and the environment. A lack of confidence in local elected officials is evident in the large number of growth control initiatives that appeared on local ballots in 2000. Unless there is consensus on state-level activities, growth and land use policies seem destined to be decisions made at local ballot boxes.

5. The growth of the Latino population could result in major political changes, since many Latinos have expressed more trust than other groups in government.

California officially became a majority-minority state in 2000, as the Latino and Asian populations continued to expand. In twenty years, Latinos will be the largest racial and ethnic group, and they are predicted to account for half of the state's population by mid-century. Latinos have started to make a mark on politics by voting in greater numbers, by largely supporting Democrats, and by gaining office in federal and state legislative races. In policy preferences, Latinos have been more likely than others to favor an active government. They are more trusting of government, more willing for government to become involved in business and personal decisions, and more optimistic about the government's ability to shape California's future.

At the same time, it is important to note that Latinos are not yet achieving anything close to their real potential in terms of influence in the political realm, and lack of socioeconomic and educational progress may limit their voting participation. Will there be major strides in the educational and income levels of Latinos, which generally accompany increased voter participation? The answer to this question may in large part determine the future of voter distrust and election outcomes in California.

6. California has become an un-party state, rather than a one-party state: the major political trends in force are an increasing number of independent voters and a more prevalent reliance on citizens' initiatives.

The Democrats continued to be on a roll in the 2000 elections. This success was not the result of increased Democratic registration and party-line voting. Rather, it reflects the increase in independent voters and the Democrat's success in focusing on issues that independent voters care about in times of surplus and plenty—schools and programs that provide for future health and well-being. Meanwhile, Republicans have lost ground by remaining with the issues that were their strong suits with independent voters in the past: defense, crime, and fiscal restraint. Still, when the economy falters and budget deficits once again become the norm, the state's elections may well return to a more competitive two-party status. The loosely affiliated independent voters, who are highly distrustful of government and political parties, can easily shift their allegiances as they have before.

Meanwhile, voter distrust deepened and expanded in scope in the aftermath of the 2000 presidential election controversy. Voters became more distrustful of voting, elections, and the political process itself. They also expressed frustration over the state's initiative process, offering the opinion that initiatives had become confusing, abused, and all-too-often driven by special—particularly moneyed—interests.

Yet the state's residents were even less impressed with their legislators' ability to make good laws and public policies. Californians have been telling us for years in our statewide surveys that they could do a better job than the paid professionals in Sacramento and that they would thus prefer to make all of the important decisions at the ballot box through the initiative process. The fact that their state elected officials signed off on what is now almost unanimously viewed as a flawed effort to deregulate the state's electricity industry only served to reinforce people's negative view of the representative system of government. Now, the choice between representative democracy and direct democracy was seen as a decision about the lesser of two evils.

Some observers have opined that the deregulation debacle can be laid at the door of term limits, which put inexperienced elected officials in the position of making important decisions about issues that they knew little about. Such excuses do not fly with the public, which prefers to keep its legislators on a short leash.

7. In many ways, the electricity problem underscored the state's lack of readiness for the future and the reasons why voters distrust their government.

On a consistent basis, throughout prosperity and recession, many Californians have said they do not trust the government to do what is right. They prefer a smaller government that does less over a larger government that does more. Some wonder how much the government can actually accomplish when it comes to resolving problems. Others complain that the government interferes too much in their private lives, gets in the way of business, and keeps the market from working more efficiently. The state's electricity crisis did not, in and of itself, cause voters to distrust their government, but it did reinforce their low expectations of the government's performance.

The long run of prosperity from the mid-1990s through the 2000 election ended on a sour note. A flawed deregulation plan from the governor and state legislature five years earlier led to a statewide crisis in the supply and cost of electricity by the end of 2000. The state government was forced to intervene, and it used the large budget surplus that was supposed to provide money for schools and infrastructure to keep the lights on. In this one brief moment, the hopes for addressing future problems with surplus monies vanished as quickly as the coffers emptied. In short, the electricity problem exacerbated Californians' crisis of confidence in their government. It symbolized to many people what was most worrisome about their state: an inability of its government leaders to think ahead and plan for what will be needed as population growth and demographic change rapidly alter the face of California.

The electricity issue was defined by the public from the start as a government-induced problem due to state interference and deregulation of the electricity industry. So how did people want to fix the problem? Ironically, despite their lack of confidence and their desire for less government interference, the public's first response was to suggest that the government reregulate the electricity market. Moreover, when the governor allowed the state to step into the electricity business, the public showed little sign of opposition. As for the governor asking the president for help, the idea of the federal government intervening in a state problem sounded just fine to most residents. Indeed, the public would welcome any efforts by Washington to place a cap on the price of electricity supplied by out-of-state producers.

However, by summer 2001, earlier attitudes had reasserted themselves. Most Californians said they wanted the state government to get out of the electricity business. Lacking a belief that their government could rewrite the state's electricity laws without inflicting further damage, many wanted the voters to decide what policies should be adopted. Even though it appeared that their government had averted a serious crisis, and investigations were pointing to the fact that electricity market manipulation had occurred, Californians still had little faith that their elected officials could do the right thing, could perform their duties efficiently, and could be responsive to people's needs. For years, Californians will be reminded of their government's mistakes in the energy arena—as the state pays for billions in bond debts through higher electric bills to consumers and as the utility companies and their shareholders and employees limp out of their financial limbo. The need to restore faith and credibility in government has never been more evident—but how can this possibly be done?

MAKING CALIFORNIA'S DEMOCRACY WORK BETTER

Improving both the process and the inclusiveness of California's democracy might go a long way toward restoring public trust in government. The following list provides some recommendations that might help avert a further crisis in confidence with respect to candidates who are elected to state office, initiatives that become state law, and the perceived trustworthiness of government officials.

1. *Bring modern technology to the election process.*
A visit to a California polling place on Election Day is like a stroll into the Twilight Zone. It is as if we are transported into the nineteenth century—no machinery, no electricity. We are checked in through paper lists of eligible voters and then are handed ballots that we complete with pens or punch machines. We drop the ballots in cardboard boxes. Californians have increasingly traded this scene for the convenience of filling out a ballot at home and dropping it in the mail. Today, about one in four voters take the absentee-ballot route, far more than the system was ever intended to handle. We now know that pretechnology voting systems are fraught with problems and errors. California's polling places and absentee ballots are no exceptions. Had California's presidential election been a close one, we would have been the laughing stock of the nation. It was a month from Election Day before all of the California ballots were hand-counted, largely due to the volume of paper absentee ballots. The state government must offer incentives and pressure to move the voting operations of all counties into the high-tech modern era, including touch-screen voting in polling places and absentee voting online.

2. *Encourage voter registration and participation.*
When all is said and done, the most we can expect these days is for half of the state's eligible adults to participate in presidential elections. Fewer show up for gubernatorial races and state primaries, and even fewer for local elections. Why worry? Well, because voter turnouts today are far lower than even in the recent past, and they show signs of declining even more. The state has two problems that lead to low voter turnout: Many people are not registering to vote, and many people who are registered to vote are not casting ballots. These two issues can and should be addressed so that more Californians will vote. For many Californians, elections do not become interesting until the final weeks of a campaign. By the time they focus, it is too late to register to vote. Like other states, California could allow people to register to vote in the days immediately preceding the election or on Election Day itself. How about expanding the locations and making registration an easier task? In order to get more people to cast ballots, more options should be made available. Why does voting have to take place at a local polling place on Election Day? Shopping malls, stores,

banks, public libraries, and government buildings could be outfitted with touch-screen voting systems so that people could log in and cast their ballots at times and places that are convenient. Why is it easier to buy a lottery ticket than to vote? Only because politicians are reluctant to change the rules, fearful that the outcome may favor their opponents, while low turnout continues to imperil democracy.

3. Strive for a more representative electorate and office holders.
California has now become a majority-minority state. Moreover, it will become a mostly Latino state in the early 2020s if current projections hold. The electorate is changing—the percentage of white voters has declined 10 points over the last decade, while the number of Latino and Asian voters has been climbing. Elected officials in the state are also becoming a more racially and ethnically diverse group. However, the changing diversity in the political composition of the state has been minimal, and there are reasons to think it may soon stall out. Asians have been slow to gravitate to politics, even as they assimilate into the state's high-tech economy, higher education, and home ownership. Latinos have lagged behind in political participation, because lower income and education levels seem to be major hindrances. Moreover, many young adults of all races and ethnicities have simply tuned out the political scene. Someone has to nurture the state's political process toward greater social diversity. Without any help, the electorate and elected officials may remain distinctly different from the public. This process need not be solely in the hands of the major political parties, especially given the large number of people who are inclined to register as independent voters. The state's nonprofit organizations have the resources and credibility to participate in this activity, which would amount to a massive public education campaign and community outreach efforts. But what better way to invest in the state's future than to create a more inclusive electorate and government?

4. Take a "mend it, don't end it" approach to citizens' initiatives.
Critics see direct democracy as a threat to the power and influence of representative democracy, which they consider a superior system of governance. For this reason, many elected officials and political observers would like to see the initiative process just go away. All of this negativity directed toward the initiative process will not stop it from becoming a more important element in state policymaking. A more constructive effort would

be to have the seasoned politicians and policy experts working to improve the initiative system. There are plenty of areas that need fixing, and the public readily admits that it is time to change this much-beloved "fourth branch" of government. Is the system badly broken? Probably it is. There are too many initiatives qualifying for the ballot, too many written in a confusing manner, too many that pass and yet are determined by the courts to be invalid or illegal, and too much involvement in the process by big money and special interests. However, there is no shortage of good ideas for reforming the process—for example, the proposals offered in the mid-1990s by the California Constitution Revision Commission and, more recently, by the Speaker's Commission on the California Initiative Process. What is now needed is a concerted, bipartisan effort to make the initiative process better.

5. Reform the campaign finance system.
It was former Speaker Jesse Unruh who coined the phrase "money is the mother's milk of politics." Money is also the corrosive force that is destroying people's confidence in both their elected officials and the citizens' initiative process. The public assumes that campaign contributions have a negative influence on state policymaking, and too much of the news they hear out of Sacramento corroborates this belief. Even before the 2000 election was over, state elected officials were busy filling their campaign war chests for the 2002 elections with funds from the companies they were supposed to be regulating. In the 2000 elections, we saw a new trend emerge in the arena of campaign finance: high-tech millionaires using their fortunes to push their favorite policy idea through as an initiative. It is not as though special interests have not always been players. Rather, it is the concept of individuals using their money to change the state's constitution and laws without enduring the scrutiny of public office. The progress to date in campaign finance reform is disappointing. Consider these two election outcomes in California: both parties ganged up to defeat Proposition 25, a tough campaign finance initiative in March 2000; then, both parties were able to push through their own campaign finance law in November 2000, Proposition 34, which rolled back the disciplined restrictions that voters had enacted years ago. Without true limits on campaign finance, the voters will become even more alienated from and angry with their government and elected officials, and they will eventually become cynical even about the initiative process.

SEPTEMBER 11: WHAT WE LEARNED ABOUT TRUST
IN GOVERNMENT

Americans reacted with shock, anger, and grief after the twin towers of
the World Trade Center collapsed in New York and a wing of the Pentagon was in flames in Washington, D.C., on a day that shall live in in-
famy—September 11, 2001. Three airplanes piloted by hijackers pur-
posely crashed into these symbols of American economic power and
military might. In an unprecedented step, all flights originating from and
entering the United States were cancelled. School children were sent
home and workplaces and downtowns were emptied as a precaution
against further attacks. The stock market and air travel were suspended
for days. Special procedures were undertaken to ensure the safety of the
president, the vice president, and congress. At this writing, about 3,100
casualties were counted among the plane crash victims, the workers in
the targeted buildings, and the fire and police personnel involved in the
rescue operations. In the early hours of the worst terrorist attack in U.S.
history, people strained to comprehend the horror that had occurred and
turned to worrying about what terrorist attacks on America would be
next.

The president concluded, "We are at war," and told other nations that
they were either "for us or against us" in a battle involving a new kind
of twenty-first-century war with an unknown, invisible, and menacing
enemy. Some even compared the terrorist attacks on that frightful day
to the attack on Pearl Harbor. In the weeks after September 11, the federal government began a "war on terror" on two fronts. On the domestic
scene, it worked to track down suspected terrorists and increased security in airports and likely targets of attack. On the international scene,
the government sent the U.S. military to Afghanistan to hunt down
Osama Bin Laden and his Al Qaeda network—the presumed master-
minds of the terrorist attacks, who were in hiding there—and to put an
end to the Taliban regime in the country that had given refuge to those
involved in the worst terrorist attack on American soil.

Americans reacted as they typically do in times of war, during serious
emergencies, or after national tragedies. They rallied around their country and its most visible leaders. The national surveys taken in the weeks
after September 11 indicated near-unanimous support for the president
and whatever actions government officials said were needed to assure
the safety and security of the nation. Most Americans had said they were
dissatisfied with the way things were going in the country in surveys

taken before September 11; afterward, most respondents indicated that they were satisfied. The normal partisanship in approval ratings had been suspended; Democrats, Republicans, and independent voters all agreed that their government and its officials were doing well. Americans seemed eager to express their support for efforts to defeat a common enemy, and they did so when asked to respond in public opinion surveys.

In California, we saw trends that closely paralleled those found in the national surveys. In two post–September 11 surveys in the fall of 2001, six in ten residents said the state was headed in the right direction, which was a reversal of the mood of the public a few months earlier. Eight in ten Californians approved overall of the job the president was doing in office, a 33-point increase since July, and even more liked his handling of terrorism and security issues. Six in ten state residents rated the performance of Congress as excellent or good in December, a 21-point increase since October 2000. The governor's and state legislature's ratings showed smaller gains; about half of adults approved of their job performance overall in December 2001 and January 2002.

One shift in attitudes that took public opinion experts by surprise was a dramatic increase nationally in reports of trust in the federal government. In the immediate aftermath of September 11, solid majorities of Americans said that they trusted the federal government to do what is right "always" or "most of the time." Such a positive response to this question had not been seen in forty years. Some believed that the terrorist attacks may be a socially transforming event that could end the long-standing distrust in government; this belief fit with a school of thought at the time that America would recover but would "never be the same" after September 11. Perhaps, then, the new normalcy would include a level of trust in the government that was a throwback to earlier times.

Most political observers attributed the spike in confidence to the public's shock and concern toward a catastrophic event. They expected the trust in government to be temporary in nature, and they made similar predictions about the record-high approval ratings for the president. Indeed, there formerly have been dramatic examples of such attitude changes. During the Persian Gulf War, the president's approval ratings skyrocketed, and then they plunged within a few months. National surveys in the late fall of 2001—only two months after the terrorist attacks—found that trust in the federal government had already dropped below a majority, even while eight in ten Americans continued to approve of their president's job performance. Still, the level of trust in government was high by recent standards, although also reflecting a dramatic decline in this attitude within a few weeks time.

What can we learn about changes in trust in government attitudes from the September 11 attacks? First, people may be reluctant to make negative statements about their government in times of great peril—either because they want to reassure themselves that they are in good hands or because they are reluctant to speak out and to appear to be disloyal and even suspicious in their views. More important, increasing trust offers reaffirming evidence of the strong link between postmaterialist values and distrust in government in our times: when the public's sense of security is lost—perhaps people felt more vulnerable than ever before in the wake of the September 11 attacks—many people gravitate to the idea that government will meet their basic needs, such as their safety from terrorism. As the threat recedes, though, the focus on quality of life and common feelings of distrust in government are likely to resurface—unless government takes action that changes people's opinions about its ability to be effective, efficient, honest, and responsive. Many Americans saw their government as responsive after September 11, but that alone will not create permanent opinion changes; new evidence about efficiency, honesty, and effectiveness are also needed.

If the public had broadly changed its opinions toward government, then we should see attitude changes toward the government's role, state government, and proposals involving taxes and spending. Such attitude changes may take many months or even years to fully assess, but the preliminary evidence suggests that they have not occurred.

The same surveys that indicated a growing trust in federal government after September 11 also showed that most Americans still preferred a smaller government with fewer services. In our January 2002 survey, Californians expressed more trust in the federal government to do what is right than they had a year earlier, while overall trust in the state government was unchanged. Californians seemed to hold on as stubbornly as ever to the view that state and local governments should give them something for nothing. When asked about the state budget deficit, for instance, their responses after September 11 followed the pattern we had seen earlier. Residents wanted the state government to give "high priorities" to education, health, and welfare spending in light of a budget deficit. Yet most residents preferred for the state government to reduce spending and avoid any tax increases as the solution to a huge budget deficit. The 2002 election would offer many opportunities to test the staying power of distrust in government after September 11. As of this writing, the indications are that we should not expect a sea change in the public's attitudes toward its government and toward spending and tax issues.[1]

FINAL THOUGHTS

If Californians could not find enough reasons to feel good about their government in the near-perfect circumstances surrounding the 2000 elections, they never may—unless, that is, there is a concerted effort to change from the inside the things that trouble people about their governments. Perhaps in times of external threat or national emergency, as Americans experienced after the terrorist attacks in the fall of 2001, there is a strong tendency for people to rally around their top leaders and the federal government. But that may prove to be an initial, narrow, and short-lived reaction to crisis, rather than a solid and permanent bond between the people and their government, unless there is a deep reservoir of trust to carry the newfound positive feelings forward and into more normal circumstances. Moreover, the nationalistic and patriotic feelings that are expressed in times of national crisis, as we saw in the wake of terrorist attack on American soil, may not trickle down to the state and local government levels.

The idea of reform-from-within leading to a government that lives up to the public's expectations of responsiveness, honesty, efficiency, and effectiveness holds the most promise for California. Only this can break the cycle of distrust that places government officials in the unenviable position of lacking the resources needed to tackle problems—the public's trust and its willingness to give elected representatives the power and money to do what needs to be done. Without the proper resources and authority, further public failures and disappointments by state and local governments are inevitable. Until change from within takes place, Californians will continue to use the citizens' initiative process as it was intended by its creators: as a state policymaking tool of last resort intended to hold the elected officials closely accountable to the people who have lost confidence in their judgment. In the final analysis, the largest U.S. state remains woefully unprepared for its challenging future.

1. See PPIC Statewide Surveys (2001d, 2001e, 2002) and national surveys in the months immediately after September 11 by the *Los Angeles Times* (Brownstein, 2001b); *Washington Post* and ABC News (Morin and Deane, 2001); Gallup (Newport, 2001); and the *New York Times* and CBS News (Stille, 2001).

References

Alvarez, R. Michael and John Brehm. 1998. "Speaking in Two Voices: American Equivocation about the Internal Revenue Services." *American Journal of Political Science* 42 (2): 418–452.

Associated Press. 2001. "Chronology of California's Power Crisis." April 6.

Ayon, David R. 2000. "Latinos: Once Wooed, Now Nearly Forgotten." *Los Angeles Times,* October 29.

Baldassare, Mark. 1986. *Trouble in Paradise: The Suburban Transformation in America.* New York: Columbia University Press.

———. 1992. "Suburban Communities." *Annual Review of Sociology* 18:475–494.

———, ed. 1994a. *Los Angeles Riots: Lessons for the Urban Future.* Boulder, CO: Westview Press.

———, ed. 1994b. *Suburban Communities: Change and Policy Responses.* Greenwich, CT: JAI Press.

———. 1998. *When Government Fails: The Orange County Bankruptcy.* Berkeley, CA: University of California Press and Public Policy Institute of California.

———. 2000. *California in the New Millennium: The Changing Social and Political Landscape.* Berkeley, CA: University of California Press and Public Policy Institute of California.

Baldassare, Mark, Joshua Hassol, William Hoffman, and Abby Kanarek. 1996. "Possible Planning Roles for Regional Government: A Survey of City Planning Directors in California." *Journal of the American Planning Association* 62:17–29.

Baldassare, Mark, and Cheryl Katz. 2000. *Orange County Annual Survey.* Irvine, CA: University of California, Irvine.

Baldassare, Mark, Michael Shires, Christopher Hoene, and Aaron Koffman. 2000. *Risky Business: Providing Local Public Services in Los Angeles County.* San Francisco, CA: Public Policy Institute of California.

Baldassare, Mark, and Georjeanna Wilson. 1995. "More Trouble in Paradise: Urbanization and the Decline in Suburban Quality of Life Ratings." *Urban Affairs Quarterly* 30:690–708.

———. 1996. "Changing Sources of Suburban Support for Local Growth Controls." *Urban Studies* 33:459–471.

Barabak, Mark. 2000. "Despite Polls, Bush Plans to Run All Out in California." *Los Angeles Times,* April 6.

Barber, Bernard. 1983. *The Logic and Limits of Trust.* New Brunswick, NJ: Rutgers University Press.

Barnes, Fred. 2000. "California Doesn't Matter." *Weekly Standard* 5 (43).

Bay Area Economic Forum. 2001. "The Bay Area: A Knowledge Economy Needs Power." San Francisco, CA: Bay Area Economic Forum.

Becerra, Hector, and Fred Alvarez. 2001. "Census Reflects Large Gains for Latinos." *Los Angeles Times,* May 10.

Beck, Paul Allen, Hal G. Rainey, and Carol Traut. 1990. "Disadvantage, Disaffection, and Race as Divergent Bases for Citizen Fiscal Policy Preferences." *Journal of Politics* 52 (1): 71–93.

Benson, Mitchel. 2000. "Would the Real Ronald Reagan Incarnation Please Step Forward?" *Wall Street Journal,* March 1.

———. 2001. "For Governor Davis, Worst Fear Is Electricity Ballot Initiative." *Wall Street Journal,* March 6.

Betts, Julian, Kim S. Rueben, and Anne Danenberg. 2000. *Equal Resources, Equal Outcomes: The Distribution of School Resources and Student Achievement in California.* San Francisco, CA: Public Policy Institute of California.

Block, A. G. 2000. "California Stands Apart." *California Journal,* December 1.

Bok, Derek. 1996. *The State of a Nation: Government and the Quest for a Better Society.* Cambridge, MA: Harvard University Press.

Booth, William. 2001. "California's Ethnicity Grows: State Has the Most Multiracial People." *Washington Post,* March 31.

Borenstein, Daniel. 2001. "After Power Crisis, Davis Finds It's Lonely at the Top." *Contra Costa Times,* October 7.

Bowler, Shaun, and Todd Donovan. 1998. *Demanding Choices: Opinion, Voting, and Direct Democracy.* Ann Arbor: University of Michigan Press.

Bowler, Shaun, Todd Donovan, and Caroline Tolbert. 1998. *Citizens as Legislators: Direct Democracy in the United States.* Columbus: Ohio State University Press.

Broder, David. 2000a. "A New GOP in California." *Washington Post,* March 5.

———. 2000b. "California Learning Curve." *Washington Post,* April 9.

———. 2000c. *Democracy Derailed: Initiative Campaigns and the Power of Money.* New York: Harcourt Brace.

Brownstein, Ronald. 2001a. "Energy on Agenda, but Issue Is Blame." *Los Angeles Times,* June 20.

———. 2001b. "Americans Unified in Support for Bush, War." *Los Angeles Times,* November 15.

Bustamante, Cruz M. 1999. "Remarks of Lt. Gov. Cruz M. Bustamante, Lieutenant Governor's Commission for One California." August 17, State Capitol. Sacramento: Lt. Gov's. Office.

Bustillo, Miguel. 2000. "State GOP Is Distancing Itself from Proposition 187." *Los Angeles Times,* August 7.

Cain, Bruce, Sara Ferejohn, Margarita Najar, and Mary Walther. 1995. "Constitutional Change: Is It Too Easy to Amend Our State Constitution?" In Bruce Cain and Roger Noll (eds.), *Constitutional Reform in California.* Berkeley, CA: Institute of Governmental Studies Press, pp. 265–290.

Cain, Bruce, and Elisabeth Gerber, eds. 2002. *California's Open/Blanket Primary: A Natural Experiment in Election Dynamics.* Berkeley, CA: University of California Press.

Cain, Bruce, Roderick Kiewiet, Michael Chwe, David Ely, Juani Funez-Gonzalez, Amita Shastri, and Carole Uhlaner. 1986. "The Political Impact of California's Minorities." Paper presented at Minorities in California: A Major Public Symposium. Pasadena, CA: California Institute of Technology.

Cain, Bruce, Roderick Kiewiet, and Carole Uhlaner. 1991. "The Acquisition of Partisanship by Latinos and Asian Americans." *American Journal of Political Science* 35:390–422.

Cain, Bruce, and Roger Noll. 1995. *Constitutional Reform in California.* Berkeley: California Policy Seminar.

California Association of Realtors. 2001. "Existing Single Family Median Home Price: 1990 to 2000." Sacramento, CA: California Association of Realtors.

California Constitution Revision Commission. 1996 *Executive Summary: Final Report and Recommendations to the Governor and the Legislature.* Sacramento, CA: State of California.

California Department of Education. 2000. "Eastin Releases California's SAT Scores for 2000." Press release and data tables. Sacramento, CA: State of California.

California Department of Finance. 1997. *California Demographics: Winter 1997.* Sacramento, CA: State of California.

———. 1998. "New State Projections Show No Ethnic Majority in Two Years: Total Population Nearly Doubling over 50-Year Period." Press release and data tables. Sacramento, CA: State of California.

———. 2000a. "Historical City, County, and State Population Estimates, 1991–2000, with 1990 Census Counts." Sacramento, CA: State of California.

———. 2000b. "Per Capita Personal Income: 1950 to 1999." Updated September 18. Sacramento, CA: State of California.

———. 2000c. "Race/Ethnic Population Estimates: Components of Change for California Counties April 1990 to June 1998." Sacramento, CA: State of California.

———. 2001a. "Civilian Labor Force and Employment: 1986 to 2000." Updated January 12. Sacramento, CA: State of California.

———. 2001b. "Historical Data: Budget Expenditures All Funds." Updated January 2001. Sacramento, CA: State of California.

———. 2001c. "Historical Data: General Fund Budget Summary." Updated January 2001. Sacramento, CA: State of California.

California Secretary of State. 1952. *Statement of the Vote, November 1952.* Sacramento, CA: State of California.

——. 1956. *Statement of the Vote, November 1956.* Sacramento, CA: State of California.

——. 1960. *Statement of the Vote, November 1960.* Sacramento, CA: State of California.

——. 1964. *Statement of the Vote, November 1964.* Sacramento, CA: State of California.

——. 1968. *Statement of the Vote, November 1968.* Sacramento, CA: State of California.

——. 1972. *Statement of the Vote, November 1972.* Sacramento, CA: State of California.

——. 1976. *Statement of the Vote, November 1976.* Sacramento, CA: State of California.

——. 1980. *Statement of the Vote, November 1980.* Sacramento, CA: State of California.

——. 1984. *Statement of the Vote, November 1984.* Sacramento, CA: State of California.

——. 1988. *Statement of the Vote, November 1988.* Sacramento, CA: State of California.

——. 1992. *Statement of the Vote, November 1992.* Sacramento, CA: State of California.

——. 1994. *Statement of the Vote, November 1994.* Sacramento, CA: State of California.

——. 1996. *Statement of the Vote, November 1996.* Sacramento, CA: State of California.

——. 1998a. *Statement of the Vote, June 1998.* Sacramento, CA: State of California.

——. 1998b. *Statement of the Vote, November 1998.* Sacramento, CA: State of California.

——. 2000a. "California's Crime Rate Has Been Nearly Cut in Half Since the Three Strikes Law was Enacted Six Years Ago." May 5. Sacramento, CA: State of California.

——. 2000b. *Statement of the Vote, March 2000.* Sacramento, CA: State of California.

——. 2000c. *Statement of the Vote, November 2000.* Sacramento, CA: State of California.

California Voter Foundation. 2001. "Top Ten Contributors to California Propositions." Sacramento, CA: California Voter Foundation.

Chance, Amy. 2000. "State GOP to Start Running Bush Ads Next Week." September 2.

Chance, Amy, and Emily Balzar. 2000. "California Voters Liked Gore's Grasp of Issues." *Sacramento Bee,* November 8.

Chaucer, Geoffrey. 2001. "The Prologue to Canterbury Tales." In Charles W. Eliot (ed.), *English Poetry I: From Chaucer to Gray.* The Harvard Classics, vol. 50. New York: P. F. Collier and Son, 1909–1914. Bartleby.com, 2001.

Chavez, Lydia. 1998. *The Color Bind: California's Battle to End Affirmative Action.* Berkeley, CA: University of California Press.

Citrin, Jack. 1974. "The Political Relevance of Trust in Government." *American Political Science Review* 68:973–988.

———. 1979. "Do People Want Something for Nothing?: Public Opinion on Taxes and Government Spending." *National Tax Journal* 32:113–129.

Citrin, Jack, and Samantha Luks. 1998. "The Problem of Political Trust." Paper prepared for the Pew Charitable Trusts, Philadelphia, Pennsylvania, June 15.

Citrin, Jack, and Christopher Muste. 1999. "Trust in Government." In John Robinson (ed.), *Measure of Political Attitudes*. New York: Academic Press, pp. 465–523.

Clark, Terry N., ed. 1994. *Urban Innovation*. Beverly Hills: Sage Publications.

Clark, Terry N., and Lorna Ferguson. 1983. *City Money*. New York: Columbia University Press.

Clark, Terry N., and Vincent Hoffman-Martinot, eds. 1998. *The New Political Culture*. Boulder, CO: Westview Press.

Clark, Terry N., and Ronald Inglehart. 1998. "The New Political Culture." In Terry Clark and Vincent Hoffman-Martinot (eds.), *The New Political Culture*. Boulder, CO: Westview Press.

Clark, Terry N., and Michael Rempel, eds. 1997. *Citizen Politics in Post-Industrial Societies*. Boulder, CO: Westview Press.

Clark, William A. V. 1998. *The California Cauldron: Immigration and the Fortunes of Local Communities*. New York: The Guilford Press.

———. 2001. *Immigration and the Hispanic Middle Class*. Washington, DC: Center for Immigration Studies.

Coile, Zachary. 2000. "California a Democratic Stronghold: Demographic Changes Loosen GOP's Grip on State." *San Francisco Examiner*, November 8.

Congressional Budget Office. 2001. *The Budget and Economic Outlook: Fiscal Years 2002 to 2011*. Washington, D.C.: U.S. Congress.

Covarrubias, Amanda. 1998 "Latinos Prove Powerful at Polls." *San Jose Mercury News*, November 8.

Craig, Stephen C. 1996. *Broken Contract: Changing Relationships between Americans and Their Government*. Boulder, CO: Westview Press.

Daly, Mary C., Deborah Reed, and Heather N. Royer. 2001. "Population Mobility and Income Inequality in California." *California Counts* 2 (2). San Francisco: Public Policy Institute of California.

Dardia, Michael. 1995. "The California Economy: Issues and Research Ideas." Staff briefing in June 1995. San Francisco, CA: Public Policy Institute of California.

Dardia, Michael, and Sherman Luk. 1999. *Rethinking the California Business Climate*. San Francisco, CA: Public Policy Institute of California.

Davis, Gray. 1999. "State of the State Address." January 6. Sacramento, CA: Governor of California.

Dear, Michael, H. Eris Schockman, and Greg Hise, eds. 1996. *Rethinking Los Angeles*. Thousand Oaks, CA: Sage Publications.

DeBow, Ken, and John C. Syer. 1997. *Power and Politics in California*. Boston: Allyn and Bacon.

Decker, Cathleen. 2000. "California Profile: Shift toward the Left Takes a Firm Hold." *Los Angeles Times*, November 8.

De la Garza, Rodolpho. 1987. *Ignored Voices: Public Opinion Polls and the Latino Community.* Austin, Texas: Center for Mexican American Studies.

Del Olmo, Frank. 2000. "On Latino Voters, Bush Gets It." *Los Angeles Times,* August 6.

DelVecchio, Rick. 2000. "Open Space, Urban Sprawl on Ballots around the Bay." *San Francisco Chronicle,* October 17.

DiCamillo, Mark, and Mervin Field, 1998. "Proposition 13 Twenty Years Later." May. San Francisco, CA: Field Institute.

Dionne, E. J. 1991. *Why Americans Hate Politics.* New York: Simon and Schuster.

——. 2000. "School Wars." *Washington Post,* September 26.

Dowall, David. 1984. *The Suburban Squeeze: Land Conversion and Regulation in the San Francisco Bay Area.* Berkeley, CA: University of California Press.

Erber, Ralph, and Richard Lau. 1990. "Political Cynicism Revisited." *American Journal of Political Science* 34 (1): 236–253.

Ferejohn, Sara. 1995. "Reforming the Initiative Process." In Bruce Cain and Roger Noll (eds.), *Constitutional Reform in California.* Berkeley, CA: Institute of Governmental Studies Press, pp. 313–325.

Fernandez, Kenneth, and Max Neiman. 1997. "Models of Anti-immigration Sentiment and Other Speculations Regarding the Rise of Contemporary Xenophobia." Paper presented at the 1997 Annual Meeting of the Southwest Political Science Association, New Orleans.

Field Institute. 1999. "Voting in California's 1998 General Election." January. San Francisco, CA: Field Institute.

Fischer, Claude S. 1975. "The City and Political Psychology." *American Political Science Review* 69 (2): 559–571.

——. 1984. *The Urban Experience.* New York: Harcourt Brace Jovanovich.

Fulton, William. 1997. *The Reluctant Metropolis: The Politics of Urban Growth in Los Angeles.* Point Arene, CA: Solano Press.

Fulton, William, Paul Shigley, Alicia Harrison, and Peter Sezzi. 2000. *Trends in Local Land Use Ballot Measures, 1986 to 2000.* Ventura, CA: Solimar Research Group.

Garment, Suzanne. 1991. *Scandal: The Crisis of Mistrust in American Politics.* New York: Times Books.

Gaudette, Karen. 2000. "Voters Decide Land-Use Issues in California." Associated Press, November 9.

Gay, Claudine. 2001. *The Effect of Minority Districts and Minority Representation on Political Participation in California.* San Francisco: Public Policy Institute of California.

Geissinger, Steve. 2001. "State Power Grab?" *Oakland Tribune,* January 9.

Gerber, Elisabeth. 1995. "Reforming the California Initiative Process: A Proposal to Increase Flexibility, Legislative Accountability." In Bruce Cain and Roger Noll (eds.), *Constitutional Reform in California.* Berkeley, CA: Institute of Governmental Studies Press, pp. 291–311.

——. 1998. *Interest Group Influence in the California Initiative Process.* San Francisco, CA: Public Policy Institute of California.

——. 1999. *The Populist Paradox: Interest Group Influence and the Promise of Direct Legislation.* Princeton, NJ: Princeton University Press.

Glickfeld, Madelyn, and Ned Levine. 1990. *The New Land Use Regulation "Revolution": Why California's Local Jurisdictions Enact Growth Control and Management Measures.* Los Angeles, CA: University of California at Los Angeles.

Glickfeld, Madelyn, Ned Levine, and William Fulton. 1996. *Home Rule: Local Growth, Regional Consequences.* Los Angeles, CA: University of California at Los Angeles.

Greenberg, Stanley B. 1995. *The Politics and Power of the New American Majority.* New York: Times Books.

Hajnal, Zoltan, and Mark Baldassare. 2001. *Finding Common Ground: Racial and Ethnic Attitudes in California.* San Francisco, CA: Public Policy Institute of California.

Hajnal, Zoltan, and Hugh Louch. 2001. *Are There Winners and Losers?: Race, Ethnicity, and California's Initiative Process.* San Francisco, CA: Public Policy Institute of California.

Hansen, John Mark. 1998. "Individuals, Institutions, and Public Preferences over Public Finance." *American Political Science Review* 92 (3): 513–531.

Hardin, Russell. 1996. "Trustworthiness." *Ethics* 107 (1): 26–43.

Hawthorne, Michael R., and John E. Jackson. 1987. "The Individual Political Economy of Federal Tax Policy." *American Political Science Review* 81 (3): 757–774.

Hertzberg, Robert. 2000. "Hertzberg creates Speaker's Commission on Initiative Process." October 27, Sacramento: Assemblyman Robert Hertzberg's Office.

Hillburg, Bill. 2000. "Minorities Now the Majority in California." *Los Angeles Daily News,* August 30.

Howard, John. 2001. "Davis Devises New Borrowing Plan." *Orange County Register,* October 11.

Howell, Susan, and Deborah Fagan. 1988. "Race and Trust in Government: Testing the Political Reality Model." *Public Opinion Quarterly* 52 (3): 343–350.

Inglehart, Ronald. 1998. "The Trend Toward Postmaterialist Values Continues." In Terry N. Clark and Michael Rempel (eds.), *Citizen Politics in Post-Industrial Societies.* Boulder, CO: Westview Press.

Jeffe, Sherry Bebitch. 1999. "Will Bush Save the State GOP?: Consider the Brown Family." *Los Angeles Times,* July 18.

———. 2000a. "Davis Keeps Pushing Education, but Support Is Fading." *Los Angeles Times,* January 16.

———. 2000b. "The Quackenbush Scandal: The Incredibly Shrinking Republican Bench." *Los Angeles Times,* April 23.

———. 2000c. "California's One-Party State, but Can the Democrats Rest Easy?" *Los Angeles Times,* August 13.

Johnson, Hans. 1996. "Undocumented Immigration to California: 1980–1993." *California Counts* 1 (1). San Francisco: Public Policy Institute of California.

———. 1999. "How Many Californians?: A Review of Population Projections for the State." *California Counts* 1 (1). San Francisco: Public Policy Institute of California.

———. 2000. "Movin' Out: Domestic Migration to and from California in the 1990s." *California Counts* 2 (1). San Francisco: Public Policy Institute of California.

Kasindorf, Martin. 2001. "California Dreams Itself into a Corner." *USA Today*, June 17.

Keil, Roger. 1998. *Los Angeles: Globalization, Urbanization and Social Struggles*. New York: John Wiley.

Keith, Bruce E., David B. Magleby, Candice J. Nelson, Elizabeth Orr, Mark C. Westlye, and Raymond E. Wolfinger. 1992. *The Myth of the Independent Voter*. Berkeley, CA: University of California Press.

Kerr, Jennifer. 2001. "$116 Million Spent on State School Ballot Items." Associated Press, February 7.

Korber, Dorothy. 2000. "No More Majority in State: Whites under 50 Percent, Census Says." *Sacramento Bee*, August 30.

Latino Issues Forum. 1998. "The Latino Vote 1998: The New Margin of Victory." San Francisco, CA.: Latino Issues Forum.

Legislative Analyst's Office. 1993. "Common Cents: Background Material on State and Local Government Finances." Sacramento: State of California.

———. 1995. "Cal Guide: A Profile of State Programs." Sacramento: State of California.

———. 1999a. "LAO Analysis of the 1999–2000 Budget Bill." Sacramento: State of California.

———. 1999b. "A Special Guide to K–12 Reform." Sacramento: State of California.

———. 2000a. "Cal Facts: California's Economy and Budget in Perspective." Sacramento: State of California.

———. 2000b. "LAO Analysis of the 2000–2001 Budget Bill." Sacramento: State of California.

Lesher, Dave. 1998. "Election Seen as Test of Latinos' Political Course." *Los Angeles Times*, October 21.

Levi, Margaret, and Laura Stoker. 2000. "Political Trust and Trustworthiness." *Annual Review of Political Science* 3:475–507.

Lewis, Paul. 1996. *Shaping Suburbia: How Political Institutions Organize Urban Development*. Pittsburgh: University of Pittsburgh Press.

Lewis, Paul, and Max Neiman. 2001. *Swimming against the Tide: Local Governments Confront Growth in California*. San Francisco, CA: Public Policy Institute of California.

Lipset, Seymour Martin. 1996. *American Exceptionalism: A Double-Edged Sword*. New York: W. W. Norton.

Lipset, Seymour Martin, and William Schneider. 1983. *The Confidence Gap*. New York: Free Press.

———. 1987. "The Confidence Gap During the Reagan Years: 1981–1987." *Political Science Quarterly* 102 (1): 1–23.

Lo, Clarence. 1990. *Small Property versus Big Government: Social Origins of the Property Tax Revolt*. Berkeley, CA: University of California Press.

Logan, John, and Harvey Molotch. 1987. *Urban Fortunes: The Political Economy of Place*. Berkeley: University of California Press.

Los Angeles Times/CNN Poll. 1998. June primary exit poll.

Los Angeles Times Poll. 1994. November election exit poll.

———. 1998. November election exit poll.

———. 2000a. California March primary exit poll.

———. 2000b. California November general election exit poll.

Lowery, David, and Lee Sigelman. 1981. "Understanding the Tax Revolt: Eight Explanations." *American Political Science Review* 75 (4): 963–974.

Lupia, Arthur. 1998. *The Democratic Dilemma: Can Citizens Learn What They Really Need to Know?* New York: Cambridge University Press.

MacManus, Susan. 1995. "Taxing and Spending Politics: A Generational Perspective." *Journal of Politics* 57 (3): 607–629.

Maharidge, Dale. 1996. *The Coming White Minority: California's Eruptions and the Nation's Future.* New York: Times Books.

Marelius, John. 2001. "Davis: Deregulation a Failure." *San Diego Union Tribune,* January 9.

Marinucci, Carla. 2000. "New Voters in State Are Mostly Latino." *San Francisco Chronicle,* May 1.

McConnell, Patrick. 1999. "1990s on Track to Set a Record for Immigration." *Los Angeles Times,* January 24.

McWilliams, Carey. 1949. *California: The Great Exception.* Berkeley, CA: University of California Press. (Paperback printing by the University of California Press in 1999).

Mehta, Seema. 2000. "Slow-Growth Initiatives Hit and Miss." *Los Angeles Times,* November 9.

Mendel, Ed. 2000. "California GOP Leaders Wonder When Their Tide Will Turn Again." *San Diego Union,* November 13.

Meyerson, Harold. 2001. "California's Progressive Mosaic." *American Prospect* 12 (11), June 18.

Miller, Arthur. 1974a. "Political Issues and Trust in Government." *American Political Science Review* 68 (3): 951–972.

———. 1974b. "Rejoinder to Comment by Jack Citrin: Political Discontent or Ritualism." *American Political Science Review* 68 (3): 989–1001.

Miller, Warren E., and J. Merrill Shanks. 1996. *The New American Voter.* Cambridge, MA: Harvard University Press.

Moore, Joan, and Harry Pachon. 1985. *Hispanics in the United States.* Englewood Cliffs, NJ: Prentice Hall.

Morin, Richard, and Claudia Deane. 2001. "Poll: Americans Trust in Government Grows." Washington Post, September 28.

Myers, Phyllis, and Robert Puentes. 2001. *Growth at the Ballot Box: Electing the Shape of Communities in November 2000.* Washington, DC: Brookings Institution Center on Urban and Metropolitan Policy.

National Election Studies. 1998. National Election Studies. Ann Arbor: University of Michigan.

Neiman, Max, and Kenneth Fernandez. 1998. "Dimensions and Models of Anti-immigrant Sentiments: Causes and Policy Relevance." Paper presented at the Annual Meeting of the American Political Science Association, Boston.

Neiman, Max, and Ronald Loveridge. 1981. "Environmentalism and Local Growth Control: A Probe into to Class Bias Thesis." *Environment and Behavior* 13:759–772.

Nelson Communications Group. 1999. "California 2000: Focus Group Report." Sacramento, CA: Nelson Communications Group.

Nelson, Soraya Sarhaddi, and Richard O'Reilly. 2000. "Minorities Become Majority in State, Officials Say." *Los Angeles Times,* August 30.

Newport, Frank. 2001. "Trust in Government Increases Sharply in Wake of Terrorist Attack." Gallup Poll News Service, October 12.

Nickles, Jim. 2000. "Tracy's Growth Limit May Stress Other Areas." *Stockton Record,* November 10.

Nye, Joseph S., Philip D. Zelikow, and David C. King. 1997. *Why People Don't Trust Government.* Cambridge, MA: Harvard University Press.

Office of the Secretary of Education. 2000. "2000–01 California State Budget: Education Summary." Sacramento: State of California.

Orren, Gary. 1997. "Fall from Grace: The Public's Loss of Faith in Government." In Joseph Nye, Philip D. Zelikow, and David C. King (eds.), *Why People Don't Trust Government.* Cambridge, MA: Harvard University Press, pp. 77–108.

Pachon, Harry. 1998. "Latino Politics in the Golden State: Ready for the 21st Century?" In Michael B. Preston, Bruce E. Cain, and Sandra Bass (eds.), *Racial and Ethnic Politics in California,* vol. 2. Berkeley, CA: Institute of Governmental Studies Press.

Pachon, Harry, and Louis DeSipio. 1995. *New Americans by Choice.* Boulder, CO: Westview Press.

Palen, John. 1995. *The Suburbs.* New York: McGraw-Hill.

Pasco, Jean, and Meg James. 2000. "Initiative Aimed at Halting El Toro Airport Nullified." *Los Angeles Times,* December 2.

Pena, Michael. 2000. "Alameda County Urban Growth-Control Measure Heading to Victory." *San Francisco Chronicle,* November 9.

Portes, Alejandro, and Ruben G. Rumbaut. 1990. *Immigrant America: A Portrait.* Berkeley, CA: University of California Press.

PPIC Just the Facts. 2000a. *Election 2000: Legislative Analysis.* San Francisco, CA: Public Policy Institute of California.

———. 2000b. *Election 2000: Statewide Analysis.* San Francisco, CA: Public Policy Institute of California.

———. 2001a. *The Age Gap in California Politics.* San Francisco, CA: Public Policy Institute of California.

———. 2001b. *California's Digital Divide.* San Francisco, CA: Public Policy Institute of California.

———. 2001c. *California's Likely Voters.* San Francisco, CA: Public Policy Institute of California.

———. 2001d. *Latino Voters in California.* San Francisco, CA: Public Policy Institute of California.

PPIC Statewide Survey. 1999a. *Californians and Their Government Series, January.* San Francisco, CA: Public Policy Institute of California.

———. 1999b. *Californians and Their Government Series, September.* San Francisco, CA: Public Policy Institute of California.

———. 1999c. *Special Survey on the Central Valley, November.* San Francisco, CA: Public Policy Institute of California.

———. 1999d. *Californians and Their Government Series, December.* San Francisco, CA: Public Policy Institute of California.

———. 2000a. *Californians and Their Government Series, January.* San Francisco, CA: Public Policy Institute of California.

———. 2000b. *Californians and Their Government Series, February.* San Francisco, CA: Public Policy Institute of California.

———. 2000c. *Special Survey on Californians and the Environment, June.* San Francisco, CA: Public Policy Institute of California.

———. 2000d. *Special Survey on San Diego County, July.* San Francisco, CA: Public Policy Institute of California.

———. 2000e. *Californians and Their Government Series, August.* San Francisco, CA: Public Policy Institute of California.

———. 2000f. *Californians and Their Government Series, September.* San Francisco, CA: Public Policy Institute of California.

———. 2000g. *Californians and Their Government Series, October.* San Francisco, CA: Public Policy Institute of California.

———. 2001a. *Californians and Their Government Series, January.* San Francisco, CA: Public Policy Institute of California.

———. 2001b. *Special Survey on Growth, May.* San Francisco, CA: Public Policy Institute of California.

———. 2001c. *Californians and Their Government Series, July.* San Francisco, CA: Public Policy Institute of California.

———. 2001d. *Special Survey on Land Use, November.* San Francisco, CA: Public Policy Institute of California.

———. 2001e. *Californians and Their Government Series, December.* San Francisco, CA: Public Policy Institute of California.

———. 2002. *Californians and Their Government Series, January.* San Francisco, CA: Public Policy Institute of California.

Preston, Michael, Bruce E. Cain, and Sandra Bass, eds. 1998. *Racial and Ethnic Politics in California,* vol. 2. Berkeley, CA: Institute of Governmental Studies Press.

Purdum, Todd. 2001. "Non-Hispanic Whites a Minority, California Census Figures Show." March 30.

Putnam, Robert D. 1995. "Bowling Alone: America's Declining Social Capital." *Journal of Democracy* 6:65–78.

———. 2000. *Bowling Alone: The Collapse and Revival of American Community.* New York: Simon and Schuster.

Raymond, Valerie. 1998. *Surviving Proposition 13: Fiscal Crisis in California Counties.* Berkeley, CA: Institute of Governmental Studies.

Reed, Deborah. 1999. *California's Rising Income Inequality: Causes and Concerns.* San Francisco, CA: Public Policy Institute of California.

Reed, Deborah, Melissa Glenn Haber, and Laura Mameesh. 1996. *The Distribution of Income in California.* San Francisco, CA: Public Policy Institute of California.

Reyes, Belinda, ed. 2001. *A Portrait of Race and Ethnicity in California.* San Francisco, CA: Public Policy Institute of California.

Rieff, David. 1991. *Los Angeles: Capital of the Third World.* New York: Touchstone.

Roberts, Michael L., Peggy A. White, and Cassi F. Bradley. 1994. "Understanding Attitudes toward Progressive Taxation." *Public Opinion Quarterly* 58 (2): 165–190.

Rodriguez, Gregory. 1998. *The Emerging Latino Middle Class.* Malibu, CA: Pepperdine University Institute of Public Policy.

———. 1999. "Will Bush's Latino Appeal Work in California?" *Los Angeles Times,* September 5.

———. 2000. "The Democrats' Fixation on the Aggrieved Minority." *Los Angeles Times,* August 13.

Rogers, Paul. 2001. "Governor Davis Regaining Public Favor." *San Jose Mercury News,* June 23.

Rose, Craig D. 2000. "San Diego Gas and Electric Customers to Get Temporary Break." *San Diego Union Tribune,* September 6.

Saavedra, Tony, and Ronald Campbell. 2000. "'90s See Surge in Minority Growth." *Orange County Register,* August 30.

Samuelson, Robert. 1995. *The Good Life and Its Discontents: The American Dream in the Age of Enlightenment, 1945–1995.* New York: Times Books.

Sandel, Michael. 1996. *Democracy's Discontent: America in Search of a Public Philosophy.* Cambridge, MA: Harvard University Press.

Schevitz, Tanya. 2000. "California Minorities Become Majority." *San Francisco Chronicle,* August 30.

Schneider, William. 2001. "California Left Twisting in the Political Wind." *Los Angeles Times,* May 20.

Scholz, John T., and Mark Lubell. 1998a. "Trust and Taxpaying: Testing the Heuristic Approach to Collective Action." *American Journal of Political Science* 42 (2): 398–417.

———. 1998b. "Adaptive Political Attitudes: Duty, Trust, and Fear as Monitors of Tax Policy." *American Journal of Political Science* 42 (3): 903–920.

Schrag, Peter. 1998. *Paradise Lost: California's Experience, America's Future.* New York: The New Press.

———. 2000a. "Mississippification of California's Schools." *Sacramento Bee,* May 24.

———. 2000b. "Has California Become Irrelevant?" *Sacramento Bee,* August 7.

———. 2000c. "Reforming the Fourth Branch of Government." *Sacramento Bee,* December 13.

———. 2001. "Is California the Birthplace of the Next New Deal?" *Sacramento Bee,* June 13.

Schwieren, Bernd. 1999. "The Emerging Republican Minority: California's New Electorate and the Future of the Republican Party." Sacramento, CA. Photocopy.

Scott, Allen J., and Edward Soja, eds. 1998. *The City: Los Angeles and Urban Theory at the End of the Twentieth Century.* Berkeley, CA: University of California Press.

Scott, Steve. 2000. "Competing for the New Majority vote." *California Journal,* January 1.

Sears, David O., and Jack Citrin. 1982. *Tax Revolt: Something for Nothing in California.* Cambridge, MA: Harvard University Press.

Sears, David, Tom Tyler, Jack Citrin, and Donald Kinder. 1978. "Political System Support and Public Response to the Energy Crisis." *American Journal of Political Science* 22 (1): 56–82.

Shapiro, Robert Y., and John T. Young. 1989. "Public Opinion and the Welfare State: The United States in Comparative Perspective." *Political Science Quarterly* 104 (1): 59–89.

Shields, Mark. 2000. "California's Wilson is a Gift That Keeps on Giving." *Seattle Post-Intelligencer,* September 25.

Shires, Michael. 1999. *Patterns in California Government Revenues Since Proposition 13.* San Francisco, CA: Public Policy Institute of California.

Shires, Michael, John Ellwood, and Mary Sprague. 1998. *Has Proposition 13 Delivered?: The Changing Tax Burden in California.* San Francisco, CA: Public Policy Institute of California.

Silva, Fred. 2000. *The California Initiative Process: Background Material.* San Francisco, CA: Public Policy Institute of California.

Silva, Fred, and Elisa Barbour. 1999. *The State-Local Fiscal Relationship in California: A Changing Balance of Power.* San Francisco, CA: Public Policy Institute of California.

Skelton, George. 1998. "Now Latinos Are Changing the Face of Both Parties." *Los Angeles Times,* November 23.

———. 2000a. "Though Wounded, California's GOP Is Not Slain." *Los Angeles Times,* July 31.

———. 2000b. "What's up, California?: A Guide to the Peculiar Political Mindset of the Golden State." *Los Angeles Times,* August 13.

———. 2000c. "Endless Bad News Frays the Nerves of State's GOP." *Los Angeles Times,* September 21.

———. 2000d. "State Republicans Find Waking up Is Hard to Do." *Los Angeles Times,* November 13.

Sonenshein, Raphael. 1993. *Politics in Black and White: Race and Power in Los Angeles.* Princeton, NJ: Princeton University Press.

Sonstelie, Jon, Eric Brunner, and Kenneth Ardon. 2000. *For Better or for Worse?: School Finance Reform in California.* San Francisco, CA: Public Policy Institute of California.

Stanton, Sam. 2001. "Power Crunch: How Californians Got Burned." *Sacramento Bee,* May 6.

Steinberg, James, David Lyon, and Mary Vaiana. 1992. *Urban America: Policy Choices for Los Angeles and the Nation.* Santa Monica, CA: RAND.

Sterngold, James. 2001. "Governor Pledges to Save California from Power Crisis." *New York Times,* January 9.

Stille, Alexander. 2001. "Suddenly, Americans Trust Uncle Sam." *New York Times,* November 3.

Tafoya, Sonya, and Hans Johnson. 2000. *Graying in the Golden State: Demographic and Economic Trends of Older Californians.* San Francisco, CA: Public Policy Institute of California.

Tamaki, Julie, and Miguel Bustillo. 2001. "Tough Times Predicted for State Budget." *Los Angeles Times,* October 9.

Taub, Daniel. 2001. "California's Economy May Suffer Even as Power Crisis Recedes." Bloomberg.com, October 8.

Teaford, Jon C. 1997. *Post-Suburbia: Government and Politics in the Edge Cities.* Baltimore: The Johns Hopkins University Press.

Tobar, Hector. 1998. "In Contests Big and Small, Latinos Take Historic Leap." *Los Angeles Times,* November 5.

Tolchin, Susan J. 1996. *The Angry American: How Voter Rage is Changing the Nation.* Boulder, CO: Westview Press.

Uhlaner, Carole, Bruce Cain, and Roderick Kiewiet. 1989. "Political Participation of Ethnic Minorities in the 1980s." *Political Behavior* 11:195–231.

Uhlaner, Carole, and F. Chris Garcia. 1998. *Foundations of Latino Party Identification: Learning, Ethnicity, and Demographic Factors among Mexicans, Puerto Ricans, Cubans, and Anglos in the United States.* Irvine, CA: Center for the Study of Democracy.

Unz, Ron. 2000. "How the Republicans Lost California." *Wall Street Journal,* August 28.

U.S. Census. 2001. *2000 Census of Population.* Washington, D.C.: U.S. Census.

Verdin, Tom. 2000. "Minorities Now the Majority in California." Associated Press, August 30.

Vernez, George. 1992. "Needed: A Federal Role in Helping Communities Cope with Immigration." In James B. Steinberg, David W. Lyon, and Mary E. Vaiana (eds.), *Urban America: Policy Choices for Los Angeles and the Nation.* Santa Monica, CA: RAND, pp. 281–296.

Vorderbrueggen, Lisa. 2000. "Growth Initiatives: 35 Measures Boost Slow-Growth Plans around the State." *Los Angeles Times,* November 9.

Voter News Service. 1990. November election exit poll.

———. 1992. November election exit poll.

———. 1994. November election exit poll.

———. 1996. November election exit poll.

———. 1998. November election exit poll.

———. 2000. November election exit poll.

Walters, Dan. 1992. *The New California: Facing the 21st Century.* Second Edition. Sacramento, CA: California Journal Press.

———. 1998. "Latinos Emerge as Power Bloc." *Sacramento Bee,* November 15.

———. 2000a. "Ethnicity Again Concerns GOP." *Sacramento Bee,* August 3.

———. 2000b. "Democrats Roll to State Victory." *Sacramento Bee,* November 9.

———. 2000c. "Growth Control a Gordian Knot." *Sacramento Bee,* November 24.

———. 2001. "Great California Energy Crisis May Be Heading for a Climax." *Sacramento Bee,* June 19.

Warren, Mark. 1992. "Democratic Theory and Self-transformation." *American Political Science Review* 86 (1): 8–23.

———. 1996. "Deliberative Democracy and Authority." *American Political Science Review* 86 (1): 46–60.

———, ed. 1999. *Democracy and Trust.* New York: Cambridge University Press.

Weintraub, Daniel. 2001. "The Initiative: Time to Reform the Reformers Tool." *Sacramento Bee,* February 25.

Weisberg, Jacob. 1996. *In Defense of Government: The Fall and Rise of Public Trust.* New York: Scribner.

Willis, Doug. 2000. "Surge in Latino Voters Changing California Electorate." Associated Press, May 7.

Woolfolk, John. "Census: Whites Minority in State." *San Jose Mercury News,* August 30.

Yankelovich, Dan. 1983. *New Rules: Searching for Self-fulfillment in a World Turned Upside Down.* New York: Random House.

———. 1991. *Coming to Public Judgment: Making Democracy Work in a Complex World.* Syracuse, NY: Syracuse University Press.

———. 1999. *The Magic of Dialogue: Transforming Conflict into Cooperation.* New York: Simon and Schuster.

Index

Compositor:	Impressions Book and Journal Services, Inc.
Text:	10/13 Sabon
Display:	Sabon
Printer and binder:	Maple-Vail Manufacturing Group